THE MARSHALL CAVENDISH
ILLUSTRATED ENCYCLOPEDIA OF
WORLD WAR II

Volume 8

**An objective, chronological and comprehensive history
of the Second World War.**

Authoritative text by
Lt. Colonel Eddy Bauer.

Consultant Editor
Brigadier General James L. Collins, Jr., U.S.A., Chief of Military
History, Department of the Army.

Editor-in-Chief
Brigadier Peter Young, D.S.O., M.C., M.A., F.S.A. Formerly head
of Military History Department at the Royal Military Academy,
Sandhurst.

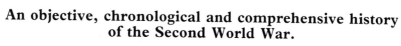

Marshall Cavendish New York & London

Editor-in-Chief Brigadier Peter
  Young, D.S.O., M.C., M.A., F.S.A.
Reader's Guide Christopher Chant, M.A.
Index Richard Humble
Consultant Editor Correlli Barnett,
  Fellow of Churchill College, Cambridge
Editorial Director Brian Innes
Illustrators Malcolm McGregor
  Pierre Turner
Contributors Correlli Barnett, Brigadier Michael Calvert, Richard Humble,
  Henry Shaw, Lt.-Col. Alan Shepperd, Martin Blumenson, Stanley L. Falk,
  Jaques Nobécourt, Colonel Rémy, Brigadier General E. H. Simmons
  U.S.M.C. (ret'd), Captain Donald Macintyre, Jonathan Martin, William
  Fowler, Jenny Shaw, Dr. Frank Futrell, Lawson Nagel, Richard Storry,
  John Major, Andrew Mollo.
Cover Design Tony Pollicino
Production Consultant Robert Paulley
Production Controller Patrick Holloway
Cover illustration The end of war;
  Corporal C. Dunn, U.S.M.C., raises the U.S. Flag over Yokosuka Naval
  Base in Japan.

C16342

Reference Edition Published 1981

Published by Marshall Cavendish Corporation
147 West Merrick Road, Freeport, N.Y. 11520
©Orbis Publishing Ltd. 1980, 1979, 1978, 1972
©1966 Jaspard Polus, Monaco

Printed in Great Britain by Jarrold and Sons Ltd.

Bound in Great Britain by Cambridge University Press

Cataloguing in Publication Data

Marshall Cavendish Encyclopedia of World War II.
  1. World War, 1939–1945—Dictionaries
  I. Young, Peter, *1915–*
  940.53'03'21   D740

  ISBN 0-85685-948-6 (set)
  ISBN 0-85685-956-7 (volume 8)

Picture Acknowledgements
1961: Blitz Publications; 1962: U.S.I.S.; 1963: Robert Hunt Library; 1964:
U.S.I.S.; 1964/1965: U.S.I.S.; 1966: Keystone; 1967: U.S.I.S.; 1968/1969:
U.S.I.S.; 1969: Keystone; 1970: Keystone; 1971: Imperial War Museum,
Keystone; 1972/1973: Orbis/Pierre Tilley; 1974: Keystone; 1974/1975: Imperial
War Museum; 1975: Imperial War Museum; 1976: U.S.I.S.; 1977: Keystone;
1978: Orbis; 1979: Robert Hunt Library; 1980: I.W.M., Robert Hunt Library;
1981: Keystone; 1982/1983: U.S. Army; 1984: John Hilleson, Keystone, Blitz
Publications; 1985: U.S.I.S., Keystone; 1986: I.W.M./Camera Press; 1987:
Novosti; 1988: Novosti; 1989: Novosti; 1990: Orbis, Robert Hunt Library; 1991:
Novosti; 1992/1993: Novosti; 1993: Novosti; 1994: Novosti; 1995: Orbis/Alan
Rees, *Time & Tide*, London, Kukryniksy; 1996: Novosti; 1997: Novosti; 1998:
Keystone; 1999: Novosti; 2000: Keystone; 2001: Keystone; 2002: Novosti; 2003:
Novosti; 2004/2005: Orbis, 2006: Novosti; 2007: Novosti; 2008/2009: Novosti,
Robert Hunt Library; 2009: Novosti; 2010: Novosti; 2011: Orbis; 2012: Camera
Press/Holmès–Lebel; 2013: Novosti, Keystone; 2014: Novosti; 2015: Robert Hunt
Library; 2016: U.S.I.S.; 2017: U.S.I.S.; 2018/2019: Keystone; 2020: U.S. Army;
2021: Robert Hunt Library; 2022: Keystone; 2023: *Daily Express, Simplicissimus,
Lustige Blätter*; 2024: Popperfoto; 2025: U.S.I.S. 2026: *Lustige Blätter, Klad-
deradatsch, Kladderadatsch;* 2027: Robert Hunt Library; 2028: Keystone;
2028/2029: U.S.I.S.; 2029: U.S. Army, Keystone; 2030: Keystone; 2031: U.S.I.S.;
2032: Keystone; 2034: U.S.I.S.; 2034/2035: U.S.I.S., Associated Press; 2035:
Lustige Blätter 2036: *Kladderadatsch, Kladderadatsch, Lustige Blätter;* 2036/2037:
U.S.I.S.; 2037: *Simplicissimus;* 2038: U.S.I.S.; 2039: Popperfoto, Orbis/Alan Rees;
2040: U.S.I.S.; 2041: Keystone; 2042/2043: Keystone; 2043: Keystone; 2044: Or-
bis/Alan Rees, Keystone; 2045: Documentation Française; 2046: *Daily Mail*, Lon-
don; 2047: Orbis; 2048: U.S.I.S., France-Libre; 2049: Keystone; 2050:
Etablissements Cinématographiques des Armées; 2051: Keystone; 2052: Or-
bis/Alan Rees; 2053: Archives de la Musée de la Guerre, U.S.I.S.; 2054/2055:
Documentation Française; 2055: Camera Press; 2056: Ullstein; 2057: Blitz
Publications; 2058/2059: Raphoen; 2059: *Punch*, London; 2060: Orbis; 2061:
Punch, London; 2062: *Nebelspatter*, Denver Post; 2062/2063: U.S.I.S.; 2064: U.S.
Army; 2065: Camera Press; 2066: U.S.I.S.; 2066/2067: U.S.I.S.; 2068: Documen-
tation Française, Orbis/Alan Rees; 2069: U.S. Army; 2070/2071: Keystone; 2072:
Mathilde Rieussec, U.S.I.S.; 2073: Keystone; 2074: U.S. Army; 2075: U.S. Army,
Keystone; 2076: Imperial War Museum; 2077: Orbis; 2078/2079: Imperial War
Museum; 2079: Keystone; 2080: J. Hilleson Agency; 2081: Imperial War
Museum; 2082: Orbis; 2083: U.S. Army; 2084: Imperial War Museum; 2085: Or-
bis/Alan Rees; 2086: U.S. Army; 2087: I.W.M./Camera Press; 2088/2089:
Keystone; 2090: Keystone, I.W.M./Camera Press; 2090/2091: Keystone; 2092:
Keystone; 2093: U.S.I.S.; 2094: U.S.I.S., Imperial War Museum; 2095: Keystone;
2096: U.S. Army; 2097: Orbis; 2098/2099: Keystone; 2100: U.S.I.S., Keystone;
2101: British Official Photograph; 2102/2103: Keystone; 2103: Keystone; 2104:
Orbis; 2105: I.W.M./Camera Press; 2106/2107: I.W.M./Camera Press; 2107:
Keystone; 2108: Keystone; 2109: Orbis; 2110: Camera Press; 2111: Keystone;
2112: Orbis; 2113: Associated Press; 2114/2115: Keystone; 2116: Associated Press;
2117: I.W.M./Camera Press; 2118: Keystone, I.W.M./Camera Press, Keystone;
2118/2119: Keystone; 2119: Keystone; 2120: Keystone; 2121: Keystone;
2122/2123: Camera Press; 2123: U.S.I.S.; 2124: U.S.I.S.; 2125: Orbis; 2126:
Keystone; 2126/2127: Blitz Publications; 2127: Keystone; 2128: Orbis/Alan Rees;
2129: Keystone; 2130/2131: Imperial War Museum; 2131: Keystone,
I.W.M./Camera Press; 2132: Orbis; 2133: Keystone; 2134: Keystone; 2135: U.S.
Army; 2136/2137: Fox Photos; 2137: Documentation Française; 2138/2139:
I.W.M./Camera Press; 2139: Novosti; 2140: Keystone; 2141: Associated Press;
2142: U.S. Air Force; 2142/2143: Imperial War Museum; 2144: Orbis; 2145:
Associated Press; 2146: Keystone; 2147: Orbis; 2148: I.W.M./Camera Press; 2149:
I.W.M./Camera Press; 2150/2151: I.W.M./Camera Press; 2152/2153:
I.W.M./Camera Press; 2154/2155: I.W.M./Camera Press; 2156: Keystone; 2157:
Keystone, I.W.M./Camera Press, Keystone; 2158: Keystone; 2159:
I.W.M./Camera Press, I.W.M./Camera Press, Popperfoto; 2160: Popperfoto;
2161: Novosti; 2162: Bibliothek für Zeitgeschichte/K. Adenauer, Orbis/Alan Rees;
2163: Keystone; 2164: Orbis; 2165: Novosti; 2166: Novosti; 2167: Orbis;
2168/2169: Blitz Publications; 2170: Orbis/Alan Rees, Blitz Publications; 2171:
Novosti; 2172/2173: Novosti; 2173: Keystone; 2174: Novosti; 2175:
I.W.M./Camera Press; 2176: I.W.M./Camera Press, Novosti; 2177:
I.W.M./Camera Press; 2178: U.S. Army; 2179: U.S. Army; Popperfoto,
I.W.M./Camera Press; 2180: I.W.M./Camera Press, Keystone; 2181: U.S. Army;
2182: Popperfoto; 2183: Popperfoto; 2184: Dr. A. Bernfes; 2185: Camera Press;
2186: Novosti, Camera Press; 2187: I.W.M./Camera Press, Novosti, Novosti;
2188: Novosti; 2189: Keystone, Novosti; 2190/2191: Keystone; 2192: Musée de la
Guerre, Vincennes/Dorka; 2193: Popperfoto, Novosti; 2194/2195: F.N.D.I.R.P.;
2196/2197: Popperfoto; 2197: Popperfoto; 2198: Popperfoto; 2199: Popperfoto;
2200: Keystone, Fox Photos; 2201: Novosti; 2202: Popperfoto, I.W.M./Camera
Press; 2203: Orbis/Alan Rees; 2204/2205: Novosti; 2204: Keystone; 2206: U.S. Army; 2207: Keystone, Deutsches Museum; 2208: I.W.M./Camera Press, Duetsches
Museum; 2209: Deutsches Museum; 2210/2211: Keystone, Deutsches Museum;
2212/2213: Keystone; 2213: Keystone, Keystone, I.W.M./Camera Press;
2214/2215: Deutsches Museum; 2216: Keystone, I.W.M./Camera Press; 2217:
Keystone; 2218/2219: Blitz Publications; 2220: Keystone; 2221: U.S. Army;
2222/2223: Keystone; 2224: Imperial War Museum, U.S. Air Force; 2224/2225:
Imperial War Museum; 2225: Keystone; 2226/2227: U.S. Army; 2228: Keystone;
2229: Bibliothek für Zeitgeschichte/K. Adenauer; 2230: I.W.M./Camera Press,
Keystone; 2231: Keystone; 2232: Orbis/Alan Rees; 2233: Keystone; 2234: U.S. Ar-
my; 2234/2235: U.S. Air Force; 2235: U.S. Air Force; 2236: I.W.M/Camera Press,
Popperfoto; 2237: U.S. Army; 2238/2239: I.W.M./Camera Press; 2240: Imperial
War Museum.

Contents of Volume Eight

CONTENTS OF VOLUME EIGHT

WORLD WAR II

△ *A bridge blown by American engineers erupts up into the sky as the Allies pull back.*

CHAPTER 135
The Ardennes gamble

It is now well known that the "Battle of the Bulge", the offensive often known as Rundstedt's, was in reality forced upon him, and that the rôle played by O.B. West in the attack begun on December 16 was limited to that of passing on to Army Group "B" the instructions of Hitler, Keitel, and Jodl at O.K.W.

It was quite clear to Rundstedt, Model, and even to Sepp Dietrich, that the objectives assigned to Operation *"Herbstnebel"* ("Autumn Fog") were far too ambitious for the Wehrmacht's limited capabilities, and they tried to convince the Führer of this. On the other hand they agreed with him – and history bears out their judgement – that if the Third Reich was not to be annihilated in less than six months, they would have to go over to the offensive, the Western Front being the only theatre where this might be possible. Italy was not vital to the Western Allies, even if the terrain and the season had made such an operation there successful; and in the East, it was generally agreed that they would not be able to force a decisive result. According to Major-General Gehlen's calculations, Stalin had something like

520 infantry divisions and more than 300 armoured and mechanised brigades at his command, and so could lose up to 30 divisions, or retreat up to 150 miles, without suffering a decisive defeat. In any case, what could be the advantage to the Germans of advancing once more to the Dniepr or the Dvina, if in the meantime the Western Allies broke through the *Westwall* and occupied the Ruhr and Saar basins?

The German chiefs thus agreed unanimously on a counter-offensive in the West, being fully aware of the logistical difficulties and man-power shortage by which Eisenhower was being plagued. However, there was deep disagreement between the Führer and his front-line generals on how far to carry the offensive. Hitler maintained that they ought to go all out, and inflict on Eisenhower a defeat as crushing as that suffered by Gamelin when the Panzer divisions had pushed through to the Somme estuary in 1940. And the fact that the Ardennes mountains were so lightly held seemed to provide him with an opportunity identical to the one he had exploited in May 1940 – we now know that he did in fact send to

Liegnitz for the documents pertaining to *"Fall Gelb"*. The plan was being prepared at H.Q. in absolute secrecy–and neither Rundstedt nor Model knew of it. Three armies were to take part: the newly formed 6th S.S. *Panzerarmee,* commanded by Colonel-General Dietrich; the 5th *Panzerarmee* under General Hasso von Manteuffel, which was withdrawn from the Aachen front (neither Model nor Rundstedt was informed of the rôle it was going to play); and the 7th Army, under General Brandenberger, which was then in the Eifel sector.

According to O.K.W.'s plan, the 5th and 6th *Panzerarmee* were to get to the Meuse in 48 hours; after this Sepp Dietrich, crossing the river north of Liège, would aim for Antwerp, via Saint Truiden and Aarschot, whilst Manteuffel, crossing the river on both sides of Namur, would aim for Brussels. The 7th Army would pivot round at Echternach and thus cover the operation against any Allied counter-attack coming from the south. With Manteuffel and Dietrich intercepting their communications at Namur and Antwerp, the whole of the Allied 21st Army Group, and most of the 12th Army Group, would be attacked on two fronts and annihilated, with the destruction of 37 of the 64 divisions that Eisenhower deployed at that time.

On October 24, Lieutenant-Generals Krebs and Westphal, chiefs-of-staff of Army Group "B" and of O.B. West respectively, had an interview with the Führer, who informed them of the plan which he had conceived, and whose execution was provisionally fixed for November 25. Both at Koblenz and at Field-Marshal Model's H.Q., the *Führer-befehl* had been severely criticised by those who would have to carry it out, as– and Krebs and Westphal had already hinted as much on a previous visit to O.K.W.–the plan bore no relationship to the resources being made available to them. Since, however, they were both in favour of a strategic counter-attack, on November 3 they submitted a counter-proposition to Hitler, better suited to the capabilities of Army Group "B", and called the "little solution" *(kleine Lösung).*

Instead of embarking on the very risky task of recapturing Antwerp, they suggested that it would be better to take advantage of the salient that the American 1st and 9th Armies had created in the *Westwall,* east and north-east of Aachen, and then envelop it in a pincer movement, enabling Dietrich to break out of the Roermond region and Manteuffel out of the Eifel region. If such an attack were completely successful, 20 Allied divisions would be destroyed and Model could then perhaps exploit Bradley's defeat and strike out for Antwerp.

As can be seen, Model, who had conceived this plan, and Rundstedt, who had forwarded it to O.K.W. with his approval, looked upon the operation as a mere sortie, just as the commander of a besieged 18th century fortress would suddenly make a night attack on the besieging forces, forcing them to start their siege preparations anew. But such an operation gained only a few weeks' respite and, sooner or later, unless help was forthcoming from elsewhere, surrender would be inevitable. Understandably then, Hitler angrily rejected such a solution, for what he needed was not a short respite,

◁ *Heavily laden German troops dash across a road in the Ardennes.*

but a decisive military victory in the West. So, as early as November 1, he had written at the head of his orders to O.B. West, that "the intention, the organisation, and the objective of this offensive are irrevocable". On receiving the counter-proposition of Model and Rundstedt, he got Jodl to reply within 24 hours that "the Führer has decided that the operation is irrevocably decided, down to its last details".

However, none of the H.Q. staff had solved any of the difficulties which the men in field command of the operation had felt obliged to point out. As Rundstedt explained on October 25, 1945, whilst being interrogated by Major Shulman of Canadian 1st Army Intelligence:

"When I was first told about the proposed offensive in the Ardennes, I protested against it as vigorously as I could. The forces at our disposal were much, much too weak for such far-reaching objectives. It was only up to one to obey. It was a nonsensical operation, and the most stupid part of it was the setting of Antwerp as the target. If

▽ *American vehicles captured by the Germans in Belgium. By the skilful and daring use of such captured equipment, the Germans hoped to sow distrust and worry in the Allied rear areas.*

we reached the Meuse we should have got down on our knees and thanked God – let alone try to reach Antwerp."

Hitler paid no more heed to Sepp Dietrich than he had to Model and Rundstedt, his only concession being to put back the date of the offensive from November 25, first to December 10, then to December 16. He also agreed to Manteuffel's suggestion to replace the three-hour artillery barrage that he had ordered by an artillery attack of only 45 minutes.

The forces assemble

The operation forced O.K.W. to redeploy its western forces. To free Model of any worries concerning his right wing, an Army Group "H" was organised, responsible for operations between the North Sea and Roermond, and commanded by Colonel-General Student, who relinquished his 1st Parachute Army to General Schlemm.

The 15th Army relieved the 5th *Panzerarmee* on the Roer, being relieved in turn between the North Sea and Nijmegen by a 25th Army under the command of General Christiansen.

According to General von Manteuffel,

at 0530 hours on December 16, 21 German divisions of all types launched their attack on the American line between Monschau and Echternach, on a 90-mile front. From north to south, the forces involved were:

1. 6th S.S. *Panzerarmee:* LXVII Corps (General Hitzfeld), with the 272nd and 326th *Volksgrenadier* Divisions; I S.S. Panzer Corps (General Priess), with the 277th and 12th *Volksgrenadier,* 3rd Parachute, and 1st and 12th S.S. Panzer Divisions; and II S.S. Panzer Corps (General Bittrich), with the 2nd and 9th S.S. Panzer Divisions.

2. 5th *Panzerarmee:* LXVI Corps (General Lucht), with the 18th and 62nd *Volksgrenadier* Divisions; LVIII Panzer Corps (General Krüger), with the 116th Panzer and 560th *Volksgrenadier* Divisions; and XLVII Panzer Corps (General von Lüttwitz), with the 2nd Panzer, Panzer-*"Lehr"*, and 26th *Volksgrenadier* Divisions.

3. 7th Army: LXXXV Corps (General Kniess), with the 5th Parachute and 352nd *Volksgrenadier* Divisions; and LXXX Corps (General Beyer), with the 276th and 212th *Volksgrenadier* Divisions.

It should be noted that although the four *Waffen*-S.S. Panzer divisions had been brought up to full strength, with a total of

△ *A section of U.S. infantry moves up into a Belgian village under cover of a Sherman tank.*

General Joseph "Sepp" Dietrich was born in 1892 in Bavaria. He was an early member of the Nazi Party, and soon after the Nazis' rise to power became a member of the *Reichstag* and of the Prussian assembly. Later he commanded Hitler's bodyguard and helped raise certain S.S. divisions. In 1942 he was given command of a corps on the Eastern Front and thereafter served in a variety of positions as a Panzer leader. He commanded the 6th *Panzerarmee* in the Ardennes.

Hasso Freiherr von Manteuffel was born into a military family in Potsdam on January 14, 1897. Educated in the Prussian cadet corps, he served in World War I. After the war he specialised in armoured warfare. In World War II he held a number of commands in France and the East. Following the July Plot he was still regarded as politically reliable and given the command of the 5th *Panzerarmee* during the Ardennes offensive. In April 1945 he led the 3rd *Panzerarmee*.

640 Panther and Pzkw IV tanks available to Dietrich, Manteuffel's three Panzer divisions had only been restored to about two-thirds of their full strength, about 320 tanks in all. And in fact, if they had been at full strength, the fuel problem would have been even more acute than it was. According to the plan, the Panzers should have attacked with sufficient petrol for five refuellings, which would have given them a range of up to 170 miles; on the day of the attack, they had only enough for two refills, as for camouflage reasons Hitler had forbidden the creation of fuel dumps close to the line. More important, he had made no allowances either for the difficult terrain or for the very bad weather. On December 28, describing the failure of the Ardennes offensive to his generals, Hitler described as follows the misfortunes that befell the 12th *"Hitlerjugend"* Panzer Division on the roads of the Ardennes:

"Only the first wave of the 12th S.S. Panzer Division's tanks was in action, whilst behind them there was an enormous convoy jammed solid, so that they could go neither forward nor back. Finally, not even the petrol could get through. Everything was stationary, and the tanks' engines were merely idling. To avoid frost damage, etc., the engines had to be run all night, which also had the advantage of keeping the men warm. This created enormous petrol requirements. The roads were bad. They could only use first gear . . . there was no end to it."

Skorzeny's special forces

Among the special forces used during this operation, mention should be made of the so-called 150th Panzer Brigade, made up of about 2,000 men conversant with American army slang, using jeeps and even old Sherman tanks rescued from the battlefield. The brigade had a double purpose: firstly, small patrols were to infiltrate the enemy lines and cause panic by spreading alarmist rumours and sabotaging telephone communications and signposts; then, when the breakthrough was being exploited, small motorised columns would be sent out to capture the Meuse bridges and hold them until the rest of the armour arrived.

This "Trojan horse" invented by Hitler was placed under the command of Otto Skorzeny, who had been promoted to colonel after capturing Admiral Horthy. The stratagem, which was quite contrary to the Geneva Convention, had some initial success because of its surprise element, but the counter-measures immediately devised by the Americans were most effective. Germans captured in American uniforms were immediately tried and shot, although some of them had only taken part in the operation when threatened with a German firing-squad.

The paratroops who spread confusion deep behind the American front line, even as far as France, never numbered more than 1,200, discounting the dummies used, and were commanded by Lieutenant-Colonel Heydte; but the pilots of the Junkers Ju 52s from which they were to jump were so badly trained that three-quarters of them jumped behind the German lines. The Allies thought they had been entrusted with the task of killing Eisenhower, but post-war research has revealed how groundless these suppositions were, although they did interfere with the normal functions of the Allied high command.

Inadequate reserves

Behind the first wave of troops, there were eight reserve divisions, seven of which were subject to O.K.W. orders. Model thus found himself with very little chance of exploiting any slight advantages he might gain without referring to Hitler. In addition there were two newly formed Panzer brigades, but that was all.

Theoretically, the attack was to be supported by 3,000 bombers and fighter-bombers, but on the first day a mere 325 planes took off, of which 80 were jets. Hitler could not bring himself to expose German towns to Allied air attacks by depriving them of fighter cover.

On December 10, O.K.W. left Berlin for Ziegenberg near Giessen, where, in preparation for the 1940 Blitzkrieg against France, a command post—never used—had been set up. It was here that two days later, having first made them hand in their pistols and brief-cases, Hitler harangued the commanders of the units engaged in this action. "There were about 30 generals including divisional commanders," writes Jacques Nobécourt. "They had been brought from Koblenz during the night by bus, twisting, turning, and going back on its tracks to deceive them regarding the

route being followed. All along the wall of the lecture hall stood S.S. men keeping an eagle eye on all present."

"No one in the audience dared move, or even take out a handkerchief," wrote Bayerlein, commander of the Panzer-*"Lehr"*, who thought Hitler looked ill and depressed.

"For two solid hours Hitler spoke, using no notes." Although we do not have the authentic verbatim account of his speech, the French version presented by Raymond Henry takes up 11 pages of his book. In it, Hitler once more reminded his listeners of the steadfastness of Frederick the Great refusing to surrender in 1761, in spite of the heavy pressure exerted on him by his brother, his ministers, and his generals; and Hitler spoke of the weakness of the coalition opposing Germany:

"On the one hand the ultra-capitalist states, on the other ultra-marxist states; on the one hand a great empire, the British Empire, slowly dying; on the other a colony just waiting to take over. Countries whose aims are becoming more and more different day by day. And if you watch closely, you can see differences arising hour by hour. A few well-struck blows and this artificial common front could come crashing down at any moment."

When Hitler had finished, Rundstedt assured him of the devoted loyalty of all his generals.

In the Allied camp

Amongst the Allies, the battle of the Ardennes was and has been the subject of considerable argument. It allowed Montgomery once more to lay claim to the title of head of Allied land forces, and even today the discussion rages between supporters of the American supreme commander and of his brilliant but independent second-in-command; just as for 20 years after the disappointing Battle of Jutland, there were divisions between supporters of Admiral Beatty, and those of Admiral Jellicoe. In his *Memoirs,* published in 1958, Montgomery expresses himself with his usual freedom, whereas Eisenhower, both during his tenure of the White House and during his later retirement, maintained a discreet silence.

We are here simply concerned with two questions: the first concerns the Allied forces holding the Ardennes, the second concerns the surprise offensive of December 16, 1944.

It must first be noted that with his right wing north of Trier and his left in the Losheim gap, south of Monschau, Major-General Middleton, commanding the American VIII Corps, held an 80-mile front with only four divisions. The 4th and 28th Divisions had been badly mauled in the unsuccessful attack on the

△ *Patton on a inspection tour. Unlike most of his compatriots, Patton realised that a major offensive through the Ardennes might be coming, and had already started laying contingency plans for switching his 3rd Army's axis of advance from east to north. This would take the German offensive in the flank and crush it.*

American transport finds it heavy going in the early winter mud of 1944.

Roer dams; the 9th Armoured Division (Major-General John W. Leonard) had never been under fire, nor had the 106th Division (Major-General Alan W. Jones) which had only taken over the Schnee Eifel sector of the front on December 11, after trailing all through France and southern Belgium in freezing rain and open lorries.

Bradley's dilemma

But did the Americans have any choice? In his *A Soldier's Story,* General Bradley explains the situation in a perfectly convincing way: to give Middleton more troops would have meant taking troops away from the two groups due to attack, to the north and south, in November. Even as it was, Hodges and Simpson had only 14 divisions between them for their 60-mile front north of the Ardennes, whilst to the south, Patton had only nine divisions, stretched over a 90-mile front. The Americans were so short of troops that the offensive was put back a week so that they could get back from Montgomery just one division they had lent him to mop up the Scheldt estuary. And to concentrate the 3rd Army's attack on a narrow front, the Americans had to transfer part of Patton's sector to Devers's 6th Army Group. If they had

wanted to reduce the risks of a German attack against Middleton's thinly held Ardennes positions, the Americans could have cancelled Patton's offensive, as Montgomery had suggested, and even dug in along the front for the winter. Both these alternatives were, to Bradley, out of the question. Middleton's forces would be stretched as thinly as possible, risking the chance of an enemy attack, and the Americans would throw all available divisions into the November offensive. Thus troops were taken away from the Ardennes to reinforce the winter offensive. It was a calculated risk which Bradley had decided to take, and one to which he stuck both then and afterwards.

Eisenhower, whilst claiming his due share of responsibility, justifies Bradley:

"The responsibility for maintaining only four divisions on the Ardennes front and for running the risk of a large German penetration in that area was mine. At any moment from November 1 onward I could have passed to the defensive along the whole front and made our lines absolutely secure from attack while we awaited reinforcements. My basic decision was to continue the offensive to the extreme limit of our ability, and it was this decision that was responsible for the startling successes of the first week of the German December attack."

It seems quite clear, after this, that the calculated risk about which Eisenhower

and Bradley talk was not something dreamed up after the event to excuse the weaknesses of their actions.

Hitler underestimated

It must be admitted, however, that Eisenhower and Bradley calculated things very tightly, as neither imagined for one minute that Hitler would fix Antwerp as the objective for his Panzers. And, of course, their reasoning followed the same lines as that of Model, Rundstedt, and Manteuffel, who all declared that the plan was impracticable and would have the most catastrophic consequences.

When he became aware of enemy troop concentrations, Colonel Dickson, head of General Hodges's Intelligence staff, said on December 10 that the defence of the Reich was based on the following strategy: the halting of the Allied offensive, followed by a counter-attack, with all forces concentrated between the Roer and the Erft.

In other words, Dickson assumed that if there was a counter-attack, it would follow the lines of the "little solution" that Rundstedt and Model had unsuccessfully suggested to Hitler, since more ambitious plans were far beyond the Wehrmacht's capabilities.

The Allies were thus quite aware that

German troops had been brought into position in readiness for a counter-attack, but they thought that these concentrations would form a flank attack on Hodges's troops preparing to attack Cologne, and that it would be combined with the breaching of the Roer dams. Later, Dickson's assumption was taken as being the correct one, and it was only on the day before the attack took place that Allied Intelligence found out that rubber boats and other craft had been assembled on the German side of the River Our.

Oddly enough, Colonel Koch, head of the American 3rd Army's Intelligence staff, was more worried than Dickson about the American situation; he even managed to get General Patton to share his apprehension, since on December 12 the latter ordered his chief-of-staff to work out "a study of what the Third Army would do if called upon to counter-attack such a break-through". And on the night of December 15-16, when he knew that the enemy was observing radio silence, he said "I want you, gentlemen, to start making plans for pulling the Third Army out of its eastward attack, change the direction ninety degrees, moving to Luxemburg and attacking north."

With all the information before us, Bradley was probably right when he said that although the Allies may have been wrong about the enemy's intentions, their estimate of his capabilities at that time was on the whole correct. For–and events were to bear this out in the following weeks–against forces as large as the Allies', Rundstedt did not have the resources necessary to ensure the success of an offensive strategy.

Thus, because they had failed to reckon with Adolf Hitler's megalomania, the Allied chiefs were caught badly napping on December 16–not least Field-Marshal Montgomery, who on the very morning of the German offensive had summed up the enemy's possibilities of action in the following words:

"The enemy is at present fighting a defensive campaign on all fronts, his situation is such that he cannot stage major offensive operations. Furthermore, at all costs he has to prevent the war from entering on a mobile phase; he has not the transport or the petrol that would be necessary for mobile operations, nor could his tanks compete with ours in the mobile battle."

▽ *Lieutenant-General Leonard T. Gerow. As a major-general, Gerow commanded the American V Corps, which was holding the sector of the Ardennes front attacked by the right wing of Dietrich's 6th* Panzerarmee.

CHAPTER 136
Battle of the Bulge

On the first day of the offensive, the 6th S.S. *Panzerarmee* attacked with its infantry divisions, keeping its Panzers in reserve to exploit the initial success. On the right it came up against the American 2nd and 99th Divisions, of V Corps, still commanded by Major-General Leonard Gerow; the 2nd Division was an experienced, battle-hardened unit which overcame its surprise very quickly, whereas the 99th Division, which had never before seen major action, had more difficulty in recovering its composure. In the end, V Corps managed to hold on to the Elsenborn ridge in spite of all enemy attacks. But Dietrich easily broke through the Losheim gap, lightly held by the 14th Armoured Division, which opened up the road to Stavelot, and in addition enabled him to turn the left flank of the 106th Division.

On the very same day this division was pierced on its left by the 5th *Panzerarmee*'s attack, which also threw back the 28th Division towards Clervaux (Clerf). The two regiments of the 106th Division holding the Schnee Eifel plateau were in imminent danger of being surrounded.

The 7th Army, reduced to four divisions, had to be satisfied with pivoting

▽ Yet again, the qualitative inferiority of Allied armour was demonstrated during the "Battle of the Bulge".

around Echternach, instead of including Luxembourg in its plan of attack, as originally planned. Although it had to yield some ground, the American 4th Division, which made up Middleton's right flank, was less severely tested than the 28th.

The Allied response

When the first news of the German attack reached S.H.A.E.F., Bradley was in Versailles, conferring with General Bedell Smith, Eisenhower's chief-of-staff. A few hours later, a further report indicated that the American 1st Army had identified eight German divisions.

Eisenhower and Bradley immediately realised the implications of this offensive, but the reserves available to them on December 16 were even less than those available to General Gamelin on May 13, 1940. They were in fact limited to XVIII Airborne Corps (Major-General Ridgeway), two of whose divisions, the 82nd and the 101st, were being reformed near Rheims, after two months' action in the Nijmegen salient. This corps was immediately alerted, and the 9th and 3rd Armies received orders to make their 7th and 10th Armoured Divisions respectively available to the 1st Army.

In a few days' time Eisenhower would also be able to call upon the 2nd Armoured Division, which had just landed in France, as well as the 87th Division and the 17th Airborne Division, which

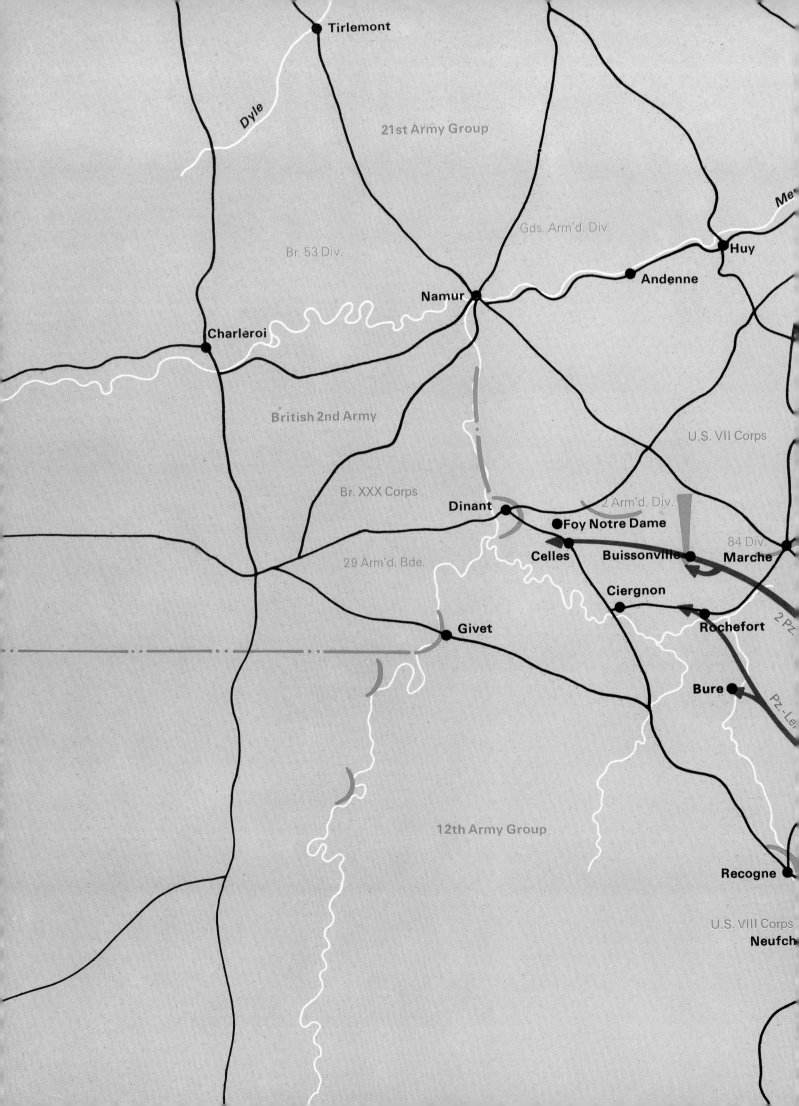

Tirlemont

Dyle

21st Army Group

Gds. Arm'd. Div.

Me

Huy

Br. 53 Div.

Andenne

Namur

Charleroi

British 2nd Army

U.S. VII Corps

Br. XXX Corps

2 Arm'd. Div.

Dinant

84 Div.

Foy Notre Dame

Celles

Buissonville

Marche

29 Arm'd. Bde.

Ciergnon

2 Pz.

Givet

Rochefort

Pz. Le

Bure

12th Army Group

Recogne

U.S. VIII Corps

Neufch

were still in England, but about to embark for France. Even then it would take time for them to come into the line, In addition, although the successes of Skorzeny's commandos and von der Heydte's paratroopers were very slight, rumour greatly magnified them. Above all, the bad weather of that week reduced Allied air strikes almost to nothing. But "low cloud" and "thick fog" were phrases that the weather forecasters repeated with monotonous regularity throughout the week December 16-23.

The Germans waver

In the public mind the Ardennes campaign is summed up in the one word: Bastogne, and rightly so, since Brigadier-General A. C. McAuliffe and his 101st Airborne Division fought heroically around the little town, although the behaviour under fire of the 7th Armoured Division and its commander, Brigadier-General Robert Hasbrook, was also worthy of the highest praise. Between December 18 and 22, the defensive position of Saint Vith compelled the 5th *Panzer-armee* to disperse its energies, and the town was only evacuated after an express order.

It is true that on December 19, in the Schnee Eifel plateau region, two regi-

ments of the 106th Division were trapped, and 6,000 men had to surrender, but everywhere else the Americans stood up gallantly under all the attacks. As Jacques Mordal very rightly says:

"The great merit of the American troops was that despite the surprise and initial disorder, a few commanders and a few handfuls of troops were found who saved the situation by holding on grimly to certain vital positions; and it may be said that rarely has the fate of so many divisions depended on a few isolated engagements. A mere handful of artillerymen firing their few guns saved Bütgenbach on December 16, and prevented the complete isolation of the 2nd and 99th Divisions. A battalion of sappers was to save Malmédy; and a company of the 51st Engineer Combat Battalion stopped the advance of the leading elements of *Kampfgruppe* 'Peiper'. They blew up the Trois-Ponts bridge across the Salm, and forced Peiper to go back via Amblève, and find a further bridge at Werbomont,

◁ *German troops pass a knocked-out American motor transport column.*
▽ ◁ *German soldiers help themselves to clothing and equipment from American dead. Note the bare feet of the corpse on the left.*
▽ *A Königstiger or Tiger II heavy tank advances through the heavily-forested Ardennes hills.*

where the pioneers of the 291st Battalion fought heroically to prevent his crossing; for the second time the German troops saw a bridge being blown up in front of them, and they also suffered severe losses from air attacks launched in spite of the bad weather.

"Stavelot, lost on December 17, was recaptured two days later. The battle went on in the sunken valley of the Amblève, where after five days of hard combat, Peiper, out of fuel, was forced to leave behind all his equipment and withdraw the few hundred men remaining on foot, in the snow, and following impossible tracks."

Slow advance

On the German side, Dietrich made the big mistake of stubbornly trying to take the Elsenborn ridge, whose defences had been greatly strengthened by the transfer to General Gerow of that first-class fighting unit, the American 1st Division; thus the 12th *"Hitlerjugend"* S.S. Panzer Division was halted around Bütgenbach. As for the celebrated *"Leibstandarte"*, it became separated from its advanced

elements, which had pushed forward into the Amblève valley, on Colonel Peiper's orders. In short, four days after the initial attack, the 6th *Panzerarmee* was still far from the Meuse bridges–which it should have reached within 72 hours.

Bastogne reached

On Dietrich's left, Manteuffel had shown more tactical flair, being further helped by the fact that General Hodges was finding it more difficult to reinforce his VIII Corps in Luxembourg than between Elsenborn and Trois-Ponts; Clervaux and Wiltz fell easily, thus opening up the way to Bastogne. Faced with this most unexpected development–for after all, it had been thought that Dietrich's forces would have the starring rôle in this offensive–Model and Rundstedt recommended the immediate transfer of II S.S. Panzer Corps from the 5th to the 6th *Panzerarmee*, following the principle that successful operations ought to be exploited in preference to the less successful.

But Hitler refused categorically to allow this transfer; no doubt because he dreaded admitting, even implicitly, the failure of Dietrich and the *Waffen*-S.S., and did not want to place one of the Nazi Party's armed units under the command of the Wehrmacht generals for whom for a long time he felt nothing but mistrust, and even hate.

Had Eisenhower known that his adversary was making this tactical mistake, he would probably have refrained from taking some of the measures which marked his intervention on December 19. But with all his reports from the front indicating that Bastogne and the 101st Airborne Division were practically surrounded, he decided that the time had come to throw all his authority into the struggle. So, at 1100 hours on December 19, he convened a meeting with Bradley and Devers, together with Patton.

Eisenhower decides on his counter-offensive

According to his memoirs, Eisenhower opened the meeting by declaring that "the present situation is to be regarded as one of opportunity for us and not disaster. There will be only cheerful faces at this conference table."

And in fact these confident phrases represented exactly the calm coolness that Eisenhower really felt on that important day. Thus the American historian Ladislas Farago, in his biography of General Patton, which he bases upon numerous unpublished documents and eye-witness accounts, has written:

"The historic Verdun conference of 19th December 1944 was, I submit, one of the high points of Dwight D. Eisenhower's generalship in the war. He was variously described as having been pale and nervous, showing not only signs of the strain but also an intimate kind of concern, as if he worried about his personal future in the aftermath of this crisis. Actually, Ike was in top form, concise and lucid, holding the conference with iron hands to its key issue–the Allied counter-attack. It was obvious to all that he knew what he wanted and was the full master of the situation. He had in full measure that special inner strength which always filled him when he was called upon to make *absolute* decisions."

◁ *The penalty of failure: men of Otto Skorzeny's special commando, caught in American uniforms, are prepared for the firing squad.*
▽ ◁ *American prisoners are marched off to the rear past a column of advancing German armour. Note the faces of the prisoners, deliberately rendered unrecognisable.*
▽ *The tide begins to turn: a Tiger II tank knocked out during the bitter fighting for the small town of Stavelot.*

The German *Panzerjäger* Tiger or *Jagdtiger* tank destroyer

Weight: 70.6 tons.
Crew: 6.
Armament: one 12.8-cm PaK 80 L/55 gun with 38
rounds and one MG 34 machine gun.
Armour: hull front 100-mm, sides and rear 80-mm, and
belly and decking 40-mm; superstructure front 250-mm,
sides and rear 80-mm, and roof 40-mm.
Engine: one Maybach HL 230 P30 inline, 700-hp.
Speed: 23.6 mph on roads and 12 mph cross-country.
Range: 100 miles on roads and 75 miles cross-country.
Length: 34 feet 11½ inches.
Width: 11 feet 10¾ inches with battle tracks, and 10 feet
8¾ inches with narrow tracks.
Height: 9 feet 3 inches.

The main decision taken was to move the six divisions of General Patton's III and XII Corps from the Saar front to the Echternach–Diekirch–Bastogne front, at the same time subordinating VIII Corps to the 3rd Army. This meant that the right flank of General Devers's army group would be extended from Bitche to Saarbrücken. Such a manoeuvre had already been discussed at 3rd Army H.Q., so that a single telephone call made from Verdun by its commander was enough to get it started. According to Farago, this order, which meant the moving of 133,178 vehicles over a total of some 1,500,000 miles, was carried out in five days. During this time, the 3rd Army's rear echelons transported 62,000 tons of supplies, the Intelligence staff distributed thousands of maps of the new sector, and the communications section put down 40,000 yards of telephone cable.

And all this was achieved in snow and on roads covered with black ice. This proves that Patton may have been a swashbuckler (that very day he said to Bradley: "' Brad, this time the Kraut's stuck his head in the meatgrinder.' With a turn of his fist he added, 'And this time I've got hold of the handle.'''), but he was also a thinker, and an organiser of the highest class. This combination of intellect and dash made Patton unique.

On December 20, Eisenhower placed Montgomery in charge of the northern flank of the German penetration (with the U.S. 1st and 9th armies under his command), and gave Bradley the southern flank. As he reported to the Combined Chiefs-of-Staff: with the enemy thrusting towards Namur, "our front is divided into two main parts on each of which we must act aggressively and with our full capabilities."

▽ *An American mortar crew in action. With its lightweight and simple construction, the mortar was an ideal infantry weapon.*

▷ German prisoners from a Volksgrenadier regiment await removal to a P.O.W. camp.
▽ The aftermath of the Ardennes gamble: a dead German soldier lies in the street of a Belgian town.
▽ ▷ American troops prepare for the counter-offensive that was to end any hope of German success.

Bastogne hangs on

On the morning of December 19, the 101st Division entered Bastogne, joining up with those elements of the 9th and 10th Armoured Divisions defending the town. The next day, XLVII Panzer Corps, following its instructions, bypassed the town to north and south, leaving the 26th *Volksgrenadier* Division the job of laying siege to it. When the commander of this formation, Lieutenant-General Heinz Kokott, called upon General McAuliffe to surrender, he received the rudest of replies: "Nuts". The garrison's high morale was kept up, firstly, by the wholehearted support of the town population under their mayor, Monsieur Jacmin, and secondly by the sound of III Corps' guns announcing the beginning of the counter-attack in the south.

On the northern half of the bulge, an attack by the 30th Division, called by the Germans "Roosevelt's S.S.", enabled Hodges to close up the Amblève valley sector by lengthening the position held by V Corps. However, by sending in II S.S. Panzer Corps to the left of I S.S. Panzer Corps, Dietrich succeeded in revitalising the offensive, forcing Hasbrook to evacuate Saint Vith on December 21. The intervention, firstly of XVIII Airborne Corps (although reduced to the 82nd Airborne Division), and secondly, of General Collins's VII Corps, comprising the 75th, 83rd, and 84th Divisions, and the 3rd Armoured Division, enabled a continuous front to be re-established on a line Manhay – Grandmenil – Hotton – Marche.

Montgomery steps in

In carrying out his tasks as commander of the 21st Army Group, Montgomery had a few difficulties with his American subordinates. His main aim was to prevent the Germans from crossing the Meuse, and provided this was done he was not very worried by the loss of a small Ardennes village here or there. He conducted the campaign according to the methods of 1918: plug the gap then, when quite ready, counter-attack. Hodges, Collins, and Ridgeway, on the other hand, hated giving up ground, and wanted to make the enemy feel the weight of their strength. To guard against every eventuality, the meticulous Montgomery established General Horrocks's British XXX Corps, comprising the 43rd, 51st, and 53rd Divisions, and the Guards Armoured Division half-way between Namur and Brussels, thereby greatly facilitating the American 1st Army's movements, which up to December 24, had involved 248,000 men and 48,000 vehicles.

By December 22, at Koblenz, Rundstedt had decided upon immediate withdrawal from the engagement, already running into trouble. Of course, Hitler, at

△ △ *3rd Army infantry advance to the relief of beleaguered Bastogne.*
△ *A soldier of the 3rd Army works his way forward under a barbed wire fence about five miles from Bastogne.*

△ An American dug-in mortar emplacement. From left to right the members of the crew are Private R. W. Fierdo of Wyahoga Falls, Ohio; Staff Sergeant Adam J. Celinca of Windeor, Connecticut; and Technical Sergeant W. O. Thomas of Chicago, Illinois.
▷ M4 Shermans of the 40th Tank Battalion lined up outside St. Vith.
△▷ The ruins of St. Vith after its recapture by the U.S. 7th Armoured Division.
▷▷ En route from Hunnange to St. Vith: men of Company C, 23rd Armoured Battalion, 7th Armoured Division.

Ziegenberg, refused to ratify this suggestion; he thought that if they threw in the O.K.W. reserves, especially the 9th Panzer and 3rd and 15th *Panzergrenadier* Divisions, they would be able to resume the offensive, or at least capture Bastogne, the main thorn in their side.

Allied air power to the fore

On December 23, an anti-cyclone brought with it a week of brilliant sunshine over the whole of the Ardennes front. The Allied air forces were immediately unleashed, flying 2,000 missions on the first day, and 15,000 in the next three days. On Christmas Eve, at a cost of 39 planes lost, 2,000 American bombers, escorted by 900 fighters, attacked the airfields near Frankfurt and the communications networks of Kaiserslautern, Bad Munster, Koblenz, Neuwied, and Euskirchen. At the same time, other air attacks were successfully launched on the enemy's

rear and on certain battlefield objectives. Last, but not least, 961 Dakotas and 61 gliders were able to drop 850 tons of supplies and ammunition to beleaguered Bastogne.

On the darker side, the small town of Malmédy, already in American hands, was twice bombed in error. Whilst the 6th *Panzerarmee* was now exhausted, the 5th managed to advance yet again some 25 miles on a line Saint Hubert–Rochefort–Dinant, moving north-west.

This movement laid bare Patton's left flank, and Eisenhower transferred to the 3rd Army the 87th Division, the 11th Armoured Division, and the 17th Airborne Division. Thus, by December 24, 32 Allied divisions were in action or in reserve on the Ardennes front, against 29 German divisions calculated by S.H.A.E.F. to be involved.

2nd Panzer Division wiped out

Faced with this further deterioration of the situation, Rundstedt renewed his plea that the offensive be abandoned. He was very strongly supported this time by General Guderian, who knew that in the East, Soviet forces were massing on the Vistula bridge-heads. Once again the Führer refused categorically, in spite of the arguments of his H.Q., only too aware of the disasters that his obstinacy would inevitably bring. In the meantime Lieutenant-General von Lauchert's 2nd Panzer Division had reached Ciney, Beauraing, and Celles, in contact with the British 29th Armoured Brigade, and only six miles from the Meuse at Dinant. On Christmas Day, it suffered a flank attack at the hands of the American 2nd Armoured Division (Major-General Harmon), which had just been transferred to VII Corps. The effect was one of total surprise, and the disaster was no less complete. By the end of the day, Lauchert's losses were as follows: 1,050 prisoners, 2,500 killed, 81 tanks (out of a total of 88), seven assault guns, all his artillery (74 pieces), and 405 vehicles. That day the American 2nd Armoured Division certainly lived up to its nickname of "Hell on Wheels". Confronted with this crushing blow, Manteuffel could only withdraw his XLVII Panzer Corps to Rochefort.

△ As the weather improved, Allied air power began to play a decisive part in the battle, not only offensively with strikes against German armour, but also defensively with supply drops. Here part of the massive Dakota fleet passes over a Sherman on its way to drop food and ammunition into Bastogne.
▷ Men of the U.S. 1st Army dig in on the northern side of the salient driven into the Allied front by the German attack.
▽ British troops, who were met by the Germans at the furthest extent of their penetration to the west. The leading Sherman is fitted with a 17-pounder gun, far superior to the more usual 75- and 76-mm guns.

Patton relieves Bastogne

Patton's 3rd Army had a little more difficulty in relieving Bastogne, as the German 5th Parachute Division under Lieutenant-General Hellmann, on the right of the German 7th Army, put up a very spirited resistance. It was not until December 26 that the American 4th Armoured Division under Major-General Gaffey managed to link up with the beleaguered garrison, and even then it was only by means of a narrow corridor a few hundred yards wide.

Half-success into defeat

Faced with these defeats, Hitler disengaged. But was he deceiving himself, or trying to deceive others? On December 28, haranguing his generals who were about to take part in Operation *"Nordwind"*, against the American 7th Army, he pretended to be satisfied with the results of *"Herbstnebel"*:

"There is no doubt that our short offensive has had the initial result of greatly easing the situation along the whole front, although unfortunately it has not had quite the great success we expected. The enemy has been forced to abandon all idea of attack; he has been compelled to regroup his forces completely, and put back into action troops completely worn out by previous engage-

ments. His strategic intentions have been completely thwarted. The psychological factor is against him, for public opinion is bitterly critical. He now has to assert that an end to the fighting cannot be envisaged before August, perhaps before the end of the year. We have therefore a complete reversal of the situation, which was certainly not considered possible a fortnight ago."

What does all this mean? Probably that Hitler would have been far better advised to have taken his head out of the "meatgrinder", when the results were in his favour. However, instead of rapidly withdrawing his 5th and 6th *Panzerarmee* behind the *Westwall*, he insisted

△ *Private Frank Vukasin of Great Falls, Montana, reloads his Garand M1 beside the corpses of two Germans during the 83rd Division's attack towards Houffalize.*

▽ *The bitterness of the fighting for Bastogne can be gauged from this photograph of German dead caught by American machine gun fire after their protecting tanks had been knocked out.*

▽ *American manpower tells: as the German effort flagged for lack of replacements, Eisenhower was able to keep a constant supply of men and* matériel *flowing into the threatened sector.*

on their trying to hold the Ardennes salient in impossible conditions, so turning his half-success of December 16 into a clear failure. That this is so is clear from the losses of the two sides: in manpower the Americans had suffered 76,890 casualties to the Germans' 81,834; in tanks 733 to 324; and aircraft 592 to 320. Whereas the Americans could replace their matériel losses with little difficulty, the Germans could not.

When one realises that German possibilities of rebuilding the Wehrmacht's strength were slowly diminishing, and that on January 12, 1945 Stalin unleashed his fifth and last winter offensive, there is no doubt that

these figures confirm the German defeat, not only in the Ardennes, but on the whole of the Western Front.

To the despair of Guderian the abandonment of Operation "Herbstnebel" did not mean a reinforcement of the Eastern Front forces, for Hitler saw "Herbstnebel" as only the first of a set of offensives in the West. The first, aimed at the recovery of Alsace and Lorraine, was propounded by Hitler to his generals on December 18. "Our first objective", he said, "must be to clean up the situation in the West by offensive action."

In this mood of total fantasy, Germany's Supreme Commander brought in the New Year, 1945.

East Prussia invaded

Previous page: *A battery of*
Soviet 203-mm howitzers
prepares to fire the opening
barrage of the final offensive of
the war in the East. The
Russians massed 43 divisions of
artillery to give the 1st
Belorussian and 1st Ukrainian
Fronts a superiority of nearly
eight to one in guns and
mortars.

January 12, 1945 saw the Red Army pour out in a great torrent over the bridgeheads it had won the previous summer on the left bank of the Vistula. Two days later it was assaulting the German positions on the Narew and the defences of Eastern Prussia which, three months earlier, had defied the efforts of Zakharov and Chernyakhovsky. Two months later Konev crossed the Oder both above and below Breslau (Wrocław), Zhukov reached it between Frankfurt and Küstrin (Kostrzyn), Rokossovsky was at its mouth and Vasilevsky was about to take Königsberg.

To the Wehrmacht, the Third Reich, and Hitler, defeated also on the Western Front, this was the death blow. It was to mean the end of nine centuries of conquest, occupation, and civilisation by the Germans of the whole area between the Oder-Neisse line and the eastern frontiers of Germany as drawn up at Versailles. By May 8, 1945 nearly eight million inhabitants of East Prussia, Pomerania, and the borderland between Brandenburg and Silesia had fled their homes before the invading Soviets. Over three and a half million more Germans were to be driven out of these same areas between 1945 and 1950. The defeat of Germany's military might was thus to bring about the greatest movement of peoples since the collapse of the Roman Empire.

109 divisions in the West . . .

We turn now to the forces with which Germany fought the Red Army in the last stage of their merciless duel.

At the turn of the year O.K.W. had 288 divisions, including 45 Panzer and *Panzergrenadier*. This number does not, however, include the divisions in course of formation under *Reichsführer* Heinrich Himmler, C.-in-C. of the *Ersatzheer* since the attempt on Hitler's life of July 20, 1944. In any case, this grandiose total is misleading, as all formations were under-strength and short of equipment.

124 of these divisions were under O.K.W.:

O.B. West (France) under Rundstedt:	74
O.B. *Süd* (Italy) under Kesselring:	24
O.B. *Süd-Ost* (Bosnia and Croatia) under Weichs:	9
Crete, Rhodes, and dependencies:	2
20th Mountain Army (Norway) under Rendulic:	15

Take away from this total the *Süd-Ost* forces fighting the Yugoslav Liberation Army and the six divisions of Colonel-General Rendulic keeping the Russians out of Narvik in the area of Lyngenfjord, and we see that the Western fronts between them were engaging 109 German divisions, or some 40 per cent of Germany's military strength at the end of 1944.

. . . and 164 in the East against massive opposition

This gave O.K.H. 164 divisions with which to fight the Red Army on a front running from the Drava at Barcs on its right to the Gulf of Riga in the area of Tukums on its left. Army Group "South" in Hungary (General Wöhler) had 38 divisions, including 15 Panzer or *Panzergrenadier*. In the Kurland bridgehead Colonel-General Schörner had 27 divisions, including three Panzer. This left 99 divisions for Army Groups "A" and "Centre" to hold the front between the southern slopes of the Carpathians and Memel on the Baltic.

▽ *A troop of SU-76 assault guns grinds across the frost-covered plains of north Germany.*

Gehlen's warning

When Major-General Gehlen reported his conclusion that a powerful enemy offensive was imminent against Army Groups "A" and "Centre", Guderian expressed his dissatisfaction with the deployment of the German forces. He wanted Kurland to be evacuated and no more reinforcements to be sent to the Hungarian theatre of operations. In his opinion, the essential thing was to protect Germany from the invasion now threatening her and, to this end, to keep the enemy out of the approaches to upper Silesia, to Breslau, Berlin, Danzig, and Königsberg.

He put this to Hitler and his O.K.W. colleagues at Ziegenberg on December 24. But, as we have pointed out before, Gehlen's report left the Führer incredulous. Worse still, when Guderian had got back to Zossen, south of Berlin, where O.K.H. had moved after the evacuation of Rastenburg, he was informed that during his return journey he had been deprived of IV S.S. Panzer Corps, which

was now to go to the Hungarian front. The corps was in Army Group "Centre" reserve behind the Narew, and this group's mobile reserves between the Carpathians and the Baltic were thus reduced at a stroke from 14 to 12 divisions, or, if they were all up to strength, by 1,350 armoured vehicles.

Guderian warns Hitler and Jodl

In spite of this snub, Guderian went back to Ziegenberg on January 1, 1945 in the hope of getting O.K.W. to see things his way. In his view, the centre of gravity of German strategy had to be brought back to the Eastern Front. But when Himmler was about to unleash the *"Nordwind"* offensive which was to follow *"Herbstnebel"*, with Saverne as its objective, Jodl was as unenthusiastic about Guderian's ideas as Hitler had been. "We have no right," he pointed out to him, "to give up the initiative we have just regained;

△ *An SU-100 roars through the blasted and deserted remains of a German town. The heroic image of the armoured warrior making new conquests with each campaign was now returning to plague the Germans.*

1990

we can always give ground in the East, but never in the West."

Shown the door for the second time, Guderian nevertheless made a third attempt to see Hitler to remind him of his responsibilities towards the Eastern Front. As the days passed without any decision being made, the Russians completed their preparations and, according to Gehlen's reckoning, their "steam-roller", now building up its pressure, had at least: 231 infantry divisions, 22 tank corps, 29 independent tank brigades, and three cavalry corps, supported by air forces that the Luftwaffe could not hope to match.

After taking the advice of Colonel-Generals Harpe and Reinhardt, commanders of Army Groups "A" and "Centre", against which the threat was mounting, Guderian drew up the following programme and presented it to Hitler on January 9:

1. Evacuation of the Kurland bridge-head.
2. Transfer to the East of a number of armoured units then fighting on the Western Front.
3. Abandonment of the line of the Narew and withdrawal of Army Group "Centre" to the East Prussian frontier, which was shorter and better protected.
4. Evacuation of the Army Group "A" salient between the bridge at Baranów and Magnuszew through which, according to Gehlen, 91 Soviet infantry divisions, one cavalry corps, 13 tank corps, and nine tank brigades were ready to break out.

In presenting these proposals, Guderian might have had in mind Jodl's opinion that some ground could still be sacrificed in the East. But he had hardly put before Hitler the comparative table of opposing forces which accompanied the plan, than the Führer broke out into a spate of abuse and sarcasm. A violent scene then took place which Guderian has described as follows:

"Gehlen had very carefully prepared the documentation on the enemy situation, with maps and diagrams which gave a clear idea of the respective strengths. Hitler flew into a rage when I showed them to him, called them 'absolutely stupid' and demanded that I send their author immediately to a lunatic asylum. I too became angry then. 'This is General Gehlen's work,' I said to Hitler. 'He is one of my best staff officers. I wouldn't

have submitted it to you if I hadn't first agreed it myself. If you demand that General Gehlen be put into an asylum, then send me to one too!' I curtly refused to carry out Hitler's order to relieve Gehlen of his post. The storm then calmed down. But no good came of it from a military point of view. Harpe's and Reinhardt's proposals were turned down to the accompaniment of the expected odious remarks about generals for whom 'manoeuvre' only meant 'withdraw to the next rearward position'. This was all very unpleasant."

What threat?

As in Hitler's eyes the Soviet threat was insignificant, not to say non-existent, the measures to meet it proposed by Guderian were therefore completely meaningless. A strictly logical conclusion, such as madmen are liable to arrive at after starting from radically wrong premises, led Hitler to give Guderian this meagre food for thought for his return journey to Zossen: "The Eastern Front must fend for itself and make do with what it has got." Could it be that Guderian was right when he said that Hitler the Austrian and Jodl the Bavarian were indifferent to the threat to Prussia? That might be somewhat far-fetched, but one might equally well suppose that Guderian the Prussian was ready to accept defeat in the West if the 6th *Panzerarmee*'s reinforcements were to be taken out of the Ardennes and given to him to block the Soviet advance towards Berlin. The least we can say is that events confirmed this latter assumption.

In any event it is clear that, reasoning *a priori* as was his custom and despite always being contradicted by events, Hitler took it that Stalin's intention was to deploy his main effort in the Danube basin towards Vienna, the second capital of the Reich, then Munich. On the other hand, after allowing IX S.S. Mountain Corps to become encircled in the so-called fortress of Budapest, it now seemed to Hitler that he should extricate it again as a matter of urgency.

So if the Eastern Front was required to go it alone, the Führer did not give any priority to dealing with Soviet advances towards Königsberg and Berlin or providing any of the resources necessary to stop them.

△ General I. D. Chernyakhovsky, one of the Red Army's brightest stars and commander of the 3rd Belorussian Front until his death in action on February 18.
◁ △ Members of the Volkssturm line up for an inspection. The equivalent of Britain's Home Guard, they formed a last line of defence against the numerically superior Russian forces.
◁ ▽ General Guderian: he argued in vain against Hitler's lunatic theories.

△ Marshal of the Soviet Union A. M. Vasilevsky, who assumed command of the 3rd Belorussian Front on Chernyakhovsky's death. He was on the spot to co-ordinate the final attacks of the 1st Baltic and 3rd Belorussian Fronts in the crushing of East Prussia.

△ *A German freighter on the
run from Danzig is caught by
the Red Air Force. Though
Hitler's "stand and fight"
orders severely hampered the
garrisons along the Baltic
coast, they received heroic
support from the navy.
Warships gave close support, and
the merchant marine
evacuated over two million
refugees.*

German strength

On January 12, 1945 German forces were
deployed between the Carpathians and
the Baltic as follows:
1. Army Group "A" (Colonel-General J.
   Harpe), with the 1st *Panzerarmee*
   (Colonel-General G. Heinrici), 17th
   Army (General F. Schulz), 4th *Pan-
   zerarmee* (General F. Gräser), and
   9th Army (General S. von Lüttwitz).
2. Army Group "Centre" (Colonel-
   General G. Reinhardt), with the 2nd
   Army (Colonel-General W. Weiss), 4th
   Army (General F. Hossbach), and 3rd
   Panzerarmee (Colonel-General . E.
   Raus).

The Soviet steamroller

1. Enormous manpower
On January 1, 1945 *Stavka*'s strength,
according to Field-Marshal von Man-
stein, was as follows: 527 infantry and
43 artillery divisions, and 302 tank and
mechanised brigades, totalling 5,300,000
men, to the Germans' 164 divisions
(1,800,000 men) on the Eastern Front.

2. The JS-3 tank
In the last six-month period, Soviet
armoured strength had increased from
9,000 to about 13,400 vehicles, in spite of
battle losses. This was all the more
remarkable in that the Russians had
changed over from the heavy KV-85 to
the Stalin tank. This weighed 45 tons and
its 122-mm gun was the most powerful
tank gun of the war. It had a 600-hp
diesel engine, a range of 120 miles, and a
top speed of 25 mph. The Soviets also
continued to build self-propelled guns,
and in particular their SU-85, 100, and 152
vehicles were to take heavy toll of both
German permanent and field fortifications.

3. Zhukov's and Konev's enormous resources
If we refer to Alexander Werth's version
of *The Great Patriotic War*, Volume 5,
we see that *Stavka* allotted to Marshals
Zhukov and Konev, commanders of the
1st Belorussian and 1st Ukrainian Fronts

respectively, the following forces:

1. 160 infantry divisions;
2. 32,143 guns and mortars;
3. 6,460 tanks and self-propelled guns; and
4. 4,772 aircraft.

The air forces were divided into two air armies, one to each front. The 16th Air Army (General S. I. Rudenko) was under Marshal Zhukov and the 2nd (General S. A. Krasovsky) under Marshal Konev. *Stavka* had thus done things well and the 1st Belorussian and 1st Ukrainian Fronts had a superiority over the German Army Group "A", according to Werth, of:

(a) 5.5 to 1 in men;
(b) 7.8 to 1 in guns and mortars;
(c) 5.7 to 1 in armoured vehicles; and
(d) 17.7 to 1 in aircraft.

If we realise that the superiority of the 2nd and 3rd Belorussian Fronts (respectively under Marshal Rokossovsky and General Chernyakhovsky) must have been similar, it will be realised that, rather than trying to create a bogey with which to frighten Hitler, Gehlen was on the contrary somewhat modest in his calculations.

Churchill urges Stalin on

The start of the Soviet fourth winter offensive had been fixed for January 20. In fact, it started on the 12th on the 1st Ukrainian Front as the result of an urgent approach to Stalin by Churchill. When he got back from S.H.A.E.F. on January 6, a visit to which we shall refer again, the British Prime Minister sent a very detailed telegram to the Kremlin in these terms:

"The battle in the West is very heavy and, at any time, large decisions may be called for from the Supreme Command. You know yourself from your own experience how very anxious the position is when a very broad front has to be defended after temporary loss of the initiative. It is General Eisenhower's great desire and need to know in outline what you plan to do, as this obviously affects all his and our major decisions. Our Envoy, Air Chief Marshal Tedder, was last night reported weather-bound in Cairo. His journey has been much delayed through no fault of yours. In case he has not reached you yet, I shall be grateful if you can tell me whether we can count on a major Russian offensive on the Vistula front, or elsewhere, during January, with any other points you may care to mention. I shall not pass this most secret information to anyone except Field Marshal Brooke and General Eisenhower, and only under conditions of the utmost secrecy. I regard the matter as urgent."

Approached in these terms, Stalin did not have to be asked twice. Before 24 hours had passed, he replied to Churchill in exceptionally warm terms. Only the weather conditions, he said, preventing the Red Army from taking advantage of its superior strength in artillery and aircraft, were holding back the start of the offensive:

"Still, in view of our Allies' position on the Western Front, GHQ of the Supreme Command have decided to complete preparations at a rapid rate and, regardless of weather, to launch large-scale offensive operations along the entire Central Front not later than the second half of January. Rest assured we shall do all in our power to support the valiant forces of our Allies."

In his memoirs Churchill thought: "It was a fine deed of the Russians and their chief to hasten their vast offensive,

△ Marshal of the Soviet Union Georgi K. Zhukov. After his conspicuous part in the defence of "Mother Russia" he was now heading the Russian advance to Berlin right across the centre of Poland: south of Warsaw, via Lódź and Poznań, to the Oder between Frankfurt and Küstrin.

△ Colonel-General N. I. Krylov, commander of the Russian 5th Army, in the 3rd Belorussian Front led by the brilliant General I. D. Chernyakhovsky.

no doubt at a heavy cost in life."

We would agree with him, though not with Boris Telpukhovsky of the Moscow Academy of Sciences, who in 1959 was inspired to write as follows about this episode in Allied relations:

"In December 1944 on the Western Front the Hitler troops launched an offensive in the Ardennes. With the relatively weak forces at their disposal they were able to make a break-through, which put the Anglo-American command in a difficult position: it even began to look as though there would be a second Dunkirk. As a result on January 6 Churchill approached Stalin with a request for help for the troops fighting in the West."

After quoting from the two telegrams given above, he concludes: "Faithful to undertakings given to his Allies and unlike the ruling Anglo-Americans, who knowingly and willingly delayed the opening of the Second Front, the Soviet Government brought forward the starting date of their offensive from January 20 to 12."

In the face of these statements by the Soviet historian, it must be pointed out that ten days before January 6, Hitler had personally acknowledged in the presence of his generals at Ziegenberg that Operation *"Herbstnebel"* had failed. Twelve days previously Patton had freed Bastogne and it was even longer since the ghost of a new Dunkirk had been

laid once and for all. It should also be remembered that the sending of Air Chief-Marshal Tedder, Eisenhower's second-in-command at S.H.A.E.F., to Moscow was decided before the start of the German offensive in the Ardennes and that his presence there was aimed at co-ordinating the final operations of the Allies in the West with those of the Soviets coming from the East, and to arrange their link-up in the heart of Germany. This was Eisenhower's version as given in his memoirs. Not only does this version seem more acceptable but it is confirmed by President Roosevelt's message to Stalin dated December 24:

"In order that all of us may have information essential to our coordination of effort, I wish to direct General Eisenhower to send a fully qualified officer of his staff to Moscow to discuss with you Eisenhower's situation on the Western Front and its relation to the Eastern Front. We will maintain complete secrecy.

"It is my hope that you will see this officer from General Eisenhower's staff and arrange to exchange with him information that will be of mutual benefit. The situation in Belgium is not bad but we have arrived at the time to talk of the next phase . . . An early reply to this proposal is requested in view of the emergency."

On that same day Churchill, who "did not consider the situation in the West bad", pointed out to his Soviet

▽ *While Zhukov pressed on through the centre of Poland, to the south the 1st Ukrainian Front under Marshal Konev, seen here taking a look at the German forward positions through a screen of branches, was driving forward along the Kielce–Radomsk–Breslau axis to take the Silesian industrial basin.*

Legend:
- FRONT LINE ON JANUARY 12 1945
- FRONT LINE ON FEBRUARY 6
- FRONT LINE ON APRIL 16
- 1ST PHASE RUSSIAN ATTACKS
- 2ND PHASE RUSSIAN ATTACKS
- XXXXX FRONT BOUNDARIES
- GERMAN RETREATS
- XXXXX ARMY GROUP BOUNDARIES
- -XXXX- ARMY BOUNDARIES
- GERMAN POCKETS
- UPPER SILESIAN INDUSTRIAL BASIN

◁ *Germany invaded: the conquest of East Prussia by the 2nd and 3rd Belorussian Fronts, and the advance of the 1st Belorussian and 1st Ukrainian Fronts from the Vistula to the Oder.*

▽ *With the Russians on the Oder, only 50 miles from Berlin, the Russians were now truly hammering at the gate with the dit-dit-dit-dah of the opening of Beethoven's 5th Symphony, used by Allied propagandists as it is also V in morse.*
▽ ▽ *Hitler and Goebbels are swept out of southern Poland by a broom of Russian bayonets.*

opposite number that Eisenhower could not "solve his problem" without prior information, albeit not detailed, of *Stavka*'s plans. As we see, this telegram of Churchill's dated January 6 did not look like an S.O.S.

4th *Panzerarmee* defeated

From January 12 to 15, the Soviet offensive extended from the Baranów bridgehead on the Vistula to Tilsit on the Niemen, finally covering a front of 750 miles. On D-day the Baranów bridgehead was 37 miles deep and held by XLVIII Panzer Corps, part of the 4th *Panzerarmee*. It had three weak infantry divisions (the 68th, 168th, and 304th) strung out along a front twice as long as it would normally cover. Each division was down to six battalions, having each had to give up one to form a corps reserve.

Corps reserve had in addition 30 tank destroyers and one company of 14 self-propelled 8.8-cm guns.

Some 12 miles from the front, in the area of Kielce–Pińczów, was the O.K.H. reserve: XXIV Panzer Corps (General Nehring: 16th and 17th Panzer Divisions). Harpe had opposed, to the best of his ability, the positioning of this unit so near to the front line, but Hitler had stuck to his decision, refusing to believe that the Soviet tanks could cover 12 miles in a day, such an idea smacking of defeatism in his opinion. And so Harpe and Gräser (4th *Panzerarmee*) must not be allowed to use up this precious reserve too soon. Like Rommel during "Overlord" they were expressly forbidden to engage it without a formal order from the Führer. Now Hitler was at Ziegenberg near Giessen and, as usual, unobtainable before 1100 hours.

Marshal Konev had ten armies, including three tank, plus three independent tank corps and three or four divisions of artillery. He had formed a first echelon of 34 infantry divisions and 1,000 tanks which he pushed into the bridgehead, giving him at the centre of gravity of the attack a superiority of 11 to 1 in infantry, 7 to 1 in tanks, and 20 to 1 in guns and mortars.

At 0300 hours on January 12, the Russians started their preparatory fire on the German positions: this stopped an hour later, and the Russians then made a decoy attack which drew the fire of XLVIII Panzer Corps and revealed the position of the German batteries. The Russians, with 320 guns per mile, then crushed the German guns with a con-

centration of unprecedented violence. Zero hour for the infantry and tanks was 1030 hours: two waves of tanks followed by three waves of infantry set out to mop up the pockets of resistance left behind by the T-34's and the JS's. They were supported by self-propelled guns firing over open sights.

By early afternoon the tanks had overrun the German gun positions and destroyed the few left after the morning shelling. By nightfall they had covered between nine and 15 miles; they carried on in spite of the darkness.

In less than 24 hours the 4th *Panzerarmee* had suffered a strategic as well as a tactical defeat, as Konev threw into the

▽ *The German night sky is lit up by a Russian Katyusha rocket barrage. Though not particularly accurate, the barrage fired by a Katyusha battery could blanket an area with as much explosive as three or four field artillery regiments' concentrated fire.*

breach his 3rd Guards Tank Army (Colonel-General Rybalko) and 4th Guards Tank Army (Colonel-General Lelyushenko), with the task of cutting off the Germans retreating from Radom and Kielce when they had crossed the Pilica. He sent his 5th Guards Army (General A. S. Zhadov) towards Czestochowa and set Kraków and the upper Silesia industrial basin as the objectives of the armies of his left.

9th Army cut to shreds

On January 14, it was the turn of Zhukov and his 1st Belorussian Front to come into the battle. The Soviet 33rd and 69th Armies (respectively under Generals V. D. Zvetayev and V. J. Kolpakchy) ran into two German divisions as they broke out of the Puławy bridgehead. The 5th Shock Army (General N. E. Berzarin) and the 8th Guards Army (General V. I. Chuikov) found themselves facing three as they in their turn advanced from the Magnuszew bridgehead. Thus, by evening on D-day the German 9th Army was broken up for good, cut to pieces even. This allowed the Russians to loose the 1st and 2nd Guards Tank Armies (Colonel-General M. E. Katukov and Colonel-General S. I. Bogdanov), sending the former off along the axis Kutno–Poznań and the latter along the axis Gostynin–Inowrocław–Hohensalza.

Chernyakhovsky's offensive

On January 13 and 14, the 2nd and 3rd Belorussian Fronts, supported by the 4th and 1st Air Armies (Generals K. A. Vershinin and T. T. Khriukin), attacked the German Army Group "Centre". In this duel between Marshal Rokossovsky and General Chernyakhovsky and Colonel-General Reinhardt, the Russians used 100 divisions, giving them a superiority of three to one. Even so, the battle raged for two days, in stark contrast to what had happened on the Vistula. General A. V. Gorbatov, commander of the Soviet 3rd Army, who had the job of driving the Germans out of their positions in the Pultusk area on the Narew, has left an account of the bitterness of the fighting: on the opening day, in spite of an "initial barrage of un-

precedented violence" he had only advanced "three to seven kilometres in the main direction, two to three the secondary direction and one to one and a half during the night's fighting". On January 14 in particular, Gorbatov had to face furious counter-attacks by the "Grossdeutschland" Panzer Corps which he describes as follows:

"A struggle of unparalleled violence and ferocity developed on the second day: this too was foggy. The enemy threw in all his reserves plus his 'Grossdeutschland' Panzer Division (sic). The latter had been on the southern frontier of East Prussia in the area of Willenberg, and our Intelligence service had failed to pick them up. Taking advantage of the fog, within 24 hours it had concentrated in the area of the break-through with the task of re-establishing the situation in our army sector, then in that of the nearest formation on our left. We had decided to attack again at 0900 hours, but the enemy prevented us. At 0820 he laid down an artillery barrage with 23 batteries of guns and 17 batteries of mortars, some six-tube Nebelwerfers and some heavy howitzers. At 0830 he then counter-attacked the troops which had got through into his defences. In two hours seven counter-attacks were driven off. At mid-day the German Panzer division came into action. By evening we had had 37 counter-attacks. Fighting died down only at nightfall."

On the other leg of the right-angle formed by Army Group "Centre", Chernyakhovsky's efforts were concentrated on the Schlossberg–Ebenrode front. He broke into the 3rd Panzerarmee's positions but, against Germans now fighting on their own soil, was unable to

△ *Soviet commanders. From left to right these are Lieutenant-General K. F. Telegin, the third member of the military council of the 1st Belorussian Front with Zhukov and Colonel-General M. S. Malinin, the chief-of-staff; Colonel-General V. I. Chuikov, head of the 8th Guards Army; and Lieutenant-General M. I. Kazakov, head of the 69th Army. The military council was a peculiarly Russian concept: all major orders at front and army level had to be signed by the three members of the military council of the formation in question. The council consisted of the commander, his chief-of-staff, and a political member. This last was an army commissar or civilian party member. After October 1942 the political member was given a military rank.*

achieve anything like the successes won by Zhukov and Konev in Poland, where they were now exploiting their early victories.

New conflict between Hitler and Guderian

On January 16, Hitler finally abandoned what Guderian called his "little Vosges war" and returned to his office in the Chancellery. Here he made two decisions which brought a show-down with the O.K.H. Chief-of-Staff. First of all he stuck to his order to transfer the *"Grossdeutschland"* Panzer Corps from Army Group "Centre" to Army Group "A" and send it over to Kielce, where it was to attack the flank of the Russian tank forces advancing on Poznań. Guderian repeated the arguments he had put forward the previous evening on the phone, but in vain.

"They would not arrive in time to stop the Russians and they would be withdrawn from the defences of East Prussia at a time when the Russian offensive was reaching its peak. The loss of this formation would give rise to the same catastrophe in East Prussia as we had had on the Vistula. Whilst we were struggling for a final outcome, the divisions up to full fighting strength would still be on the trains: the *'Grossdeutsch-land' Panzergrenadier* and the Luftwaffe 'Hermann Göring' Panzer Division of the *'Grossdeutschland'* Panzer Corps, under General von Saucken, the staunchest of commanders."

It was no good, as usual, and events bore out the gloomiest of forecasts: not only did the German 2nd Army cave in and Rokossovsky set off for Elbing as ordered, but the *"Grossdeutschland"* Panzer Corps arrived at Lódź under a hail of Soviet shelling and only saved its neck by a prompt retreat. Reduced to a moving pocket, together with XXIV Panzer Corps, it nevertheless managed to filter back through the Soviet columns and to cross over to the left bank of the Oder.

▽ *Soviet M1942 76.2-mm gun in action. This was the standard Russian divisional artillery weapon, and could be used either as a conventional weapon or as an anti-tank gun. Compared with equivalent British and American weapons, the 25-pounder and 75-mm, which had ranges of 13,400 and 13,600 yards, the Russian gun had the considerably better range of 15,000 yards.*

Hitler may have satisfied Guderian's demand by announcing that he would go over to the defensive on the Western Front, but he aroused his indignation by ordering to Hungary the best of the formations salvaged in this manner, in particular the 6th S.S. *Panzerarmee*. In Guderian's opinion, the Hungarian railways could not cope with the traffic and it would take weeks before Army Group "South" could go over to the counterattack as Hitler had ordered, whereas Sepp Dietrich's Panzers could concentrate on the Oder in ten days. Beaten on the military question, the Führer counterattacked on the grounds of the economy, maintaining "that Hungarian petroleum deposits and the nearby refineries are indispensable after the bombing of the German coal hydrogenation plants, and have become decisively important for the conduct of the war. No more fuel means your tanks can't run or your planes take off. You must see that. But that's the way it is: my generals understand nothing of the economy of war!"

Hitler's reasoning was clearly not devoid of foundation as petroleum, until uranium came along, was the life-blood of war. But his chief-of-staff's calculations turned out to be correct, since the 6th *Panzerarmee* had to wait until March 6 before it could launch its offensive on the Hungarian front. Even so, its intervention north of the Carpathians was hardly likely to have prevented Zhukov from reaching the Oder between Küstrin and Frankfurt. Diverting it to the south made the Soviet invasion easier.

the Swords to his Knight's Cross from Hitler, and unpacked his bags in his new command post than on January 26 he received the order to go to East Prussia and take over immediately the command of Army Group "Centre". Unfortunately for this group, in spite of the valour of its new commander, nothing could be done to stave off the impending disaster.

△ *Colonel-General P. S. Rybalko* (seated), *commander of the 3rd Guards Tank Army, follows the progress of his forces, part of Konev's 1st Ukrainian Front.*
Overleaf: *A German officer, clad in a snow-suit, finds it heavy going in the winter snows of 1944–45.*

Changes in the German command

The catastrophe in Poland demanded a scapegoat. Hitler chose one in the person of Colonel-General Harpe, C.-in-C. Army Group "A", forgetting that he had himself ordered the imprudent stationing of XXIV Panzer Corps in O.K.H. reserve very close to Harpe's lines. This was the root of the trouble, as Hitler realised, but only after dismissing Harpe's warnings.

Harpe was replaced by Colonel-General Schörner, and Rendulic, Schörner's colleague, received command of Army Group "North", which had just driven off strong Soviet attacks in the Kurland bridgehead. Scarcely had Rendulic left Oslo, received

Hitler at fault again

It cannot, of course, be argued that Reinhardt could have forced Rokossovsky and Chernyakhovsky to give up their offensive if he had had the use of the *"Grossdeutschland"* Panzer Corps. There is no doubt, however, that by depriving him of this formation, Hitler virtually condemned Army Group "Centre" to inescapable defeat, a defeat which reached the proportions of a strategic catastrophe, involving the total destruction of 28 German divisions.

In planning the offensive, *Stavka* had given the 3rd Belorussian Front the task of destroying the enemy forces in Tilsit and Insterburg, then of making for Königsberg. The 2nd Belorussian Front was to overcome the enemy resistance in the Przasnysz–Mława area and then

advance along the axis Deutsch-Eylau–Marienburg–Elbing. This would prevent the Germans driven out by Chernyakhovsky from crossing the Vistula, and they would then fall into the hands of Rokossovsky. Apart from slight variations this was the manoeuvre attempted by Rennenkampf and Samsonov in August 1914 against East Prussia, which ended up in their defeat at Tannenberg and the Masurian Lakes. Here, however, all resemblance between the two campaigns ceases. Chernyakhovsky and Rokossovsky were younger and more energetic than their predecessors in the Tsar's army. Trammelled by the despotic authority of the Führer, Reinhardt on his side had none of that perfect freedom of action which von Hindenburg enjoyed under the Kaiser and Moltke.

Rokossovsky's advance

In spite of the German 2nd Army's resistance, the 2nd Belorussian Front's attack began again on January 16, favoured by a bright spell which allowed efficient support by General Vershinin's planes. Two days later the Russian forward troops were engaged some 21 miles from their point of departure, in the area of Przasnysz and Ciéchanow. Forty-eight hours later Rokossovsky took Mława and Dzialdowo (Soldau), reached the East Prussian frontier, which he then crossed, and launched his 5th Tank Army towards its objective at Elbing. From then on things moved quickly, and Hitler only just had time to blow up the monument to the German victory at Tannenberg and to have the mortal remains of Field-Marshal von Hindenburg and his wife exhumed.

On the same day the 3rd Belorussian Front had overcome the 3rd *Panzerarmee*, which finally succumbed on January 19. By the 21st, the Russians had taken the fortified position along the Inster, with the little town of Insterburg, and Tilsit, where Lieutenant-General Rein's 69th Division had held out, almost to the last grenadier, Rein himself sharing the fate of his men. A few days later Chernyakhovsky had his right at Labiau, at the edge of the frozen lagoon of the Kurisches Haff, his centre at Wehlau, on the west bank of the Alle less than 31 miles from Königsberg, and his left from Gołdap to Lyck in the Masurian Lakes area.

The trap closes on Army Group "Centre"

On January 17, when it became clear that Rokossovsky's battering-ram would destroy his 2nd Army, Reinhardt had asked permission to pull back the 4th Army from its 140-mile wide front (Nowogród–Augustów–Gołdap) to a line Ortelsburg–Lötzen–Masurian Lakes canal. This would save three divisions, which would make up for the loss of the *"Grossdeutschland"* Panzer Corps and stave off a break-through. Quoting his "five years experience of warfare", Hitler refused this sensible request; Reinhardt could not bring himself to remind Hitler of the sinister experience of Vitebsk.

Three days later, when the German 2nd Army positions had been breached and Chernyakhovsky had been successful at Tilsit on the Inster, Lieutenant-General Heidkämper, chief-of-staff of Army Group "Centre", noted in his diary: "To keep the 4th Army in its present exposed position now appears grotesque. At 2030 hours the C.-in-C. (Reinhardt) again puts before the Führer the reasons for its immediate withdrawal. *'Mein Führer'*, he began, 'in my anxiety for the safety of East Prussia, I venture again to turn to you. According to my appreciation of the situation, we shall tomorrow face an attack on the whole of East Prussia. Examination of a captured map reveals that the 5th Guards Tank Army, with four tank corps, is to make for Danzig. The strength of our 2nd Army is so depleted that we cannot withstand this attack. The second strategic danger is in the 3rd *Panzerarmee,* which the enemy has broken into. If the Guards Tank Army is able to force its way through we shall be caught in the rear: here we have no resources at all.'"

There followed long exchanges between Reinhardt and Hitler. The latter, never short of arguments, advised Reinhardt to use the *Volkssturm* militia against the Soviet tanks and told him that the 4th Panzer Division had been withdrawn from Kurland, loaded on five liners, and was expected to reach him very soon. This would be followed very shortly by 20 infantry battalions from Denmark. It was for these reasons that he opposed Reinhardt's request, and when at mid-day on January 21 he finally agreed, the fate of Army Group "Centre" had been sealed.

By remaining in its allotted positions on January 17, 4th Army suffered the inevitable encirclement, with 350,000 men trapped around the strongpoint of Lötzen, where supplies were reckoned to be enough for one division for 70 days. The commander, General Hossbach, realising the impossibility of his position, tried to fight his way out, down towards the Vistula. He was thus knowingly disobeying O.K.H.'s orders, but he had the approval of Colonel-General Reinhardt, who saw in this a chance of saving the 3rd *Panzerarmee* as well.

Holding off Chernyakhovsky on the line Sensburg–Rastenburg–Friedland–left bank of the Pregel, Hossbach, after 125 miles of forced marches in five days through snowstorms, nevertheless failed to get to Elbing before the Soviet 5th Guards Tank Army. The latter had reached the shore of the Frisches Haff near the little town of Tolkemit on

▽ *The cold took a terrible toll of the exhausted German forces.*

January 27 and had cut the last link between East Prussia and the rest of the Reich. Further south, XXVI and VI Corps (Generals Matzky and Grossmann) had attacked the previous night and got as far as Preussisch-Holland, 12 miles south of Elbing.

On the one hand Rokossovsky was thus able to avoid the opposition intended for him and consequently to reinforce his strength. On the other the secret evacuation of East Prussia by Hossbach, with the connivance of Reinhardt, was denounced to Hitler by Erich Koch, the *Gauleiter* of the province. The Führer dreaded the setting up in Königsberg of a government of "Free Germany" once the Russians were in the town. It was here that Frederick I, the Elector of Brandenburg, had been crowned in 1701. It therefore had to be held at any price, even at the cost of 28 divisions.

And so Reinhardt was relieved by Rendulic on January 27. Three days later Hossbach was ordered to hand over command of the 4th Army to General Friedrich-Wilhelm Müller. Stalin had, of course, no intention of setting up a Free German Government (even one devoted to him and presided over by General von Seydlitz-Kurzbach) in Königsberg, which had been allotted to the Soviet Union by the Teheran Conference, and which he was going to rename Kaliningrad. Was this just mistrust on Stalin's part, or did he think it best to leave things as they were?

The Russians gather momentum

Whilst the ring was closing round the 3rd *Panzerarmee* and the 4th Army, and what was left of the 2nd Army was powerless to prevent the forces of the 2nd Belorussian Front from crossing the lower Vistula, Colonel-General Schörner's savage energy was unable to hold back the onrush of Marshals Zhukov and Konev, though their losses, the strain on their equipment, and the stretching of their lines of communication eventually slowed the Russians down to advances of less than half a mile in places.

On January 15, between the Baranów bridgehead and the Carpathians, the 4th Ukrainian Front came into action with 18 infantry divisions and two tank corps. At Jaslo it easily broke through the thinly-held line of the 1st *Panzerarmee* and set off for Kraków without hindrance.

On January 16, Guderian noted, the Russian advance "gathered extraordinary speed". In effect, on the 1st Belorussian Front the 4th Tank Army, having passed through Jedrzejów the night before, reached Czestochowa on the 17th in two stages, covering a total distance of 70 miles. On its right the 3rd Guards Tank Army reached Radomsko from Kielce (50 miles). It was therefore to be concluded that all organised resistance had ceased in front of Lelyushenko's and Rybalko's forces.

Kraków falls to Konev

This explains how Konev was able to take Kraków by an outflanking movement, so that on January 19 the Poles found it left virtually intact. The same procedure, in an operation which he

▽ *Cossack cavalry stop to water their mounts . . .*

shared equally with Petrov's 4th Ukrainian Front, gave him the industrial labyrinth of upper Silesia with its factories only slightly damaged. And, a more difficult task, he had managed to prevent the Germans from sabotaging them.

The ruins of Warsaw abandoned

On the 1st Belorussian Front the advance proceeded at an equally fast pace. On January 16 Zhukov's right having seized Modlin, where the Bug joins the Vistula, the Warsaw garrison of four incomplete battalions and a few artillery batteries sought and obtained O.K.H.'s approval to abandon the ruins of the city and escape encirclement. This common-sense decision put Hitler in a state of indescribable fury. In spite of Guderian's vehement protests, he arrested three officers of the operations staff and had Guderian himself undergo a wearisome interrogation by Kaltenbrunner.

By January 19, the 1st and 2nd Guards Tank Armies had reached their first objectives. Konev advanced from Gostynin to Inowrocław then to Bydgoszcz (Bromberg). On January 23, having covered 90 miles in four days, he occupied the latter without resistance. On the left, Colonel-General Bogdanov took a week to cover the 110 miles from Kutno to Poznań. The old fortress of Poznań, dating back to the Prussian era, had been hastily re-armed and put under the command of Major-General Mattern. The 2nd Guards Tank Army had better things to do, and so by-passed it and drove on: next stop Frankfurt on the Oder.

On the same day, the left of the 1st Belorussian Front took Lódz, and south of it advanced to make contact with the 1st Ukrainian Front. Remnants of re-treating German units of Army Group "A" mingled with the advancing Russians. "The enemy," Guderian said, "had virtually nothing in front of him. Only the moving pockets of XXIV and the *'Grossdeutschland'* Panzer Corps moved on westwards, fighting all the time, imperturbable, picking up a host of smaller units as they went along. Generals Nehring and von Saucken carried out a military exploit during these days every bit worthy to be recounted by a new Xenophon."

Marshals Zhukov and Konev now had no difficulty in overcoming the resistance put up by Colonel-General Schörner to

▷ A Panther tank in East Prussia: certainly one of the finest tanks of the war.
▽ Grenadiers of the Grossdeutschland Corps march towards the front, pulling a light anti-tank gun.

The Russian KV-85 heavy tank

Weight: 45 tons.
Crew: 5.
Armament: one 85-mm M1944 gun with 71 rounds and three 7.62-mm DT machine guns with 3,276 rounds.
Armour: hull nose and front 75-mm, sides 65-mm, and rear 60-mm; turret front, sides, and rear 110-mm, and mantlet 95-mm.
Engine: one V-2K inline, 600-hp.
Speed: 25 mph.
Range: 205 miles.
Length: 22 feet 6 inches
Width: 11 feet 4 inches.
Height: 10 feet 10 inches.

Further down the Oder, Generals Nehring and von Saucken had managed to escape from the pursuing 1st Belorussian Front and had crossed back over the river at Glogau (Głogów). Zhukov's two Guards Tank Armies covered a good 60 miles along the Poznań–Berlin axis, where two weak divisions, without artillery, had been sent to prop up what was left of the German 9th Army. Without halting at the small garrison of Schneidemühl (Pila), which they by-passed, they reached the Oder at Küstrin in the early days of February. This brought them opposite Frankfurt, around which bridgeheads on the left bank were soon established. And so Zhukov's forward troops were now only 50 miles as the crow flies from the New Chancellery bunker.

The German hecatomb

On the 30th day of the offensive, Moscow published the first figures from Konev's and Zhukov's victories: 70 German divisions destroyed or cut to pieces; 295,000 men killed and 86,000 taken prisoner; 15,000 guns and mortars, 34,000 vehicles, and 2,955 tanks destroyed or captured. If it is realised that the mobile reserves behind Army Group "A" consisted of five Panzer and two *Panzergrenadier* divisions, the last figure seems to bear no relation to reality. As for the ratio of killed to prisoners, as Alexander Werth has pointed out, it belies the statements of the Soviet propagandist Ilya Ehrenburg, who described to his readers "Germans running away like rabbits". And Werth also recalls the confidential statement of an officer from the front who said to him "In some places their resistance reminds me of Sebastopol: those German soldiers can be quite heroic at times."

At the same time, Zhukov was in front of Küstrin and 335 miles from his point of departure, whilst Konev in Silesia was 300 miles from his. Logistic considerations now became of prime importance to the two marshals' tank armies, especially as they had greatly outdistanced the infantry following them on foot. And so February, March, and early April were devoted to small-scale operations only, though these were important as they led to the mopping up of East Prussia and the deployment of the Red Army on what is now called the Oder-Neisse line, ready for the final offensive.

△ *A column of Russian T-34/85 medium tanks arrives in Heiligenbeil, on the Frisches Haff, only about 25 miles from Königsberg.*

slow their advance. On January 18, the 72nd Division was wiped out near Piotrków, then the 10th Panzer, 78th, and 291st Divisions succumbed trying to block the way into Silesia to the Soviet tanks. They were no more of an obstacle than the Oder would be. By the end of January the forward troops of the 1st Ukrainian Front had reached the Oder above Oppeln (Opole) and on either side of Breslau (Wrocław) had established two vast bridgeheads at Brieg (Brzeg) and Steinau (Scinawa) on the right bank. This marked the beginning of the encirclement of the Silesian capital.

CHAPTER 138
Advance to the Oder

Marshal Rokossovsky's break-through towards Elbing and the crushing defeat of the German 2nd Army (which was driven back to Danzig) left the left wing of Army Group "A" uncovered, and west of a line running north-south through Toruń the whole of Pomerania lay open to the Soviet invader. In mid-January there was little more than a handful of troops, mostly infantry, to defend it.

To close this enormous breach, Guderian got Hitler to approve the formation of an Army Group "Vistula", but the two men were violently opposed on the question of who was to command it. The reshuffling of commands in the Danube theatre meant that the general staff of Army Group "F" were out of jobs, as also was Field-Marshal von Weichs, whom Guderian described as "a man who is as intelligent as he is brave and upright and one certainly cut out to master such a difficult situation, insofar as it can be mastered." But Weich's profound religious feelings disqualified him in Hitler's eyes. So, despite Guderian's violent protests, this delicate command was given to *Reichsführer*-S.S. Heinrich Himmler. Himmler had no religious feelings, to be sure, but during Operation *"Nordwind"* in lower Alsace he had shown both ineptitude and hesitation in command. What was worse, Hitler refused Guderian's proposal that the staff of Army Group "F" should come under his control. Himmler was thus able to recruit his own from amongst his cronies, and as chief-of-staff he chose Lieutenant-General Lammerding of the *Waffen*-S.S.,

whose name will for ever be linked with Oradour-sur-Glane.

On January 25, Army Group "North" was renamed "Kurland", "Centre" was renamed "North", and "A" became "Centre". The general staff of the 3rd *Panzerarmee* were withdrawn from East Prussia and put under Army Group "Vistula". By emptying the depôts, schools, and training centres and sending part of Berlin's A.A. defences down to the Oder, O.K.H. was able for the last time to reconstitute some kind of coherent force with which to face the Russians.

In early February it had five army groups with a total of 135 divisions deployed as follows:

	Infantry divisions	Panzer and *Panzergrenadier* divisions	*Totals*
"Kurland"	20	2	22
"North"	19	5	24
"Vistula"	25	8	33
"Centre"	20	8	28
"South"	19	9	28
Totals	103	32	135

Surrender in the West?

In less than a month, in spite of the reinforcements we have mentioned, the number of German divisions facing the Red Army had dropped from 164 to 135. Most of these were below strength and some were down to the equivalent of an

▽ *Russian bridge-builders at work in the Oder. Only with the completion of a heavy duty bridge could the bridgehead on the west bank be considered at all secure. Note the considerably more primitive, yet nevertheless effective, construction methods of the Russians compared with the Western Allies.*

infantry regiment. Under these circumstances, Guderian understandably thought that Ribbentrop should be informed of the situation. He suggested that the two of them should approach Hitler to recommend that Germany lay down her arms in the West. Ribbentrop was unwilling, so Guderian attempted to win Hitler over to a manoeuvre which, for some weeks at least, would avert the threat to Berlin.

"I resolved," he said, "to demonstrate once more to Hitler that the Hungarian offensive had to be abandoned. Instead we would attack the Russian salient on the Oder between Frankfurt and Küstrin by going for its flanks, which were not very strong, in the south on the line Glogau–Guben and in the north of the line Pyritz–Arnswalde. I thus hoped to strengthen the defence of the capital and the interior of the Reich and gain time to conclude armistice talks with the Western powers."

But this proposal, which presupposed the evacuation also of Kurland, Norway, and Italy, merely provoked Hitler to an attack of maniacal fury.

Russian superiority overwhelming

As the 6th *Panzerarmee* finally set off for Hungary, Guderian's proposed pincer round the tank armies of the 1st Belorussian Front became impossible through lack of resources. He therefore fell back on a flank attack which was to bring into operation Army Group "Vistula". Breaking out south-east from Arnswalde, it would beat the enemy forces north of the Warta, which would protect Pomerania and force Zhukov to give up his positions before Frankfurt and Küstrin. Speed was essential, but Himmler and his staff took a week to get ready. Konev's vigorous attacks in Silesia, moreover, obliged O.K.H. to reinforce Army Group "Centre" at the expense of Army Group "Vistula".

On February 13, the 3rd *Panzerarmee* finally mounted a counter-attack, starting from Arnswalde, and scored some initial success. But it was soon compelled to go

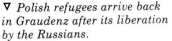

▽ *Polish refugees arrive back in Graudenz after its liberation by the Russians.*

over to the defensive, as *Stavka* turned on to it Rokossovsky's centre and left as well as Zhukov's two tank armies. With his left at Könitz and his right on the Oder at Schwedt, Colonel-General Raus was defending a front of 160 miles with only eight divisions. It is therefore not surprising that this was quickly broken by the two Soviet marshals' offensive on February 24. They had nine tank corps and no fewer than 47 infantry divisions.

Back to the Baltic

Driving on through Schlochau and Büblitz, the 2nd Belorussian Front's tanks reached the Baltic north of Köslin on February 28, cutting the German 2nd Army's last land communications with the rest of the Reich. This army now had its back to the sea, its right on the Stolpe and its left on the Nogat. A few days later Zhukov broke through to Dramburg and drove on to Treptow, in spite of the

intervention one after the other of four Panzer or *Panzergrenadier* divisions. During this fighting General Krappe's X S.S. Panzer Corps was wiped out and Raus was just able to save some 50,000 men of his army who, on March 11, were sheltering on Wolin Island. Eight days later a special Kremlin communiqué announced the capture of the port of Kolberg (now Kołobrzeg) where the 163rd and the 402nd Divisions were cut to pieces almost to the last man.

△ *German corpses litter the pavements of Brieg after its capture by the 1st Ukrainian Front. From here the southern arm of a pincer would sweep up to close the trap around Breslau.*

Konev invades Silesia

Konev's job in Silesia was to align his front with Zhukov's, according to Russian official histories today. But was it to be only this? Judging by the means employed, it seems unlikely.

On February 4, Konev launched a first attack when he broke out of the bridgehead at Brieg and advanced nearly 13 miles along the left bank of the Oder. South-east of Breslau, the Russians advanced as far as Ohlan, some 13 miles from the Silesian capital, and south down to Strehlen. A special Moscow communiqué claimed that this action brought in 4,200 prisoners.

△ *The wreckage of a Messerschmitt Bf 110 unit of the Luftwaffe, caught by a surprise Russian attack.*

A week later the 3rd Guards Tank and the 4th Tank Armies broke out from the Steinau bridgehead and advanced at Blitzkrieg speed over the plain of Silesia. On February 13, Colonel-General Lelyushenko was attacking Glogau, 25 miles north-west of Steinau. On his left, supported by a division of artillery and followed by Colonel-General K. A. Koroteev's 52nd Army, Rokossovsky had forced a crossing of the Bober at Bunzlau the night before. On February 15, after a 60-mile dash north-west, the Soviet tanks reached Guben, Sommerfeld, Sorau, and Sagan, which they lost and regained in circumstances still unknown.

So Konev's aim was not merely to align his front with Zhukov's but to cross the Neisse, roll up the front along the Oder down-river from Fürstenberg, and advance towards Berlin through Cottbus. Halted on the Neisse, either by *Stavka* or by enemy opposition, however, he closed the ring round Breslau. At the beginning of March, he was facing Schörner on the line Bunzlau – Jauer – Schweidnitz – Neïsse – Ratibor, at the foot of the mountains separating Silesia from Bohemia and Moldavia.

Mopping up East Prussia fell to the 3rd Belorussian Front, reinforced up to 100 divisions against the 24, including five Panzer, of Army Group "North", at the beginning of February. At the same date the Russians were in the outskirts of

Königsberg; from here the front moved along the course of the river Alle between Friedland and Guttstadt, then turned north-west to reach the coast near Frauenberg. This left the Germans trapped in a rectangle about the size of Brighton – Guildford – Winchester – Portsmouth. Colonel-General Rendulic did not limit himself merely to defensive operations. On February 19 he counterattacked in a pincer manoeuvre and reestablished communication, though precariously, between Königsberg and Pillau, the latter a Baltic port giving him a supply and evacuation link with the rest of the Reich less exposed than Königsberg.

Chernyakhovsky's idea had been to cut East Prussia in two from south-west to north-east, but on February 18 he was killed in front of Mehlsack by a shell splinter as he was on his way to the H.Q. of General Gorbatov, commander of the 3rd Army. Twice decorated a Hero of the Soviet Union, he was the youngest and one of the most gifted of the great Russian war leaders. In his honour the small Prussian town of Insterburg was renamed Chernyakhovsk.

Stalin nominated Marshal A. M. Vasilevsky to succeed him, while Vasilevsky's job as Chief-of-Staff of the Red Army was taken over by General A. I. Antonov.

The offensive proceeded along the same axis, in spite of obstinate German resistance, which General Gorbatov emphasises in his memoirs. The invaders' superior strength soon began to tell, however. On March 14, the Russian 3rd Army concentrated on a narrow front twice as much infantry and five times as much artillery as the Germans, gained over three miles in three days and got to within eight miles of the sea, which it finally reached on March 25. "What a sight on the coast!" Gorbatov writes. "Several square miles of lorries and vans loaded with *matériel*, food, and domestic equipment. Between the vehicles lay corpses of German soldiers. Some 300 horses were attached in pairs to a chain and many of these were dead too."

Königsberg falls

And so the German 4th Army was cut in two and trapped in two pockets. Meanwhile, on March 12, Hitler had replaced

The Russian Joseph Stalin-2 heavy tank

Weight: 45.5 tons.
Crew: 4.
Armament: one 122-mm D-25 gun with 28 rounds, one 12.7-mm DShK and two 7.62 DT machine guns.
Armour: hull glacis 110-mm, nose 127-mm, sides 89-mm, and front pannier sides 133-mm; turret front 64-mm, sides 95-mm, roof 45-mm, and mantlet 102-mm.
Engine: one V-2K inline, 600-hp.
Speed: 27 mph.
Range: 100 miles.
Length: 31 feet 7 inches.
Width: 10 feet 3 inches.
Height: 9 feet.

Rendulic as C.-in-C. Army Group "Kurland" and Colonel-General Weiss, C.-in-C. 2nd Army, was given the sad honour of presiding over the death-throes of Army Group "North". On March 30, the pocket which had formed round the little towns of Braunsberg and Heiligenbeil surrendered, yielding (if we are to believe a Soviet communiqué of the period) 80,000 dead and 50,000 prisoners. In the night of April 9-10 General Lasch, commander of the Königsberg fortress, decided to send envoys to Marshal Vasilevsky. The town had been under heavy and incessant air bombardment for some ten days, whilst the attackers, having taken the fortifications, infiltrated the streets amidst the burning buildings. No German authors we have consulted blame the commander for surrendering, though 92,000 men were taken prisoner and 2,232 guns were lost. Lasch was condemned to death in his

absence, however, and his family imprisoned.

On April 15, the Russians invaded the Samland peninsula, from which they had been driven out two months previously. Ten days later, the last remnants of the German 4th Army, now under the command of General von Saucken, evacuated the port of Pillau, which had served as a transit station for 141,000 military wounded and 451,000 civilian refugees since January 15.

Along the lower Vistula, Rokossovsky had the right of the 2nd Belorussian Front, and in particular the Polish 2nd Army (General Swierczewski) facing the six corps and 17 divisions, all very dilapidated, which the reorganisation of command in January had put into the incapable hands of the sinister Heinrich Himmler.

By February 18, on the right

▽ *A Russian SU-152 assault gun lumbers into the ruins of Königsberg, once the heart of East Prussia.*

bank of the Vistula, the Russians had reached Graudenz (Grudziadz) but it took them until March 5 to overcome the last resistance of this small town. On February 21 they took Dirschau (Tczew) on the left bank 21 miles from Danzig. On March 9, the Soviet forces which had reached the Baltic north of Köslin crossed the Stolpe and drove on towards Kartuzy, turning the right flank of the German 2nd Army, which had come under the command of General von Saucken after the transfer of Colonel-General Rendulic.

Danzig, Gdynia, and Poznań occupied

The struggle was now concentrated around Danzig and Gdynia, which the Germans had renamed Gotenhafen. In this hopeless battle the defenders brought in the pocket-battleship *Lützow* and the cruisers *Prinz Eugen* and *Leipzig,* which several times knocked out Soviet tanks with their gunfire, though their ammunition was gradually more and more severely rationed. On March 23, the Polish 2nd Army took Sopot, half-way between Danzig and Gdynia, and by the 30th it was all over. The German 2nd Army held out obstinately until May 9 in the Hela peninsula, in the Vistula estuary, and in the narrow strip of land enclosing the Frisches Haff, so that between January 15 and April 30 no fewer than 300,000 military personnel and 962,000 civilians had been embarked for Germany.

The strongpoint of Poznań gave in on February 24 after a resistance to which the Red Army paid considerable tribute. Then it was the turn of Schneidemühl and Deutsche Krone in Pomerania.

On the Oder, the fortress of Glogau, first attacked on February 13, held out until April 2. By the latter date, apart from the coastal strips held by Saucken and the Kurland bridgehead which continued to defy the Soviet assaults, the only point still holding out east of the Oder-Neisse line was Breslau. Its garrison, commanded by Lieutenant-General Niehoff, was now closely hemmed in by the 6th Army of the 1st Ukrainian Front under General V. A. Gluzdovsky.

This military tragedy was echoed by a national tragedy of massive and catastrophic proportions: the exodus of nearly eight million Germans who had taken refuge on the other side of the Oder-Neisse line at the time of the capitulation of May 8, 1945. But not all those who fled before the Soviet invasion managed to find shelter. The journalist Bernard George reckons that 1,600,000 people, mostly old men, women, and children, died of exhaustion, cold, and brutal treatment from a soldiery drunk for revenge. And so in five months, this catastrophe cost Germany more civilians than France lost soldiers in the whole of the 52 months of World War I. Much of the responsibility for this affair must naturally be laid on Hitler (and his collaborators in the government and the party) and on the party authorities in Germany's eastern provinces: *Gauleiters* Erich Koch in Eastern Prussia, Forster in Danzig and Western Prussia (the former Polish corridor), and Arthur Greiser in the Warthegau, the new German name for the provinces of Poznań, Lódź (Litzmannstadt), and Czestochowa, annexed to the Third Reich in October 1939.

Hitler had obstinately refused to consider the possibility of a Russian invasion and went into fits of furious temper when anyone dared broach the subject in his presence. All preparations, even all estimates for the evacuation of the civilian population in the threatened provinces appeared to the *Gauleiters* of Königsberg, Danzig, and Poznań a scandalous demonstration of defeatism and an intolerable attack on the dogma of the Führer's infallibility. And so in many areas the exodus was improvised actually under enemy shelling. In June 1940, when the French refugees poured out along the roads there were vehicles and petrol supplies and the weather was good. In January and February 1945, the Germans had only their animals and carts, it was snowing hard, and the temperature was 20 to 25 degrees below zero Centigrade.

In his war memoirs, Colonel-General Rendulic, who saw these pitiful convoys pass by, remarked how they were often led by French prisoners, the only able-bodied men left in the villages of East Prussia, whom the refugees praised unstintingly for their devotion. On many occasions, and this was borne out by other witnesses, they protected the women and girls from the violence of their Allies.

Much has been written in Germany about the atrocities committed by the Soviet invaders. The evidence has

△ △ *An SU-76 assault gun pushes its way through the detritus of the German retreat back towards Berlin.*
△ *German dead. Against the crushing weight of Russian guns and tanks, the German Army had little or no chance.*

2013

been doubted by some, but a Red Army officer said to Werth:

"In Poland a few regrettable things happened from time to time, but, on the whole, a fairly strict discipline was maintained as regards 'rape'. The most common offence in Poland was 'dai chasy' – 'give me your wrist-watch'. There was an awful lot of petty thieving and robbery. Our fellows were just crazy about wrist-watches – there's no getting away from it. But the looting and raping in a big way did not start until our soldiers got to Germany. Our fellows were so sex-starved that they often raped old women of sixty, or seventy or even eighty – much to these grandmothers' surprise, if not downright delight. But I admit it was a nasty business, and the record of the Kazakhs and other Asiatic troops was particularly bad."

It is hardly surprising that the Soviet soldiers, after the devastation of their villages, and after just seeing the abominations of the extermination camps of Maidenek, Treblinka, and Oswiecim (or Auschwitz) should exact revenge on the German people. On the other hand, the American, British, and French troops who discovered Ravensbrück, Bergen-Belsen, Buchenwald, and Dachau seem to have reacted differently. It would appear that neither the military nor the political authorities, normally so strict in matters of discipline, took the trouble at the time to stem this tide of bestiality. Very much to the contrary, journalists and intellectuals such as the well-known Ilya Ehrenburg incited the Red Army in the press and on the radio to dishonour their victory. And this homicidal propaganda cannot but have had the approval of the Kremlin. On April 14, as Alexander Werth reported, there was a sudden change of tone: Ehrenburg was brutally disowned in an official-looking article in *Pravda* by Comrade G. F. Alexandrov, then the licensed ideologist of the Central Committee of the Communist Party of the U.S.S.R. His "clumsy error" was not to have noticed that Stalin had just proclaimed: "Hitlers come and go, but the German people go on for ever."

It seems that the Kremlin feared that the horrors caused by the invasion might prevent the free flowering of communism in Central Europe. That was right, but it was too late.

CHAPTER 139
The Allies confer

On Tuesday September 6, 1944, Churchill and his three chiefs-of-staff left the Clyde on board the liner *Queen Mary* for Halifax, Nova Scotia. Here a special train took them to Quebec late in the morning of September 11. President Roosevelt and his military colleagues were waiting for the British party. To Winston Churchill's great disappointment Harry Hopkins had excused himself: apart from the health reasons which explained his absence (and these were real enough), he was also suffering the consequences of his loss of favour at the White House at this time.

During this Anglo-American conference, which had been named "Octagon", the discussion concerned mainly the form of participation to be taken by the British forces in the fight against Japan, after the Third Reich had been driven to unconditional surrender. Planning included operations in Burma, a possible air and naval offensive from Australia against Singapore, and putting a Royal Navy formation under the com-

mand of the American Pacific Fleet, which had just won a victory at the Marianas Islands and was about to win another at Leyte.

In the European theatre, it was decided not to withdraw a single division from the Allied forces in the Mediterranean until the result of the attack the 15th Army Group was preparing to launch across the Apennines was known; its objective was the Adige line, just short of the Piave.

Churchill, now fearful of a Russian take-over of central Europe, expressed hope at Quebec that Alexander's forces in Italy might in fact be able to reach Vienna before the Red Army.

An agreement was also made between the British and the Americans to mark off their future occupation zones in Germany. After some argument about the allocation of the Westphalian industrial basin, it was decided, according to Admiral Leahy, President Roosevelt's Chief-of-Staff, to divide the zones as follows: "(a) The British forces, under a British

△ *President Franklin Roosevelt reviews a guard of honour at the Quebec Conference, September 1944.*

△ *British troops in combat against the Japanese in the Burmese jungle. Operations in this theatre were among the points discussed at Quebec.*
▷ *The highly strategic Burma Road, cutting through the jungle terrain.*

commander, will occupy Germany west of the Rhine and east of the Rhine north of a line from Coblenz following the northern border of Hessen and Nassau to the border of the area allocated to the Soviet Government.

(b) The forces of the United States, under a United States commander, will occupy Germany east of the Rhine, south of the line from Coblenz following the northern border of Hessen–Nassau and west of the area allocated to the Soviet Government.

(c) Control of the ports of Bremen and Bremerhaven and the necessary staging areas in that immediate vicinity will be vested in the commander of the American zone.

(d) American area to have, in addition, access through the western and north-western seaports and passage through the British controlled area.

(e) Accurate delineation of the above outlined British and American areas of control can be made at a later date."

Reading this text one notices that:

1. at this time no French occupation zone was provided for;
2. Bremen and Bremerhaven were in-cluded in the American occupation zone because President Roosevelt wanted to make sure that his troops would be supplied without using French terri-tory; and
3. Berlin was not mentioned and there was no reference to the facilities which the two Western powers would require from their Soviet ally if they were to have free access to the German capital at all times.

Robert Murphy, the American diplomat who had just taken up his duties as adviser to General Eisenhower on Ger-man affairs, frequently mentioned and deplored this last point. He states in his memoirs that "no provision had been made for the Anglo-American powers to reach that city", and notes that his colleague James Riddleberger, the State Department's delegate to the European Consultative Council in London, who was equally aware of this omission, had suggested that "the occupation zones should converge upon Berlin like slices of pie, thus providing each zone with its own frontage in the capital city". Murphy also asked Riddleberger whom he had approached with his plan. The latter had told Ambassador Winant, who had been opposed to any modification of the original plan and accused Riddleberger of not having confidence in Soviet Russia. Riddleberger replied that on this he was exactly right. Winant told Murphy that the right of access to Berlin was implicit in the Western Allies presence there.

In addition, according to Murphy, the "daydreams" of Winant, the U.S. Ambassador in London, and therefore the American representative for Russo-American affairs at the European Consultative Council, relied too much on Roosevelt's usual formula: "I can handle Stalin."

The Morgenthau Plan

During the "Octagon" Conference the notorious Morgenthau Plan (named after its author, the Secretary of the Treasury) was discussed.

Since the beginning of August, Eisenhower had been requesting instructions on the attitude to be adopted after the German defeat, and the War Department sent him a note on the subject, asking him to make his observations. However, a member of Eisenhower's staff committed the double indiscretion of getting hold of a copy of this memorandum and sending it to Henry Morgenthau. Morgenthau had wormed his way into the President's favour to such an extent that he was the only member of his cabinet to call him by his first name.

After the cabinet session of August 26, 1944, James V. Forrestal, the Secretary of the Navy, noted in his valuable diary:

"The Secretary of the Treasury (Henry Morgenthau, Jr.) came in with the President with whom he had had lunch. The President said that he had been talking with the Secretary of the Treasury on the general question of the control of Germany after the end of the war. He said that he had just heard about a paper prepared by the Army and that he was not at all satisfied with the severity of the measures proposed. He said that the Germans should have simply a subsistence level of food—as he put it, soup kitchens would be ample to sustain life—that otherwise they should be stripped clean and should not have a level of subsistence above the lowest level of the people they had conquered.

"The Secretary of War (Henry L. Stimson) demurred from this view, but the President continued in the expression of

1

2

3

△ *The principal military participants in the "Octagon" Conference. Discussion here included the part Britain was to play in the war against Japan, and initial agreement was reached over Allied occupation zones in post-war Germany.*

▽ *Henry Morgenthau Jr., U.S. Secretary of the Treasury and author of the Morgenthau Plan for the treatment of Germany after the war. In this, German factories were to be dismantled, mines flooded, raw materials cut off, and the people were to live by subsistence farming. At the conference, Churchill and Roosevelt endorsed this Plan.*

this attitude and finally said he would name a committee composing State, War, and Treasury which would consider the problem of how to handle Germany along the lines that he had outlined, that this committee would consult the Navy whenever naval questions were involved."

According to the plan, Germany would not only have her factories, in particular her steel plants, dismantled, but all her raw material resources also cut off, because she would be permanently forbidden to mine coal and iron ore. Her mines were to be flooded and the German people would have to subsist on crops and cattle-breeding as in the early times of the Holy Roman Empire. Secretary of State Cordell Hull and Secretary of War Henry L. Stimson were firm in their objections, but Roosevelt remained obstinate and, leaving his diplomatic chief in Washington, took Morgenthau with him to the Quebec Conference. It is interesting to note the reception given by Churchill to this inhuman and preposterous project.

Churchill's opinion alters

In the volume of his memoirs entitled *Triumph and Tragedy,* which he wrote in 1953, Churchill tells us:

"At first I violently opposed this idea. But the President, with Mr. Morgenthau – for whom we had much to ask – was so insistent that in the end we agreed to consider it."

This is both true and false. There is no doubt that he recoiled when he learned of the Morgenthau plan, as Lord Moran heard him say on September 13 at the dinner of the Citadel Night, when the subject came up:

"I'm all for disarming Germany, but we ought not to prevent her living decently. There are bonds between the working classes of all countries, and the English people will not stand for the policy you are advocating." And he is said to have muttered: "You cannot indict a whole nation."

On the other hand, when Roosevelt and Morgenthau insisted, Churchill, in spite of what he said, not only promised them that he would examine the plan for reducing Germany to a pastoral existence, but after it had been examined by Professor Lindemann (later Lord Cherwell), put his signature to it on September 15. According to Lord Moran, Cherwell as Churchill's scientific adviser had persuaded the Prime Minister, explaining what he had not noticed at first sight, that "the plan will save Britain from bankruptcy by eliminating a dangerous competitor".

1. General H. H. Arnold
2. Air Chief-Marshal Sir Charles Portal
3. General Sir Alan Brooke
4. Field-Marshal Sir John Dill
5. Admiral E. J. King
6. General G. C. Marshall
7. Admiral of the Fleet Sir Dudley Pound
8. Admiral W. D. Leahy

It is tempting to dismiss the versions of Churchill and his doctor out of hand, as they are contradictory. However, the evidence given by Anthony Eden, now Lord Avon, supports Lord Moran's version point by point; he writes:

"On the morning of September 15th I joined the Prime Minister and the President, who were by now in agreement in their approval of the plan. Cherwell had supported Morgenthau and their joint advocacy had prevailed. Large areas of the Ruhr and the Saar were to be stripped of their manufacturing industries and turned into agricultural lands. It was as if one were to take the Black Country and turn it into Devonshire. I did not like the plan, nor was I convinced that it was to our national advantage.

"I said so, and also suggested that Mr. Cordell Hull's opinion should be sought for. This was the only occasion I can remember when the Prime Minister showed impatience with my views before foreign representatives. He resented my criticism of something which he and the President had approved, not I am sure on his account, but on the President's."

Meanwhile, Cordell Hull, on whose territory Morgenthau was trespassing, and Stimson, who refused to admit defeat, were left behind in Washington. However, they did not relax their opposition to the Morgenthau plan and on September 18,

the deputy Secretary of War, John Mc-Cloy, also condemned it to Forrestal:

"In general the programme according to Mr. McCloy, called for the conscious destruction of the economy in Germany and the encouragement of a state of impoverishment and disorder. He said he felt the Army's role in any programme would be most difficult because the Army, by training and instinct, would naturally turn to the re-creation of order as soon as possible, whereas under this programme they apparently were to encourage the opposite."

Eisenhower's view: "silly and criminal"

McCloy was not exaggerating in interpreting the feeling of the U.S. high command as he did. Already in August, when Morgenthau had visited S.H.A.E.F., Eisenhower had told him that "it would be madness" to deprive the Germans of their natural resources and he rejected all arguments to the contrary. In *Crusade in Europe* Eisenhower bluntly describes his attitude:

"I emphatically repudiated one suggestion I had heard that the Ruhr mines should be flooded. This seemed silly and

△ *The ruins of a defeated country. Reconstruction would have been practically impossible under the harsh terms of the Morgenthau plan.*

criminal to me . . . These views were presented to everyone who queried me on the subject, both then and later. They were eventually placed before the President and the Secretary of State when they came to Potsdam in July 1945."

Harry Hopkins himself joined this protest; Roosevelt and Morgenthau therefore had to shelve indefinitely the plan so accurately described by General Eisenhower. Moreover in London, the Treasury informed the Prime Minister that if German productivity were completely destroyed, she would no longer be able to pay for her imports, and England would therefore lose an important market as soon as peace came. The argument with which Morgenthau had won over Lord Cherwell was therefore entirely refuted. In these circumstances, Churchill made no bones about going back on his agreement, and was quite ready, when he wrote the penultimate volume of his war memoirs, to forget that he had given it, even in writing: he had in fact contributed to drawing up the resolution that had been formulated. The Morgenthau plan was a dead letter.

German propaganda benefits

However, the Morgenthau plan had certain consequences, even though it had been abandoned by the Western Allies. What was learned of it in Germany gave Goebbels a propaganda line which he developed on the radio with his usual diabolical skill. The Allies, he pointed out to his fellow countrymen on every possible occasion, were not only making war against the Nazis, but against the whole German people, who would be condemned to the bleakest poverty by a ruthless enemy if they were so naïve as to cease their resistance and disown their Führer; in destructive purpose, Anglo-Saxon "Jewry" was no different from the Moscow Bolsheviks. The Quebec resolution, moreover, demonstrated the error of people who, like the July 20 conspirators, thought they could spare the German people the Soviet invasion by paying for it at the price of capitulation to the West.

Moscow Conference

"Que diable allait-il faire dans cette galère?" (What on earth was he doing in this company?) One might well echo Molière's question when considering the visit Churchill made to Moscow from October 9 to 16, 1944.

According to Churchill's own account, the Soviet penetration into south-east Europe compelled him to make this journey. With Rumania's about-face, followed by the Bulgarian armistice, the launching of the Soviet autumn offensive, and "in spite of the Warsaw tragedy . . . I felt the need of another personal meeting with Stalin . . . As the victory of the Grand Alliance became only a matter of time it was natural that Russian ambitions should grow. Communism raised its head behind the thundering Russian battle-front. Russia was the Deliverer, and Communism the gospel she brought."

At this juncture, neither Bulgaria's nor Rumania's fates were of the slightest concern to Great Britain; on the other hand Churchill was very worried about what would happen to Poland and Greece. Great Britain considered herself responsible for the restoration of their governments-in-exile, if this was what their peoples really wished. And it was essential that they should be able to express themselves freely. In fact, this was far from certain since Stalin had set up a Polish government subservient to him in Lublin, and George Papandreou's Greek Government seemed to be dependent on the Communist resistance group.

On the other hand, work was not proceeding well at Dumbarton Oaks, where an inter-Allied conference was meeting for the purpose of laying the foundations of a future United Nations Organisation. The Russians clashed with the British and Americans both on the composition of the General Assembly and on the balloting method for the Security Council. Moscow was now determined that the rule of Great Power unanimity should prevail. Once again, according to Churchill in 1953, he felt he should strike while the iron was hot:

"I felt sure we could only reach good

△ *The men whose remorseless advance during the winter of 1944-45 was the background to all Allied discussions on the fate of the countries of central and south-eastern Europe: the soldiers of the Red Army.*

△ *Lord Moran, Churchill's ever-present physician. He saw Churchill every day and was able to note his reaction to events as they happened. His book* Churchill: The Struggle for Survival *thus provides valuable insight into Churchill's thoughts, especially with regard to his attitude towards the Morgenthau Plan and the settlement of the Polish question.*

decisions with Russia while we had the comradeship of a common foe as a bond. Hitler and Hitlerism were doomed; but after Hitler what?"

Churchill's initiative

Therefore Churchill took the initiative in a telegram on September 27, and proposed a visit to the Kremlin. Stalin, in his reply of September 30, welcomed the idea "warmly". Roosevelt excused himself from accompanying Churchill to Moscow as the presidential elections were imminent, and his absence from the U.S.A. at this time might well have prejudiced the result to his disadvantage. However, his ambassador in the U.S.S.R., Averell Harriman, was to replace him, taking part in the conversations as an observer, and as Roosevelt's message of October 4 stated:

"While naturally Averell will not be in a position to commit the United States—I could not permit anyone to commit me in advance—he will be able to keep me informed, and I have told him to return and report to me as soon as the conference is over."

And as he feared that his British partner might indulge in some passing whim, Roosevelt sent word to Stalin on the same day:

"I am sure you understand that in this global war there is literally no question, military or political, in which the United States is not interested. I am firmly convinced that the three of us, and only the three of us, can find the solution of the questions still unresolved. In this sense, while appreciating Mr. Churchill's desire for the meeting, I prefer to regard your forthcoming talks with the Prime Minister as preliminary to a meeting of the three of us which can take place any time after the elections here as far as I am concerned."

Churchill does not mention it in his memoirs, but he took great offence at the President's precaution, according to Lord Moran, who in his capacity as Churchill's doctor saw him every day. But what was more serious, according to Moran, by the end of September "the advance of the Red Army has taken possession of [Churchill's] mind. Once they got into a country, it would not be easy to get them out. Our army in Italy was too weak to keep them in check. He might get his

way with Stalin by other means.

"All might be well if he could win Stalin's friendship. After all it was stupid of the President to suppose that he was the only person who could manage Stalin. Winston told me that he had found he could talk to Stalin as one human being to another. Stalin, he was sure, would be sensible. He went on to speak of this proffer of friendship to Stalin as if it were an ingenious idea that had just occurred to him, and while he spoke his eyes popped and his words tumbled over each other in his excitement. He could think of nothing else. It had ceased to be a means to an end; it had become an end in itself. He sat up in bed.

"'If we three come together,' he said, 'everything is possible—absolutely anything.'"

As can be seen, there is a strong difference between Churchill's attitude in his memoirs and his reactions at the time as his doctor saw them; in 1953, when the cold war was at its height and he had just been re-elected, Churchill could not admit to his readers that he had deluded himself into thinking he could win Stalin over.

Spheres of influence

Accompanied by Anthony Eden, General Sir Hastings Ismay, his chief-of-staff, and Field-Marshal Sir Alan Brooke, the C.I.G.S., the Prime Minister travelled via Naples, Cairo, and Simferopol' and arrived in Moscow on the evening of October 9. At 2200 hours, he and Eden were conducted to Stalin's office. Stalin, accompanied by Molotov, was waiting for him. And in the absence of Averell Harriman, the four men lost no time in making a preliminary survey of the world situation.

Doubtless Harriman would not have objected to their decision to invite the Polish government to send a delegation to Moscow. But perhaps he would have thought that Churchill was unduly compromising the future as well as the U.S.A. if he had heard him tell Stalin:

"Let us settle about our affairs in the Balkans. Your armies are in Roumania and Bulgaria. We have interests, missions, and agents there. Don't let us get at cross-purposes in small ways. So far as Britain and Russia are concerned, how would it do for you to have ninety

per cent predominance in Roumania, for us to have ninety per cent of the say in Greece, and go fifty-fifty about Yugoslavia?"

And even more so if he had seen Churchill make in writing a proposal which had never been agreed by London and Washington. Churchill in fact, whilst his words were being translated, scribbled on a half sheet of paper:

"Roumania

Russia	..	..	90%
The others	..	..	10%

Greece

Great Britain	..	..	90%
(in accord with U.S.A.)			

△ △ *The "Red Orchestra" batters Nazi ears with its successes in Poland and East Prussia.*

△ ◁ *How* Simplicissimus *saw "free" Polish broadcasts from the "Soviet paradise".*

△ *John Bull tells Poland "The best solution is to give him all he steals and you'll be friends."*

△ *George Papandreou, Greek Prime Minister. In April 1944, he was brought out of Greece by the Allies to form a Greek government-in-exile in Cairo. Churchill was concerned about the fate of Greece after the war and considered Great Britain responsible for the restoration of the government-in-exile. When the Germans withdrew from Greece in October 1944, Papandreou returned to Athens as Prime Minister.*

▷ *Churchill arrives in Moscow, October 9, 1944. Concerned by the increasing Soviet penetration of south-east Europe, Churchill initiated this conference himself, determined to reach amicable agreement with Stalin over the future of the Balkans and, more important, Poland.*

Russia	..	..	..	10%
Yugoslavia		..	..	50-50%
Hungary	..	..	..	50-50%
Bulgaria				
Russia	..	..	..	75%
The others		..	..	25%"

Stalin ticked the paper passed to him by Churchill, who writes: "It was all settled in no more time than it takes to set down."

Stalin's acceptance of Churchill's proposals was not quite so casual as it seemed, but in fact reflected the acknowledged political and military realities of the situation.

In exchange for a half-sheet of paper the Western Powers, on Churchill's initiative, had abdicated all influence in Bucharest and Sofia, and implicitly left the Rumanians and Bulgarians to face the Soviet giant alone. Yet such a division of spheres of influence was only realistic in view of the Red Army's advances, as the case of Poland was to show.

In addition, it was later observed that this arrangement on October 9 did not remove the threat of Communist subversion from Greece, in spite of the percentage of that unhappy country conceded to Great Britain by the Kremlin.

In fact, though, after the war, Soviet Russia abstained from providing the Greek Communist party with very much aid in their fight against the right-wing parties, armed by the Western powers.

Tito goes it alone

The 50 per cent influence allotted to Britain in Yugoslavia dropped to zero even before hostilities ended in Europe, and Tito tore up the agreement he had concluded in the previous year with Dr. Subašić, Prime Minister of the Yugoslav government-in-exile. Obviously, in October 1944, Churchill and Eden no longer had any illusions about the future direction of Marshal Tito's policy, in spite of the Anglo-American arms deliveries which had saved him from defeat and death. Moreover, in this division of spheres of influence, it was clear that Churchill had completely forgotten Albania, on which Greece had some claims.

Eden *versus* Molotov

But before 24 hours had passed, Molotov tried to obtain from Eden some modifications of the percentages agreed on the day before. He received a curt refusal, but a note of Eden's shows that his own report of the incident was coolly received by the Prime Minister, who was wrapped up in his own illusions:

"W. rather upset by my report. I think he thought I had dispelled good atmosphere he had created night before. But I explained this was the real battle and I could not and would not give way."

His firmness was rewarded, as Molotov undertook to call on the Bulgarians to evacuate immediately the Greek and Yugoslav provinces which they had occupied by German agreement in April and May 1941. As regards Yugoslavia, Eden wrote:

"We also spoke of Yugoslavia, when Stalin said that Tito thought the Croats and Slovenes would refuse to join in any government under King Peter. He him-

self had the impression that the King was ineffective. I replied that I was sure the King had courage and I thought that he had intelligence. Mr. Churchill interjected that the King was very young.

"'How old is he?' asked Stalin. 'Twenty-one,' I answered. 'Twenty-one!' exclaimed Stalin with a burst of pride, 'Peter the Great was ruler of Russia at seventeen.' For that moment, at least, Stalin was more nationalist than communist, the same mood as had seen the disappearance for the time being of the portraits of Marx and Engels from the Kremlin rooms and their replacement by Kutuzov and Suvorov."

Poles in exile

On October 13, the Polish delegation of the government-in-exile, consisting of its Prime Minister, Stanislas Mikolajczyk, Professor Grabski, and Foreign Minister Tadeusz Romer started discussions with Stalin, Molotov, Churchill, Eden, and Harriman, who had been instructed to keep strictly to his rôle as observer. They intended to reach an agreement on two questions: firstly, the eastern frontiers of Poland; and secondly, the formation of a unified Polish government, including the London government's representatives and members of the Lublin "National Committee". Although they expected to make some territorial sacrifices to the Soviet Union, Mikolajczyk and his colleagues were aghast when they discovered that the Teheran agreement (which had been concluded behind their backs by the "Big Three") had prescribed the Curzon Line as their country's frontier; thus 48 per cent of Polish territory would be surrendered to the U.S.S.R. without the population involved being consulted about the transfer.

The Polish prime minister's protests against the acquiescence which was being demanded of him left Stalin cold and uncompromising.

After this session, the British and Poles met. Churchill lost his temper and started threatening the unfortunate Mikolajczyk:

"I pressed Mikolajczyk hard to consider two things, namely, *de facto* acceptance of the Curzon Line, with interchange of population, and a friendly discussion with the Lublin Polish Committee so that a united Poland might be established."

Δ *Averell Harriman* (right), *U.S. Ambassador in Moscow, with Anthony Eden, who accompanied Churchill to the Moscow Conference. Harriman represented Roosevelt at the conference, but was absent when Stalin and Churchill decided on spheres of influence in the Balkans.*

Overleaf:
Top left: *"And look! The nice uncle is even offering you a stool."*
Top right: *The imbalance of power late on in the war.*
Below: *Poland's pathetic plight: "And we all put our faith in this boat."*

BALANCE OF POWER

ATLANTIK CHARTA

2026

This is the version of the meeting in Churchill's memoirs, but it seems to be a typically British understatement. In fact, on the next day the Prime Minister confided to Moran: "I was pretty rough with Mikolajczyk . . . He was obstinate and I lost my temper." A few hours later Churchill returned to the subject: "I shook my fist at him and lost my temper."

It is hard to accept Mikólajczyk's account of the conversation; his memoirs were published in New York and Toronto and were not challenged by Churchill. The striking thing about Churchill's diatribes, as recounted by Mikolajczyk, is not so much their violence ("You're not a government! You're an unreasonable people who want to shipwreck Europe. I'll leave you to stew in your own juice. You have no sense of responsibility when you want to abandon the people in your care, and you've no idea of their sufferings. You've no thought for anything but your own wretched, mean, and egotistical interests.") and their threats ("We shall not part as friends. I shall tell the world how unreasonable you've shown yourselves to be . . . We'll take a stand and break away from you if you continue to

prevaricate. I'll consider opening relations with the other Poles. The Lublin government can work perfectly. They'll be the government for sure.") as his confidence that if the Polish Government gave in to the Big Three, all would be for the best in the best of all possible Europes. Churchill continued:

"Our relations with Russia are better than they've ever been. I expect them to remain so . . . we do not intend to jeopardise the peace of Europe . . . Your discussions are nothing more than criminal attempts to undermine goodwill between the Allies with your *Liberum veto*. It is a criminal act of your doing!"

Assuming this determinedly optimistic point of view, Churchill described to Mikolajczyk the advantage which would compensate Poland for the sacrifices he was calling upon her to make:

"But think what you will get in exchange. You will have a country. I will see that a British ambassador is sent to you. And there will also be an ambassador from the United States, the greatest military power in the world . . .

"If you accept the Curzon line, the United States will devote themselves most

△ *Polish troops manning a self-propelled gun are briefed by their commander. Men such as these, fighting with the Soviet forces, were now in an ambivalent position. Did they consider the possibility that their efforts to liberate their country might be furthering Soviet rather than Polish interests?*

actively to the reconstruction of Poland and will doubtless give you large loans, perhaps even without your having to ask for them. We will help you too, but we will be poor after this war. You are *obliged* to accept the decision of the great powers."

Mikolajczyk, in spite of Churchill's tone of voice, was not completely insensitive to this argument. He proposed a compromise, in which he was prepared to recognise the Curzon Line as Poland's eastern frontier, provided that the Drohobycz and Boryslaw oil wells, as well as the great historically and traditionally Polish cities of L'vov and Vilnyus on the east of the line, remained Polish. But Stalin refused to countenance any such concessions.

△ *Bierut, President of the Lublin "Committee of National Liberation". Churchill thought the Lublin Poles were "mere pawns of Russia" when he met them at the Moscow Conference.*
▷ *The Communist provisional government of Poland at a march-past in Lublin. The officers are saluting in the traditional Polish manner, with three fingers (one for the Father, one for the Son, and one for the Holy Ghost) despite their new Communist persuasion.*
△▷ *Roosevelt, on board the cruiser* Quincy *travelling to the Yalta Conference, stops off in the Great Bitter Lake to entertain King Farouk of Egypt on his birthday. This delighted Farouk, who had felt slighted by other Allied leaders.*
▽▷ *London, Washington, and Moscow recognised General de Gaulle's provisional government as the government of the French Republic at the Moscow Conference. Here, General de Gaulle is seen arriving at Moscow. He was not, however, invited to the Yalta and Potsdam Conferences.*

Combined Polish government?

In doing this, Stalin was risking nothing; on the one hand his armies had crossed the Curzon Line on the entire front between the Niemen and the Carpathians; on the other hand, the Lublin Committee delegates, Osóbka-Morawski and Bierut, stated in the presence of Churchill, Eden, and Harriman:

"'We are here to demand on behalf of Poland that Lvov shall belong to Russia. That is the will of the Polish people.'

"When this had been translated from Polish into English and Russian I looked at Stalin and saw an understanding twinkle in his expressive eyes, as much as to say, 'What about that for our Soviet teaching!'"

In their memoirs Churchill and Eden made no attempt to conceal their disgust when they heard these servile commonplaces. Nevertheless Mikolajczyk received the peremptory advice to accept these foreign agents in his government. Otherwise it would be the end of Poland.

Conduct of the war

As Roosevelt had wished, the problems relating to the articles of the future international organisation were not mentioned during the conference. The agenda was devoted to presenting, discussing, and putting final touches to the plans for the

last phase of the war in Europe and for the participation of the Red Army in the war against Japan.

Brooke on Stalin

With his usual clarity, Brooke set out the situation on the Western Front and in Italy, and explained General Eisenhower's intentions. The deputy chief-of-staff of the Red Army, General Antonov, then spoke, and Brooke noted in his diary that he was extremely pleased with the ensuing discussion.

On October 15, the war against Japan was discussed, with particular reference to the Red Army and the possibility of moving supplies via the trans-Siberian railway for an offensive in Manchuria with 60 divisions and appropriate air forces. Stalin took over from his military colleague and explained the difficulties of the project. According to Brooke:

"He displayed an astounding knowledge of technical railway details, had read past history of fighting in that theatre and from this knowledge drew very sound deductions. I was more than ever impressed by his military ability."

Complete military agreement was reached by the Big Three. This did not mean that a political agreement had been reached, however. While being allies for the duration of the war it was becoming increasingly clear that after the war Soviet Russia and the United States of America would be global rivals. With this in mind, Stalin cleverly exploited the differences between Britain and America to his own advantage.

Churchill proposes the division of Germany

With regard to a future peace settlement Churchill and Stalin agreed that Germany might be divided up and that a southern state, consisting of Baden, Württemberg, Bavaria, and Austria, would be formed. To give more stability to this Danubian confederation, Churchill wanted Hungary to join it, but Stalin, who had designs on Hungary, refused.

The only success claimed by the British Government was the *de jure* recognition by London, Washington, and Moscow of General de Gaulle's provisional government as the government of France.

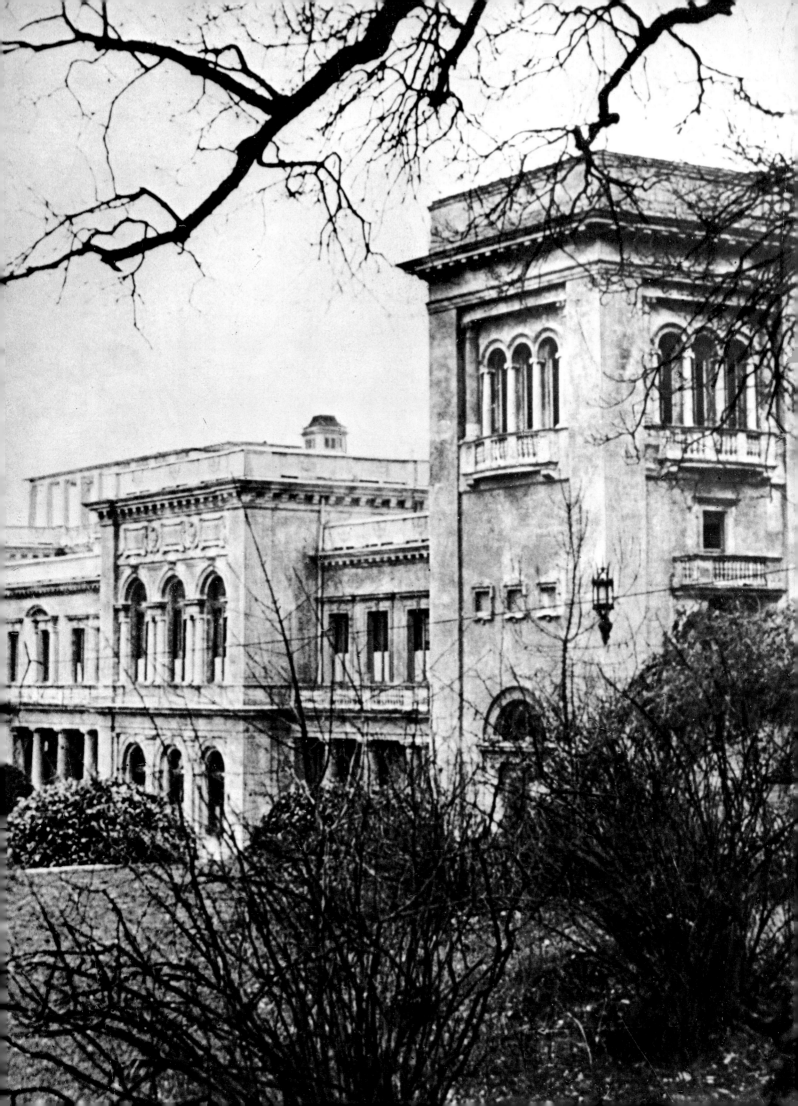

The "Big Three" confer at Yalta

Much has been written, at any rate in the West, about the "Argonaut" Conference, during which Roosevelt, Churchill, Stalin, and their chief political and military colleagues met at Yalta in the Crimea. In 1955, the State Department published a wide collection of diplomatic documents relating to the Big Three's meeting, the discussions they had together, and the resolutions and agreements they signed. Thus we can compare these authentic records with the statements of those taking part in the conference.

During the period between Churchill's Moscow journey and the Yalta conference, a number of occurrences which influenced the course of negotiations should be mentioned.

On November 7, 1944, the American people re-elected Roosevelt to a fourth term as President, admittedly by about 3,000,000 fewer votes than in 1940. Obviously, in making his choice, the American voter was relying on the adage that one should not change horses in mid-course. Nevertheless, the victor of this exhausting campaign had neglected his brief and, in addition, he was in a very poor state of health.

"The President looked old and thin and drawn; he had a cape or shawl over his shoulders and appeared shrunken; he sat looking straight ahead with his mouth open, as if he were not taking things in." This was Moran's description of him on February 3, and the next day he wrote:

"It was not only his physical deterioration that had caught their attention. He intervened very little in the discussions, sitting with his mouth open. If he has sometimes been short of facts about the subject under discussion his shrewdness has covered this up. Now, they say, the shrewdness has gone, and there is nothing left." Again, Moran noted on the 7th:

"To a doctor's eye, the President appears a very sick man. He has all the symptoms of hardening of the arteries of the brain in an advanced stage, so that I give him only a few months to live."

For personal reasons Roosevelt, before starting on his electoral campaign, had dropped his previous Vice-President, Henry A. Wallace, in favour of Harry S. Truman, the senator from Missouri. This was a stroke of luck for the free world. Truman, a man of strong character, was, however, quite unprepared for his task when on April 12, 1945 he was suddenly

called upon to take over the responsibilities of power.

Moreover the Secretary of State, Cordell Hull, had now reached retirement age. Roosevelt appointed Edward R. Stettinius in his place. Stettinius was a conscientious civil servant who knew his job thoroughly, but he was called upon to take over his duties under a President in very poor health, to say the least, and was faced by an opposite number as redoubtable and experienced in international affairs as Molotov.

Wavering support for Poland from the West

Mikolajczyk, when he returned to London, found that the majority of his government disapproved of the concessions he had felt compelled to make to the U.S.S.R. He therefore accepted the consequences, and resigned. He was succeeded by Tomasz Arciszewski, a militant social-democrat. But although he was more to the left than his predecessor, the new head of the exile government failed to move the Kremlin.

When he resigned on November 24, 1944, Mikolajczyk handed over two documents concerning the policy of the U.S.A. and Great Britain towards the future Polish state. In a letter after he had been re-elected, President Roosevelt defined the American attitude clearly and positively:

"The Government of the United States is, most determinedly, in favour of a strong Polish state, free, independent, and conscious of the rights of the Polish people, to run its internal politics as it sees fit, without any outside interference."

Certainly the U.S.A. could not depart from their traditional policy and guarantee the frontiers of the future Polish state, but they were ready to play a very large part in its economic reconstruction.

Moreover, on the previous November 2, on Churchill's instructions, Sir Alexander Cadogan, Permanent Under-Secretary of State at the Foreign Office, wrote to Romer, the Polish Foreign Minister, a letter of which the following is an extract:

"Finally you ask if His Majesty's Government will guarantee the independence and integrity of the new Polish state. On this point the reply of His Majesty's Government is that they are ready to give this guarantee conjointly with the Soviet Government. If the Government of the United States also believed that it could associate itself in this guarantee, that would be so much the better, but His Majesty's Government does not make this a condition of the guarantee, which it is ready to give conjointly with that of the Soviet Government."

It is evident that Great Britain's attitude in this declaration fell considerably short of the U.S.A.'s, as she made her guarantee of Polish independence subject to an agreement with the Soviet Union. What would happen if Stalin refused this guarantee – a guarantee that it was hardly in his interests to comply with?

Stalin recognises the "Lublin Committee"

On December 18, a statement by Secretary of State Stettinius, recalling the terms of Roosevelt's letter to Mikolajczyk, was brought to Stalin's notice. On December 27, Stalin in his reply to Roosevelt maintained that this statement had been overtaken by events; then after a long diatribe against Arciszewski and his colleagues, he added in so many words:

"I must say frankly that in the event of the Polish Committee of National Liberation becoming a Provisional Polish Government, the Soviet Government will, in view of the foregoing, have no serious reasons for postponing its recognition."

Then, in spite of a letter from Roosevelt, who said he was "disturbed and deeply disappointed" by this declaration and by the hasty Moscow decision, he proceeded to recognise the Lublin Committee on January 5, 1945; he gave Roosevelt the following explanation:

"Of course I quite understand your proposal for postponing recognition of the Provisional Government of Poland by the Soviet Union for a month. But one circumstance makes me powerless to comply with your wish. The point is that on December 27 the Presidium of the Supreme Soviet of the U.S.S.R., replying to the corresponding question by the Poles, declared that it would recognise the Provisional Government of Poland the moment it was set up. This circumstance makes me powerless to comply with your wish."

But he omitted to say that he had dictated this request for recognition to the "Polish Committee of National Liberation."

The new government moves in

It was in this sort of atmosphere that the Yalta Conference opened. Certainly Roosevelt had no intention of recognising the puppet government which Stalin controlled, and Churchill even less so. But in the meantime events had moved on. In fact just when the three delegations were holding their first session, Zhukov's advance guard reached the bend of the Oder whilst Konev's was about to take Breslau. Except for the Polish corridor, all Polish territory was in the hands of the Russians, who were everywhere set-

ting up the Lublin Committee's representatives and hunting down the partisans who had been fighting the Germans for five years under the command of the Polish government-in-exile.

The conference opens

On February 2, Roosevelt, who had arrived on the cruiser *Quincy,* and Churchill, who had flown in, met at Valletta in Malta. They joined the Combined Chiefs-of-Staff Committee, which had been in session for three days and was completing plans for the great operation to take the British and the Americans into the centre of Germany. Then the two delegations flew to the Crimea and on the evening of February 3 moved into the buildings reserved for them: the Americans into the former imperial palace of Livadia; the British five miles away in

1. *Harry Hopkins*
2. *Alger Hiss*
3. *James V. Forrestal*
4. *Robert Winant*
5. *Edward R. Stettinius*

Harry S. Truman was born in 1884. He was a Senator for Missouri when the United States entered the war, and soon entered the limelight as chairman of the Senate Special Commission looking into the National Defense Program. Truman headed the committee with tact and care, and saved the U.S. billions of dollars by pruning costs in the allocation of contracts. His success in this was instrumental in his selection by Roosevelt as Vice-Presidential running mate in the 1944 election campaign. When Roosevelt died on April 12, 1945, Truman became President. Because he had not been in his predecessor's inner circle, Truman had at first to rely on Roosevelt's cabinet in following up the policies already in operation. But as 1945 progressed, he gradually phased out Roosevelt's appointees in favour of his own. He continued to follow the general line of Roosevelt's policies, however, and pressed on with preparations for the San Francisco Conference, which was to set up the United Nations Organisation. Unlike Roosevelt, however, he soon saw what Stalin's real intentions towards Europe were, and that there was little the Western Allies could do about it. Truman attended the Potsdam Conference in July 1945, and authorised the atom bombing of Hiroshima and Nagasaki.

the Vorontzov villa. Stalin and his colleagues were to stay at the Yusupov Palace halfway between them, an arrangement obviously calculated to prevent any Anglo-American private conversations and to make *tête-à-tête* talks with Roosevelt easier.

The first such meeting took place in the afternoon of February 4, and the President was moved to get Stalin to repeat his Teheran toast (that 50,000 German officers should be shot) because Roosevelt maintained the devastation caused by the Wehrmacht in the Crimea gave him a desire for revenge.

Roosevelt chosen as chairman

A few hours later the conference opened in the Livadia Palace, and Stalin immediately proposed that there should be no rotation of chairmanship, but that Roosevelt should chair the proceedings for the whole meeting.

Arthur Conte, in his *Yalta ou le partage du monde,* has noted that this was a skilful Soviet manoeuvre, as it was not intended

American vacillation

Eden also noted that the American president was "vague and loose and ineffective", letting the discussion drift on, without being able to pin Stalin and Churchill down to firm and precise terms. The various questions on the agenda were discussed unmethodically, by fits and starts, and Harry Hopkins several times had to bring the discussion back to the subject by passing notes to Roosevelt. But the bias of these notes can easily be guessed, as in spite of the troublesome state of his health, the so-called *éminence grise* of the White House was still strongly pro-Soviet.

Secretary of State Stettinius was too new in his job to know how to assert himself usefully in the discussion. As for the fourth member of the American delegation, the diplomat Alger Hiss, whose particular responsibility was questions relating to the future United Nations Organisation, he was later condemned to five years' imprisonment on January 22, 1950 by a New York court for perjury about his Communist associations.

Another circumstance played against the two Western powers; this was the ten day period allowed by the American constitution to the President to approve or veto bills adopted by the Congress. As he could not do this by cable or radio, it was essential for him not to prolong his stay in the Crimea beyond a week. Stalin, however, was in no hurry and was ready to sell Roosevelt time in exchange for concessions.

△ ◁ *The Combined Chiefs-of-Staff Committee in session in Malta, January-February 1944, completing plans for the advance into central Germany. Roosevelt and Churchill joined the committee briefly before continuing their journey to Yalta.*
▽ ◁ ◁ *Reunion on board the cruiser* Quincy, *at anchor off Malta: Roosevelt, General Marshall (on the right), Vice-Admiral Cooke (on the left), and Admiral King (back view).*
▽ ◁ *Churchill and Roosevelt acknowledge their reception at Yalta. Molotov is on Churchill's right. Note how ill Roosevelt looks; Lord Moran said at the time that he appeared "shrunken".*
△ *Russia sits down to a nourishing meal of "little states of Europe" stew, with the comment "You can see how happy I am to swallow up the people you abandoned and I freed."*

merely as a practical working arrangement: "This also showed a remarkable appreciation of Roosevelt's psychology, by strengthening him in the awareness of his superiority. He was also dissociating himself from British imperialism. It in fact separated the British and the Americans by conferring the chairmanship on the American; Roosevelt thus had power to arbitrate, a conciliatory rôle which would naturally lead him to show increased understanding of the Russian position. Stalin immediately gave himself a big advantage while appearing to give it to Roosevelt."

Formidable negotiator

Since he had seen Stalin at work, Anthony Eden refers to his diplomatic talents in a way that reminds one of Field-Marshal Sir Alan Brooke's references to his strategic abilities:

"Marshal Stalin as a negotiator was the toughest proposition of all. Indeed, after something like thirty years' experience of international conferences of one kind and another, if I had to pick a team for going into a conference room, Stalin would be my first choice. Of course the man was ruthless and of course he knew his purpose. He never wasted a word. He never stormed, he was

Three German comments on Allied relations:

△ *Stalin, past master of the shot-in-the-neck method of execution, sets the table for the next conference with his latest invention.*

△▷ *"I have the feeling, my dear Roosevelt, that we've been left decidedly behind the marshal," says Churchill.*

▷ *Overheard during the post-war carve-up of the world: "Well, Sam, what are you doing?" "I was just thinking how I could repay you for your great help." "Incredible! I was just thinking the same thing."*

velt, Stettinius, and James) could tell one another gratefully: "After the rain comes the sun."

seldom even irritated. Hooded, calm, never raising his voice, he avoided the repeated negatives of Molotov which were so exasperating to listen to. By more subtle methods he got what he wanted without having seemed so obdurate" – the sign of a first-class diplomat.

Nevertheless, Eden also acknowledged that Molotov was a first-rate assistant to Stalin. One may well suppose that when responsibilities were assigned, the orders given to Molotov were to adopt such a harsh tone that when Stalin took over negotiations in the style so vividly described by Eden, the British and American representatives (in particular Roose-

Churchill placed in a difficult position

Under these circumstances it is not hard to see that the British delegation had no easy task, faced with the vacillations of American policy and Stalin's firm resolve to make the maximum possible advances in all parts of the world. Thus the British did not receive the immediate support of their natural allies when they proposed the immediate and simultaneous evacuation of Persia by the British and Soviet forces that had occupied the country

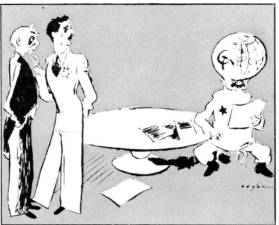

◁ *The three delegations get down to work. Stalin is seated second from left at the top, Roosevelt at the right, and Churchill at bottom left, with a cigar.*

△ *Death comments "But why argue about future supplies of cannon fodder, my dear sirs? I'm quite content with your present ones."*

▽ ◁ *Eden comments on his Russian opposite number: "Molotov clearly isn't a devious character. His territorial ambitions aren't difficult to see."*

since August 1941. Similarly, the Soviet Union succeeded in imposing its attitude about a revision, once peace came, of the Montreux Convention. This had, since July 20, 1936, laid down the law concerning the control of the Turkish narrows.

Therefore Churchill left the Crimea full of forebodings, quite the reverse of his happy mood of the previous October 9, when he landed at Moscow airport. But to the last day of his life he did his best to deny any responsibility for the inexorable process which led to the enslavement of 120 million Europeans behind the Iron Curtain. According to Churchill, everything was decided at Yalta during the conference when he was, if one can put it like that, "sandwiched" between Stalin and Roosevelt. In this way he was able to divest himself of his responsibility

in this most unjust settlement of World War II, making Roosevelt shoulder it all. But in view of the documents just quoted, it is impossible to confirm this black and white judgement, and Alfred Fabre-Luce's judgement in *L'Histoire démaquillée,*

"Churchill changed tack too late", seems more correct. All the same, he changed tack a year before Truman.

The resolutions

We may now quote the resolutions adopted by Churchill, Roosevelt, and Stalin and drawn up by Eden, Stettinius, and Molotov. We shall limit our comments to the resolutions on Poland, Germany, and the Far East.

(a) The reorganisation of Poland
Stalin conceded to the Allies that the Soviet-Polish frontier could in places run three and even five miles to the east of the Curzon Line, which he claimed had been originated by Clemenceau, although neither the British nor the Americans pointed out this obvious historical error. The Oder and the Neisse were to constitute the western frontier of the new Poland. But although, at Teheran, they had agreed on the eastern Neisse (which runs through the town of Neisse), as is clear from a question from Churchill concerning the allocation of the upper Silesian industrial basin, Stalin and Molotov claimed they had been referring to the western Neisse, which meets the Oder between Guben and Fürstenberg.

Churchill pointed out in vain that this additional modification of the German-Polish frontier would entail the further expulsion of eight million Germans. Stalin replied that the matter was now settled, as the province's inhabitants had fled from the Soviet advance, which was only half true, and they then went on to consider the agenda.

As regards Poland's political reorganisation, we must refer to Point 7 of the protocol recorded on February 11 by the foreign ministers of the Big Three. Taking into consideration the Red Army's complete "liberation" of Poland, it stated:

"The provisional government actually operating in Poland must in the future be reorganised on a larger democratic base, to include the popular leaders actually in Poland and those abroad. This new government is to be called the Polish Government of National Unity.

"Mr. Molotov, Mr. Harriman, and Sir A. Clark Kerr are authorised to form a commission to consult initially the members of the Provisional Polish Government, as well as other Polish leaders (both in Poland and abroad), with a view to the reorganisation of the actual government along the lines set out below. The Polish Government of National Unity must set about organising free and open elections as soon as possible, on the basis of a universal franchise and a secret ballot. All democratic and anti-Nazi parties will have the right to take part and put up candidates."

It can be seen that there is a great difference between this tripartite declaration and Stalin's statement to Roosevelt on May 4, 1943: "As regards the Hitlerites' rumours on the possibility that a new Polish government will be formed in the U.S.S.R., it is scarcely necessary to give the lie to these ravings."

The two Western powers did not expressly recognise the government formed from the Lublin Committee, but they took note of its existence, and the men who were to give it the character of national unity provided for by the protocol gathered round it and not round the legal government in London. No one stated how many of these men were to come from London and how many from Lublin; but this question was to be examined by a commission and Molotov, who was to be at its centre, would have much greater authority than the British and American Ambassadors in Moscow. Yalta, therefore, consummated Churchill's failure to preserve Polish independence and democracy and Stalin's success in making Poland a Communist satellite.

(b) Germany's fate
In order to snatch these concessions from his allies, in exchange for a more vague promise of "free and open elections on the basis of a universal franchise and a secret ballot", Stalin put forward the argument that in the event of a German revival the Soviet Union's security demanded the existence of an independent and friendly Poland. In this respect, it is odd to note that neither Churchill nor Roosevelt thought of pointing out to Stalin that the arrangements they had just decided on for the treatment of Germany eliminated any danger of aggression on her part for centuries to come.

Apart from the Oder-Neisse frontier which was to be imposed on Germany, Point 3 of the Yalta protocol is absolutely clear in this respect. Churchill and Eden with some difficulty secured France's right to take part in the occupation of Germany and to send delegates to sit on the Allied Control Commission charged with administering the defeated power.

The Partition of Poland

- ———— Polish boundary in 1937
- ———— Polish boundary in 1947
- ———— Curzon Line

Niemen

Vilnyus

Gdynia
Danzig

EAST PRUSSIA

U.S.S.R.

Wolin

Stettin

Oder

GERMANY

Toruń

Vistula

Bug

Warsaw

Brest-Litovsk

Frankfurt

POLAND

Görlitz

Breslau

Kraków

L'vov

Drohobycz

Stanislaw

CZECHOSLOVAKIA

HUNGARY

RUMANIA

Anthony Eden, the British Foreign Secretary at the time of the Yalta Conference, was born in 1897 and served on the Western Front in World War I. He was Minister for League of Nations Affairs in 1933 and took over from Sir Samuel Hoare as Foreign Secretary in December. He resigned as a result of the weak British attitude to Italy in 1938. Eden became Dominions Secretary, Secretary of State for War, and finally Foreign Secretary in Churchill's Coalition Government in the War. He proved himself a very able diplomat with a flair for persuasion.

As for Roosevelt, he wavered between these two opposing points of view and finally sided with Churchill; but it was agreed that the French occupation zone would be cut out of the British and American zones. It was at this point in the discussions that Roosevelt, in reply to one of Stalin's questions, made a blunder by telling him that he could not possibly obtain authorisation from Congress to maintain American troops in Europe for more than two years after the end of the war. Stalin, it can readily be imagined, found this statement most helpful to his cause.

It was agreed between Roosevelt and Stalin that Germany should pay 20,000 million dollars in reparations; half of this sum would go to the Soviet Union, which would be paid in kind in the form of a transfer of industrial equipment, annual goods deliveries, and the use of German manpower. The final settlement of reparations owed by Germany, and their distribution among the nations that suffered as a result of her aggression, would be determined by a commission in Moscow. Great Britain had reserved her position on the question of the figure of 20,000 million dollars agreed by the Soviets and the Americans.

The principle of dividing Germany up was recorded in the protocol of February 11, and was not clarified during the Yalta discussions; the commission set up under Eden's chairmanship to examine the problem received no directives from the Big Three.

However the Conference finally agreed on the borders of the Allied occupation zones in Germany, so concluding negotiations that had been in progress since the beginning of 1943.

(c) The Far East

As Russia's relations with Japan were governed by the non-aggression pact signed in Moscow on April 13, 1941, the question of Russia taking part in the war

△ *The post-war settlement of Poland agreed at Yalta. In effect the country was shifted to the west, losing her eastern areas but gaining new western ones from Germany.*

being waged by the Anglo-Americans against the Japanese was settled by a special protocol which was kept secret.

As a reward for its intervention, the U.S.S.R. was to recover the rights it had lost by the Treaty of Portsmouth (U.S.A.) in 1905 which had crowned the Emperor Meiji's victory over Tsar Nicholas II. As a consequence, it was to regain possession of the southern part of Sakhalin island, the Manchuria railway, the port of Dairen (Lü-ta) which was to be internationalised, and its lease of Port Arthur. In addition, the Russians would receive the Kurile islands, which they had surrendered to Japan in 1875 in exchange for the southern part of Sakhalin island.

It is clear that the agreement of February 11, 1945 took little account of the interests of the fourth great power, Chiang Kai-shek's China. Admittedly it was agreed that the eastern China and southern Manchuria railways would be run jointly by a Soviet-Chinese company and that China would retain "full and complete sovereignty" in Manchuria. Nevertheless the power mainly involved in this arrangement had taken no part in the negotiations, and had not even been consulted. On this matter, the agreement merely stated:

"It is agreed that the arrangements for Outer Mongolia, as well as for the ports and railways mentioned will require the assent of Generalissimo Chiang Kai-shek. The President will take the necessary measures to obtain this assent, acting on the advice of Marshal Stalin."

But the agreement did not state what would happen if the Chunking government refused its agreement. Moreover, the British and American negotiations about this arrangement lost sight of the fact that as in 1898, the Russian reoccupation of Port Arthur and Dairen in the Kuantung peninsula automatically raised the question of Korea. However, Korea does not appear in the text.

President Roosevelt relied on his own intuition, and did not heed the warnings of Ambassador William Bullitt: "Bill, I am not challenging your facts; they are correct. I am not challenging the logic of your argument. But I have the feeling that Stalin isn't that kind of man. Harry [Hopkins] says he isn't and that all he wants is his country's security. And I think that if I give him all I can give him, and ask for nothing in return, *noblesse oblige,* he won't try to annex anything and he will agree to work with me for a world of democracy and peace."

CHAPTER 140

Himmler's offensive

Before he could accept the German surrender, the offer of which was to be brought to him at Rheims by a delegation headed by Colonel-General Jodl, General Eisenhower still had to repel two attacks, one directed against his own authority, and the other against the 6th Army Group in lower Alsace.

On December 28, 1944, Eisenhower went to Hasselt, where Montgomery had set up his headquarters. He wanted to go over the plans for future operations with him, to begin as soon as the Ardennes pocket had been nipped off. Eisenhower and Montgomery had no difficulty in reaching agreement on the objective to be set for the offensive they were about

to launch. Both favoured the Ruhr. But Montgomery thought that the "major crisis" that had just been resolved authorised him to adopt the claim he had pressed at the beginning of the preceding August. He wanted control of operations, and he thought himself the more qualified to bear the responsibility since Eisenhower had put the American 1st and 9th Armies under his command. Hence his letter to "Ike", dated December 29. Point 6 of this read:

"I suggest that your directive should finish with this sentence:

"'12 and 21 Army Groups will develop operations in accordance with the above instructions.

△ *General Leclerc (wearing the képi) inspects the men and the machines of his French 2nd Armoured Division. After helping in the defence of Strasbourg during Operation "Nordwind", the division was moved south as part of the French II Corps for the crushing of the Colmar pocket.*

"'From now onwards full operational direction, control, and co-ordination of these operations is vested in the C.-in-C. 21 Army Group, subject to such instructions as may be issued by the Supreme Commander from time to time.'"

In writing this, Montgomery was disregarding the prudent advice contained in Brooke's letter of December 24 to him:

"I would like to give you a word of warning. Events and enemy action have forced on Eisenhower the setting up of a more satisfactory system of command. I feel it is most important that you should not even in the slightest degree appear to rub this undoubted fact in to anyone at S.H.A.E.F. or elsewhere."

Eisenhower rejected his subordinate's suggestion by return of post. But, even had he not done this on his own initiative, he would have been ordered to do so by General Marshall, who cabled him from Washington on December 30:

"They may or may not have brought to your attention articles in certain London papers proposing a British deputy commander for all your ground forces and implying that you have undertaken too much of a task yourself. My feeling is this: under no circumstances make any concessions of any kind whatsoever. I am not assuming that you had in mind such a concession I just wish you to be certain of our attitude. You are doing a grand job, and go on and give them hell."

The matter would have stopped there if, on January 5, 1945, Montgomery had not given a press conference on the Battle of the Ardennes, which drove the American generals to the limit of exasperation. The text of the conference was published by General Bradley and it can be said that although Montgomery polished his own image and took some pleasure in exaggerating the part played by British forces in the Ardennes, he did not criticise his allies or their leaders in any way.

The crisis reached flashpoint when Bradley informed his old friend Eisenhower that he would ask to be recalled to the United States rather than serve under Montgomery's command. In view of the rumours spread by Goebbels's propaganda services, Churchill thought he ought to step in, which he did in the House of Commons on January 18. His excellent speech made special mention of the all-important part that the U.S. Army had played in the battle and placated everyone.

Besides this, another move of the Prime Minister's contributed to relieving the tension between S.H.A.E.F. and the 21st Army Group. As operations in Italy had slowed down considerably, it was suggested that Alexander was being wasted there. So Eisenhower's deputy, Tedder, was to be recalled to ordinary R.A.F. service, his place being taken by Alexander. Though this compromise did not win Eisenhower's approval, it also came up against Montgomery's decided opposition. If he could not control operations himself, he did not want to see anybody else get the job.

Nevertheless, Montgomery's importunity had brought him within an ace of losing his own job. Only an emollient letter of apology personally from him to Eisenhower, written at the insistence of his Chief-of-Staff "Freddie" de Guingand, prevented a final showdown.

Himmler's offensive

During the night of December 31/January

▷ *Armoured vehicles (in the foreground Stuart light tanks) of the French Foreign Legion parade through the streets of Strasbourg.*
△▷ *Strasbourg Cathedral on the day of the city's liberation.*

1, Himmler, as commander of Army Group *"Oberrhein"*, unleashed Operation *"Nordwind"*, giving his troops as objective the Saverne gap. In this way the American 7th Army would be cut in two and its fighting troops in the Bitche–Lauterbourg–Strasbourg salient annihilated. After the fast advance that Patton had been ordered to make on December 19, General Patch had had to extend his left flank as far as Saint Avold and, in the threatened sector, could only field VI Corps against eight German divisions, including the 21st Panzer and the 17th *"Götz von Berlichingen"* S.S. *Panzergrenadier* Divisions.

When he had redeployed as ordered (which stretched the seven divisions of the 7th Army over a front of 90 miles), the commander of the 6th Army Group, General Devers, had naturally been concerned about what to do in the event of a German offensive. In agreement with S.H.A.E.F., he had provided in such an event for his forces to fall back on the eastern slopes of the Vosges and the Belfort gap. This implied abandoning the plain of Alsace. In the afternoon of January 1, after a telephone call from Eisenhower, he issued the order to begin the movements planned for this eventuality.

de Gaulle disapproves

As Chief-of-Staff to the French Ministry of National Defence, General Juin had been advised since December 28 of the intentions of the 6th Army Group, confirmed by S.H.A.E.F. He had immediately informed General de Gaulle. The latter, seeing the possibility approach, wrote to General Eisenhower on January 1:

"For its part, the French Government cannot allow Strasbourg to fall into enemy hands again without doing everything in its power to defend it."

At the same time, he gave General de Lattre the following order:

"In the event of Allied forces falling

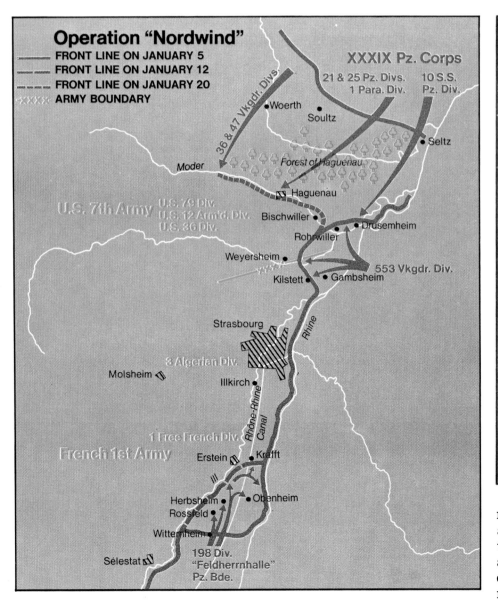

Operation "Nordwind"

——— FRONT LINE ON JANUARY 5
——— FRONT LINE ON JANUARY 12
– – – FRONT LINE ON JANUARY 20
XXXX ARMY BOUNDARY

XXXIX Pz. Corps

21 & 25 Pz. Divs.
1 Para. Div.

10 S.S.
Pz. Div.

36 & 47 Vkgdr. Divs.

Woerth
Soultz
Seltz
Moder
Forest of Haguenau
Haguenau

U.S. 7th Army
U.S. 79 Div.
U.S. 12 Arm'd. Div.
U.S. 36 Div.

Bischwiller
Drusemheim
Rohrwiller
Weyersheim
553 Vkgdr. Div.
Kilstett
Gambsheim

Strasbourg
Rhine

8 Algerian Div.

Molsheim
Illkirch

Rhône-Rhine Canal

1 Free French Div.

French 1st Army
Erstein
Krafft

Herbsheim
Obenheim
Rossfeld
Wittersheim

Sélestat
198 Div.
"Feldherrnhalle"
Pz. Bde.

△ *Operation "Nordwind",
Reichsführer-S.S. Heinrich
Himmler's ill-advised offensive
against Strasbourg.*
△▷ *General de Lattre de
Tassigny's proclamation to the
citizens of Strasbourg on
January 6, 1945. It called for
calm and confidence, and
pledged the French 1st Army
to the successful defence of the
city.*

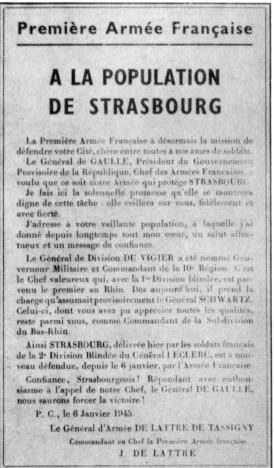

back from their present positions to the
north of the French 1st Army, I instruct
you to act on your own and take over the
defence of Strasbourg."

These letters had gone when General de
Gaulle was advised of the order to withdraw that had been circulated by
General Devers. On receiving the news,
he cabled President Roosevelt and the
Prime Minister to make clear that he was
opposed to evacuating Strasbourg and
he instructed General Juin to express the
same opinion at S.H.A.E.F.

The interview between Juin and
General Bedell Smith, who met him the
next day at S.H.A.E.F., was stormy, as
was to be expected from two such plain-
spoken men. There were even threats
about what would happen if the French
1st Army removed itself from the
authority of General Devers. All the same,
noted Juin:

"Bedell Smith, who had blanched,

nevertheless seemed to want to help
and assured me before I left that he would
try once more to convince his superior
and I secured an interview for General
de Gaulle with General Eisenhower the
next day."

On receiving the report prepared for
him by Juin, de Gaulle once more appealed
against the S.H.A.E.F. decision which,
he had just learned, affected not only
Strasbourg but the entire plain of Alsace.
In particular, he wrote to Eisenhower on
January 3:

"In any case, I must confirm that the
French Government cannot accept that
Alsace and a part of Lorraine should be
intentionally evacuated without fighting,
so to speak, especially since the French
Army occupies most of the area. To agree
to such an evacuation and in such conditions would be an error from the point of
view of the general conduct of the war,
which stems not only from the military
command, but also from the Allied governments. It would also be a serious error
from the French national point of view, to
which the government is answerable.

"Therefore I have once more to instruct
General de Lattre to use the French forces
he has to defend the positions he now

occupies and also to defend Strasbourg, even if the American forces on his left withdraw.

"From my point of view, I am extremely sorry that this disagreement has occurred at a serious moment and I should like to hope that we can resolve our differences."

In *Crusade in Europe*, General Eisenhower mentions this incident and writes that:

"At first glance de Gaulle's argument seemed to be based upon political considerations founded more on emotion than on logic and consideration."

This represents the typical reasoning of the American strategist of the time, according to whom a military leader should not consider any objective but the destruction of the enemy's organised forces, without regard for political, geographical, sentimental, or prestige aims. In short, his thought regarding Strasbourg was the same as it had been before Paris the previous summer, and as it would be before Berlin three months later. Nevertheless, against this same point of view, he had to think of the consequences that a Franco-American crisis could have on Allied relations.

Churchill sides with de Gaulle

Churchill had been alerted by de Gaulle and, accompanied by Brooke, travelled to Paris. According to Brooke, they found Eisenhower "most depressed looking" when they walked down the steps from the plane, and it is certain that, at the lunch that followed, the Prime Minister was preaching to one already half-converted. A few hours later, Generals de Gaulle and Juin met Eisenhower, in the presence of Bedell Smith, Churchill, and Brooke, who noted that very evening:

"De Gaulle painted a gloomy picture of the massacres that would ensue if the Germans returned to portions of Alsace-Lorraine. However, Ike had already decided to alter his dispositions so as to leave the divisions practically where they were and not to withdraw the two divisions that were to have been moved up into Patton's reserve."

Juin confirms this: "When General de Gaulle and I arrived at Eisenhower's headquarters at Versailles . . . Churchill was already there. As soon as we came in

he informed us that it was all settled and that Strasbourg would not be abandoned. There was not even any discussion, and the only thing that was decided was that I should go with General Bedell Smith the next day to Vittel to inform General Devers, commanding the 6th Army Group."

Moreover, the tension between Eisenhower and de Gaulle eased so much as soon as this incident was settled that Eisenhower could not restrain himself from confiding to de Gaulle the difficulties he was having with Montgomery.

The battle for Strasbourg

Both on his own initiative and in virtue of the orders he received from Paris, General de Lattre was absolutely determined to hold Strasbourg. And so, on the night of January 2-3, he promptly sent in the solid 3rd Algerian Division, under the command of General du Vigier, recently appointed governor of the city. But, in spite of this, de Lattre intended to remain as long as he could under the control of General Devers and not make difficulties

△ *G.I.s catch up with their mail and with the news while waiting for the German offensive to break on them. Although he at first advocated the abandonment of the plain of Alsace, Eisenhower was at last persuaded by General de Gaulle's political objections to change his mind and order the American 7th Army to hold the Moder line.*

"For whom tolls the bell?" "It tolls death for Hitler." And with the Allies on the Rhine and Oder, the defeat of the Third Reich and Hitler's suicide were only weeks away.

for inter-Allied strategy. That is why, at 2200 hours on January 3, he was very happy to receive the signal announcing that the 6th Army Group had received new orders.

As a result, the American VI Corps, between the Rhine and the Sarre, received orders to continue its retreat only as far as the Moder. But, on January 5, while VI Corps was digging in at this position and the 3rd Algerian Division completed its positions in Strasbourg, the 553rd *Volksgrenadier* Division crossed the Rhine at Gambsheim, between Strasbourg and the confluence of the Moder and Rhine. The next day, it was the turn of the German 19th Army to go over to the offensive, from the Colmar bridgehead. Pressing between the Ill and the Rhône-Rhine Canal, the *"Feldherrnhalle"* Panzer Brigade and the 198th Division managed to get as far as the Erstein heights, less than 13 miles from Strasbourg and 20 from the Gambsheim bridgehead that the 553rd Division had extended as far as the village of Killstett.

Around Strasbourg, attack and counter-attack followed ceaselessly. The Germans had forced the Moder a little above Haguenau and for a short time managed to establish a link with their 553rd Division. However, on January 26, they had definitely lost it again and the battle-field fell silent. O.B. West was very unhappy with the tactics Himmler had used in this offensive, for, instead of wearing down the enemy, he had wasted 11 divisions, four of them of the *Waffen*-S.S., frittering them away in piecemeal actions, ignoring the fact that the barrier of the Rhine prevented him from co-ordinating their movements. All the same, it was General Wiese who paid for the failure of *"Nordwind"*. He received the order to hand over command of the 19th Army to his comrade Rasp. As for Himmler, his flattering promotion to the command of Army Group *"Vistula"* led, on January 28, to the appointment of Colonel-General Hausser, still recuperating from the wounds he had received during the bloody fighting in the Falaise pocket, to command of Army Group *"Oberrhein"*.

In spite of Operation *"Nordwind"*, on January 15 de Lattre signed his "Personal and Secret Instruction Number 7":

"Leave the Germans no chance of escape. Free Colmar undamaged. The task consists of strangling the pocket alongside the Rhine where it receives its supplies, that is around Brisach.

"Two convergent wedges will be driven in this direction. The first will go northward and will be made by Béthouart's I Corps, which will throw the enemy off balance and suck in his reserves. Then, two days later, II Corps will go into action. This staggering is required by the time it will take to get the expected reserves into place. Its effect will be to increase the surprise of the enemy. Between the two offensive blocs, in the high Vosges, the front will remain inactive at the beginning. It will begin to move when our net along the Rhine is so tightly stretched that the fish is ready to be pulled in."

At this time, Devers and Eisenhower were so concerned about cutting off the Colmar pocket quickly that they did not hesitate to provide substantial reinforcements for the French 1st Army: the U.S. 3rd Division remained under its command, and it also received, though with certain limitations, the 28th Division and the 12th Armoured Division (Major-Generals Norman D. Cota and Roderik R. Allen), as well as the French 2nd Armoured Division under Leclerc, transferred from the Strasbourg area specifically for this purpose.

So, by January 20, 1945, the forces available to de Lattre amounted to 12 divisions, four of which were armoured. However, it should be pointed out that the 3rd Algerian Division was still engaged in and around Killstett and did not take part in the battle of Colmar and that, in the high Vosges, the newly-created 10th Division (General Billotte) was restricted to the modest rôle described above.

The German defence

Facing these forces along the 100-mile long Alsace bridgehead, the German 19th Army deployed its LXIV and LXIII Corps north and south under the command, respectively, of General Thumm and Lieutenant-General Abraham. The two corps had seven infantry or mountain divisions and the 106th *"Feldherrnhalle"* Panzer Brigade. But these forces were threadbare. Including the reinforcements attached to them, the best-equipped (the 198th Division: Colonel Barde) had exactly 6,891 men in the line, and the 716th *Volksgrenadier* Division (Colonel Hafner) had only 4,546. Furthermore, although de Lattre complained about not receiving all the supplies he thought

The American Martin B-26G Marauder medium bomber

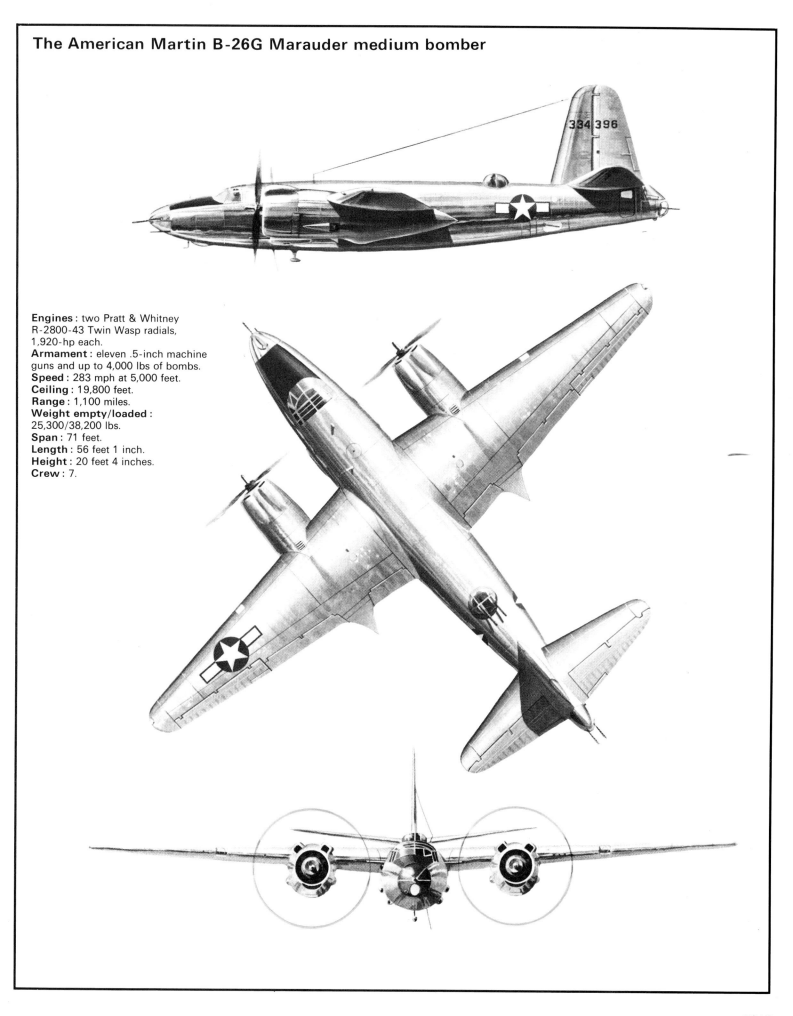

Engines : two Pratt & Whitney
R-2800-43 Twin Wasp radials,
1,920-hp each.
Armament : eleven .5-inch machine
guns and up to 4,000 lbs of bombs.
Speed : 283 mph at 5,000 feet.
Ceiling : 19,800 feet.
Range : 1,100 miles.
Weight empty/loaded :
25,300/38,200 lbs.
Span : 71 feet.
Length : 56 feet 1 inch.
Height : 20 feet 4 inches.
Crew : 7.

▷ *An M3 half-track of the French 1st Army moves into Colmar on February 2, 1945.*
▷ ▷ *A mine explodes in the path of an M10 tank destroyer of a French armoured division, fully equipped with the latest U.S. equipment.*

△ *"Our armies are marching with all despatch to the East and to the West . . ." "Is that really true?" "Yes, mein Führer, the ones on the Western Front to the East, and the ones on the Eastern Front to the West!"*

he needed, by the eighth day of battle General Rasp was reduced to ordering strict economy to his gunners: 12 15-cm and 15 10.5-cm shells per day per gun, compared with 90 155-mm and 120 105-mm shells in the French 1st Army.

Three circumstances, however, compensated a little for the numerical and *matériel* inferiority of the defenders:

1. the terrain, which was no more than "a network of streams and rivers" according to de Lattre. Within it are many woods and even more villages, among which should be mentioned the manufacturing and industrial towns of the Mulhouse region;

2. the weather. On the first day, I Corps attacked LXIII Corps in the face of a snowstorm blowing from the northeast. At night, the temperature fell to 20 and even 25 degrees Centigrade below zero. Finally, just when German resistance was softening, an unexpected rise in the temperature swelled the rivers and made the roads into sloughs of mud; and

3. though far less numerous, the Panther tanks and *"Jagdpanther"* and *"Nashorn"* tank destroyers, with their very high velocity 8.8-cm guns, were far superior to the French 1st Army's Sherman tanks and M10 tank destroyers. This superiority was emphasised by the German vehicles' wide tracks, which allowed them to manoeuvre on the snow in weather conditions with which their opponents were not able to cope.

At 0700 hours on January 20, H-hour sounded for the reinforced I Corps. Its task was to break the enemy line between Thann and the Forest of Nünenbruck, to capture Cernay, and then to push on without stopping towards Ensisheim and Réguisheim on the Ill. For this purpose, over a 14-mile front, Béthouart had the 9th Colonial Division (General Morlière) around Mulhouse, the 2nd Moroccan Division (General Carpentier) in the centre, and the 4th Moroccan Mountain Division (General de Hesdin) around Thann. In spite of the support of the tanks of the 1st Armoured Division (General Sudre), the attempt to break the enemy lines towards Cernay was not very successful, both because of the tough resistance met, aided by well-sited minefields, and because of the snowstorms which made artillery observation impossible.

On the other hand, the secondary attack, which had been entrusted to the 9th Colonial Division, took the villages of Burtzwiller, Illzach, Kingersheim, Pfastadt, and Lutterbach, a remarkable success due to the dash with which General Salan had led the infantry of this division.

On the following day, LXIII Corps counter-attacked and, on January 22, with the storm blowing worse than ever, General Béthouart expressed the opinion that they should wait for it to blow itself out. But any let-up on the part of I Corps would have prejudiced the attack of II

Corps, which was just finishing its preparations. So Béthouart was ordered to press on with his attack, and a fierce, bitter struggle was waged close to Wittelsheim, in the Forest of Nünenbruck, and for the factory towns with their potassium deposits. These towns had to be cleared one by one.

The Colmar pocket wiped out

On January 23, II Corps, still under the command of General G. de Monsabert, forced a second wedge into the German line. This was achieved with more ease than the first, even though General Rasp had got wind of the French plans.

On the right, the American 3rd Division had taken Ostheim. On the left, the 1st Free French Division had fought bitterly to capture the village of Illhausern and had formed a bridgehead on the right bank of the Ill, thus preparing to outflank Colmar to the north. But LXIV Corps stiffened its resistance and counterattacked, preventing Monsabert from any swift exploitation of his success towards Neuf-Brisach. LXIII Corps was likewise preventing Béthouart from moving on. Hidden in the woods, or even inside houses, the Panzers exacted a heavy toll from the men of the 2nd and 5th Armoured Divisions, supporting the infantry. However, on January 27, the U.S. 3rd Division reached the Colmar Canal, while General Garbay's 1st Free French Division, reinforced by Colonel Faure's paratroops, took the villages of Jebsheim and Grussenheim. Seeing how serious the situation had become, O.K.W. authorised Rasp to pull the 198th Division back over the Rhine, i.e. to give up all the ground won between Rhinau and Erstein by the attack of January 7.

Wishing to press on and complete the attack, General Devers, at the request of the commander of the French 1st Army, put XXI Corps (Major-General Frank W. Milburn) under his command, as well as the U.S. 75th Division (Major-General Porter). Milburn, who from this time on commanded all the American forces involved in the offensive, and the French 5th Armoured Division, was ordered to position his forces between Monsabert's II Corps and Billotte's 10th Division, and then push on towards Neuf-

△ *General Emile Béthouart, commander of the French I Corps. Operating on the south side of the Colmar pocket, his troops initially had a very hard time of it, and Béthouart wished to call off his attack. But de Lattre ordered him to press on regardless so that German forces would not be able to switch to the northern sector, where General de Monsabert's II Corps was about to launch its offensive.*

Brisach and also south towards Ensisheim to meet Béthouart. The offensive began again. In the evening of January 30, after a terrifying artillery bombardment of 16,438 105-mm and 155-mm shells, the United States 3rd Division (Major-General O'Daniel) succeeded in crossing the Colmar Canal, and this allowed the United States 28th Division to advance as far as the suburbs of Colmar. The division did not enter Colmar itself, for at the gates of the city, which had been left intact, General Norman D. Cota was courteous enough to give that honour to his comrade-in-arms Schlesser, commanding the 4th Combat Command (5th Armoured Division).

The United States 12th Armoured Division sped south to exploit its victory, with the intention of linking up with I Corps, which had taken Ensisheim, Soultz, and Guebwiller on February 4 and then pushed its 1st Armoured Division and 4th Moroccan Mountain Division forward.

The next day, French and American forces linked up at Rouffach and Sainte Croix-en-Plaine. Twenty-four hours later, in the light of searchlights shining towards the night sky, General O'Daniel's infantry "scaled" the ramparts of Neuf-Brisach in the best mediaeval style. Lastly, at 0800 hours on February 9, a deafening explosion told the men of the French 1st and 2nd Armoured Divisions, who were mopping-up the Forest of la Hardt, together with the 2nd Moroccan Division, that the Germans had just blown the Chalampé bridge, on the Mulhouse–Freiburg road, behind them as they pulled back over the Rhine.

And so, at dawn on the 20th day, the battle of Colmar reached its end. General Rasp left 22,010 prisoners, 80 guns, and 70 tanks in the hands of the enemy, but he had succeeded in bringing back over the Rhine some 50,000 men, 7,000 motor vehicles, 1,500 guns, and 60 armoured vehicles, which underlines his personal qualities of leadership.

As for Allied losses, the figures provided by General de Lattre will allow the reader to appreciate the cost of a modern battle. Of a total of 420,000 Allied troops involved (295,000 French, 125,000 American), casualties were as follows:

	French	American
Killed	1,595	542
Wounded	8,583	2,670
Sick	3,887	3,228
Totals	14,065	6,440

Considering just the French, de Lattre's figures also show that the infantry had taken the lion's share. On January 20, it had put 60,000 men into the line, that is about a fifth of the men in the 1st Army. On February 9, it could own to three-quarters of the losses, with 1,138 killed and 6,513 wounded. Add to these figures the 354 killed and 1,151 wounded which the battle cost the armoured units, and it becomes clear that the other arms lost only 1,022 killed and wounded. Finally, due credit must be given to the magnificent effort of the medical services under Surgeon-General Guirriec. In spite of the appalling weather they had only 142 deaths, that is 0.9 per cent of the cases received.

As a conclusion to the story of this battle, some tribute should be paid to the men who fought in it. In the *Revue militaire suisse*, Major-General Montfort has written:

"The French, under superb leadership and enjoying powerful *matériel* advantages, made a magnificent effort, fully worthy of their predecessors in World War I.

"The Germans, under extraordinarily difficult conditions and three differing requirements (operational, *matériel*, and morale), defended themselves with great ability and fought...with courage worthy of praise."

Montgomery and Eisenhower clash again

It should be noted that there had been much inter-Allied squabbling about the length of time that the battle for Colmar was taking: the Allied high command wanted this irritating pocket cleared out of the way as quickly as possible, so that all available Allied forces might be readied for the last devastating blow against Germany that would win the war in the West. The irritation caused by the Colmar delay was perhaps exacerbated by another clash between Eisenhower and Montgomery. But what increased the trouble even more was the fact that Brooke backed Montgomery with all the weight of his authority. Once more S.H.A.E.F. and the 21st Army Group were divided on the alternatives of the "concentrated push" or the "wide front". Eisenhower rejected Montgomery's in-

tention of supervising Bradley's operations, but nevertheless, on December 31, 1944, informed Montgomery of his plan of operations:

"Basic plan–to destroy enemy forces west of Rhine, north of the Moselle, and to prepare for crossing the Rhine in force with the *main effort north of the Ruhr.*"

Once the Ardennes salient had been pinched out (Point *a*), Eisenhower envisaged the following general offensive:

"*b*. Thereafter First and Third Armies to drive to north-east on general line Prum-Bonn, eventually to Rhine.

"*c*. When *a* is accomplished, 21st Army Group, with Ninth U.S. Army under operational command, to resume preparations for 'Veritable'."

In practical terms, this plan required Montgomery to force the Reichswald forest position, which bars the corridor between the Maas and the Rhine on the Dutch-German frontier, to secure the left bank of the Rhine between Emmerich and Düsseldorf, and to prepare to force a passage of the river north of its junction with the Ruhr. This sketch of a plan pleased Montgomery, who wrote:

"It did all I wanted except in the realm of operational control, and because of Marshall's telegram that subject was closed. It put the weight in the north and gave the Ninth American Army to 21 Army Group. It gave me power of decision in the event of disagreement with Bradley on the boundary between 12 and 21 Army Groups. In fact, I had been given very nearly all that I had been asking for since August. Better late than never. I obviously could not ask for more."

Nevertheless, when one considers the allotment of forces and in particular the fixing of objectives, there is no avoiding the fact that the two sides did not speak a common language any more.

Actually, Montgomery estimated that if "Veritable" was to be successful, American reinforcements should consist of five corps, (16 divisions), of which four corps (13 divisions) should be placed under the command of the American 9th Army, and the rest under the British 2nd Army. In these estimates, he seems to have been completely unaware of the principles established by his superior at the beginning of his outline dated December 31: "to destroy enemy forces west of Rhine". According to Eisenhower's clearly-expressed opinion, this required a second push from around Prüm towards the Rhine at Bonn, which would reduce the United States forces which could be detached for "Veritable"

2051

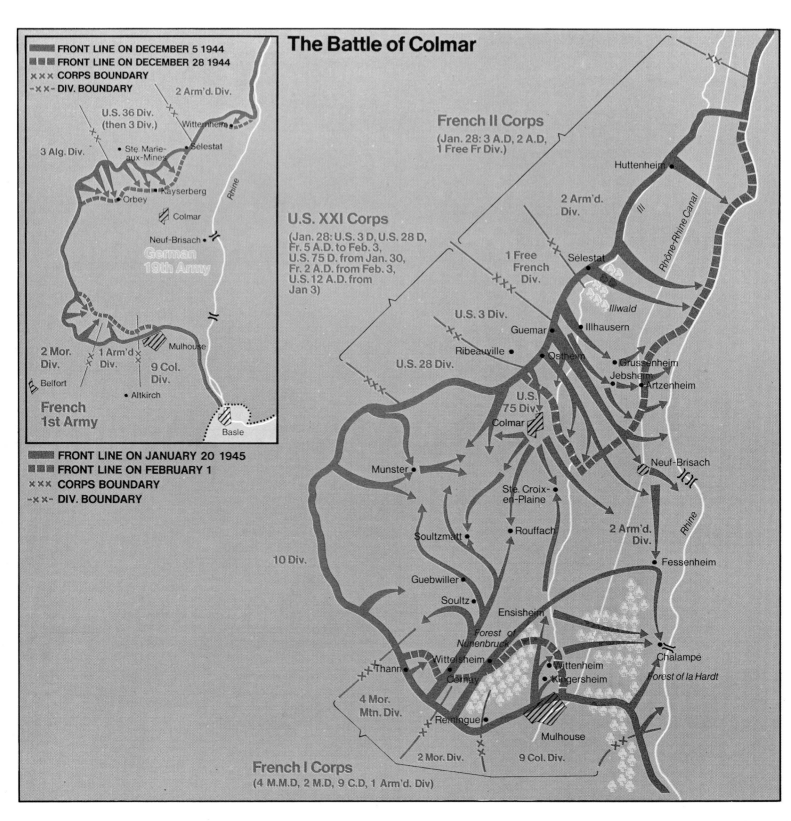

The Battle of Colmar

FRONT LINE ON DECEMBER 5 1944
FRONT LINE ON DECEMBER 28 1944
××× CORPS BOUNDARY
-×× - DIV. BOUNDARY

2 Arm'd. Div.

U.S. 36 Div.
(then 3 Div.)

3 Alg. Div.

Wittenheim

Selestat

Ste. Marie-
aux-Mines

Kayserberg

Orbey

Colmar

Neuf-Brisach

**German
19th Army**

Rhine

2 Mor.
Div.

1 Arm'd
Div.

9 Col.
Div.

Mulhouse

Belfort

Altkirch

**French
1st Army**

Basle

FRONT LINE ON JANUARY 20 1945
FRONT LINE ON FEBRUARY 1
××× CORPS BOUNDARY
-×× - DIV. BOUNDARY

French II Corps
(Jan. 28: 3 A.D, 2 A.D,
1 Free Fr Div.)

Huttenheim

2 Arm'd.
Div.

U.S. XXI Corps
(Jan. 28: U.S. 3 D, U.S. 28 D,
Fr. 5 A.D. to Feb. 3,
U.S. 75 D. from Jan. 30,
Fr. 2 A.D. from Feb. 3,
U.S. 12 A.D. from
Jan 3)

1 Free
French
Div.

Selestat

Illwald

U.S. 3 Div.

Illhausern

Guemar

Ribeauville

Ostheim

Grussenheim

Jebsheim

Artzenheim

U.S. 28 Div.

U.S.
75 Div.

Colmar

Munster

Ste. Croix-
en-Plaine

Neuf-Brisach

Rouffach

2 Arm'd.
Div.

Rhine

10 Div.

Soultzmatt

Fessenheim

Guebwiller

Soultz

Ensisheim

Forest of
Nunenbruck

Chalampé

Wittelsheim

Forest of la Hardt

Thann

Cernay

Wittenheim

Kingersheim

4 Mor.
Mtn. Div.

Reiningue

Mulhouse

2 Mor. Div.

9 Col. Div.

French I Corps
(4 M.M.D, 2 M.D, 9 C.D, 1 Arm'd. Div)

Rhône-Rhine Canal

Ill

△ *The French 1st Army's battle
to eliminate the German 19th
Army's pocket around Colmar.*

to only three corps and 12 divisions.

Montgomery was obliged to give in,
but he resumed the argument on January
20 when he heard the news that Bradley,
far from limiting himself to reducing
the Ardennes salient, intended to follow
up his attack for another fortnight.
Montgomery wrote to Brooke:

"Both Ike and Bradley are emphatic
that we should not–not–cross the Rhine
in strength anywhere until we are lined

up along its entire length from Nijmegen
to Switzerland."

Two days later, in a second letter which,
like the first, he has not quoted in his
memoirs, he harped on the same question:

"My latest information is that
S.H.A.E.F. are very worried about situation in South about Colmar and Strasbourg . . ."

As the commander-in-chief seemed
ready to reinforce this sector, it followed

that "Veritable" would be postponed indefinitely. This led him to conclude bitterly:

"I fear that the old snags of indecision and vacillation and refusal to consider the military problem fairly and squarely are coming to the front again . . . The real trouble is that there is no control and the three Army Groups are each intent on their own affairs. Patton to-day issued a stirring order to Third Army, saying the next step would be Cologne . . . one has to preserve a sense of humour these days, otherwise one would go mad."

Support for Eisenhower

Brooke was appreciative of this argument and "cordially, but very gravely", as General Eisenhower writes, expressed the view to him that putting his plan into effect would have the result of producing an "organised dispersion" of Allied forces. Eisenhower opposed this view, and events proved him right. First of all, the Germans had to be deprived of the advantage of permanent fortifications which allowed them to economise their means and then build up massive forces in the sector where the main attack would be launched:

"If, however, we should first, in a series of concentrated and powerful attacks, destroy the German forces west of the Rhine, the effect would be to give us all along the great front a defensive line of equal strength to the enemy's. We calculated that with the western bank of the Rhine in our possession we could hurl some seventy-five reinforced divisions against the German in great converging attacks. If we allowed the enemy south of the Ruhr to remain in the Siegfried, we would be limited to a single offensive by some thirty-five divisions.

"A second advantage of our plan would be the deflection of the enemy forces later to be met at the crossings of the Rhine obstacle. Moreover, the effect of the converging attack is multiplied when it is accompanied by such air power as we had in Europe in the early months of 1945. Through its use we could prevent the enemy from switching forces back and forth at will against either of the attacking columns and we could likewise employ our entire air power at any moment to further the advance in any area desired."

But although Eisenhower had refuted

Brooke's point, he was unable to convert the latter to his way of thinking. That is why he travelled to Marseilles on January 25 to explain to Marshall, who was on his way to Yalta via Malta, his plan of operations and the objections it was coming up against among the British. He had no difficulty in obtaining Marshall's complete agreement, and the latter said to him at the end of the interview:

"I can, of course, uphold your position merely on the principle that these decisions fall within your sphere of responsibility. But your plan is so sound that I think it better for you to send General Smith to Malta so that he may explain these matters in detail. Their logic will be convincing."

This was done and, after some explanations by Bedell Smith and some amendments on the part of the Combined Chiefs-of-Staff Committee, Eisenhower's plan, comprising of a double push towards the Rhine and a double encirclement of the Ruhr, was adopted and Montgomery would spare nothing to make it a success.

△ △ *American infantry move up through a snowstorm, typical of the weather that helped the Germans considerably at the beginning of 1945.*
△ *General Marshall, head of the U.S. Army, arrives in Malta en route to Yalta. Marshall sided firmly with Eisenhower in the dispute the latter was having with Montgomery.*

△ *Evidence of American artillery superiority: a destroyed German triple 2-cm self-propelled mounting.*

CHAPTER 141
Remagen Bridge

On January 16, the American 3rd and 1st Armies crushed the tip of the Ardennes salient and linked up in the ruins of Houffalize. The following day, as agreed, the 1st Army was returned to the command of Bradley, to his great satisfaction. But he was far less pleased with the task now given him, that of engaging the Germans in the wooded and hilly region of Schleiden and Schmidt, which had cost him so dear the previous autumn, and of capturing the hydro-electric system of the Raer, the Erft, and the Olef. On February 8, V Corps (under Major-General L. T. Gerow), of the 1st Army had reached its objective. That was that. At dawn, on the next day, the Germans blew up the reservoir gates; and the water rose rapidly in front of the 9th Army.

Meanwhile, the left of this army, still under the command of Lieutenant-General William H. Simpson, and the right of the British 2nd Army, under General Miles C. Dempsey, were taking out the salient which the enemy was holding between the Maas and the Raer, now an enclave between the Allied flanks. The little Dutch village of Roermond was

still held by the German 15th Army, which formed the right of Army Group "B". On January 28, this rectifying operation, a prelude to the pincer attack called "Veritable/Grenade", was brought to a successful conclusion.

Rundstedt powerless

In this duel between Field-Marshal von Rundstedt and General Eisenhower, the former had at his disposal at the beginning of February (after he had lost the 6th *Panzerarmee,* taken away to help the Hungarian front), 73 divisions, including eight Panzer or *Panzergrenadier.* But the infantry divisions had fallen to an average of about 7,000 men each. As for the armoured formations, whatever may have been the excellent quality of their *matériel,* they suffered a continual shortage of petrol because of the Allied air offensive against the German synthetic petrol plants. In other words, as had started to become evident in the battle of Colmar, the crisis in munitions was getting ever more desperate at the front. The land forces of the Third Reich, moreover, could not rely on any support from the Luftwaffe, whose jet fighters were fully engaged attempting to defend what

△ *Montgomery* (standing, right) *confers with Horrocks* (standing, left). *Note the insignia on the jeep: four stars, signifying that the owner was a general, and the badge of the 21st Army Group. This latter was a blue cross on a red shield, with two crossed golden swords superimposed.*

was left of Germany's cities against the redoubled attacks of the British and American Strategic Air Forces.

The last straw was that Rundstedt, in his office at Koblenz, was faced by a hopeless situation, and had been stripped of all initiative in the direction of operations. On January 21, he received the following incredible *Führerbefehl*, with orders to distribute it down to divisional level:

"Commanders-in-chief, army, corps, and divisional commanders are personally responsible to me for reporting in good time:

"*(a)* Every decision to execute an operational movement.

"*(b)* Every offensive plan from divisional level upwards that does not fit exactly with the directives of the higher command.

"*(c)* Every attack in a quiet sector intended to draw the enemy's attention to that sector, with the exception of normal shock troop actions.

"*(d)* Every plan for withdrawal or retreat.

"*(e)* Every intention of surrendering a position, a strongpoint, or a fortress.

"Commanders must make sure that I have time to intervene as I see fit, and that my orders can reach the front line troops in good time."

And the *Führer* further announced that any commander or staff officer who by "deliberate intent, carelessness, or oversight" hindered the execution of this order, would be punished with "draconian severity".

Allied superiority

From the Swiss frontier to the North Sea, Eisenhower had 70 divisions under his command on January 1, 1945:

	In-fantry	Ar-moured	Air-borne	Total
U.S.	31	11	3	45
British	7	4	1	12
Canadian	2	1	–	3
French	6	3	–	9
Polish	–	1	–	1
Totals	46	20	4	70

By May 8 this number would have been increased by another 15 American divisions (including four armoured), six French divisions, and two Canadian divisions (including one armoured).

Deducting six divisions fighting in the Alps or besieging German fortresses, this would give S.H.A.E.F. 87 divisions at the end of the war.

Despite the losses they had to bear, the

Allied divisions at this time were far less restricted than their German counterparts. The supply crisis, so acute in September, was now no more than an unpleasant memory. Petrol was in good supply and there was no shortage of shells at the front. The proximity fuses with which they were fitted allowed the gunners to fire shells which burst in the air, wreaking havoc among exposed troops. With reference to armour, the introduction into the United States Army of the heavy (41-ton) M26 General Pershing tank was significant. It was well-armoured, and had a 90-mm gun and good cross-country performance, the result of its Christie-type suspension and wide tracks. The Americans had rediscovered this suspension after seeing the results it gave in the service of the Germans, who had borrowed the idea from the Russians. The latter had acquired a licence to build the Christie suspension from the United States, after 1919, when the American military authorities had refused, in spite of the urging of the young Major George S. Patton, to take any firm interest in Christie and his advanced designs.

Thus the Allies' land forces were far more numerous than the Germans'. They also enjoyed powerful air support from a force which was both numerous and well-trained. Here General Devers had the Franco-American 1st Tactical Air Force (Major-General R. M. Webster), in which the French I Air Corps (Brigadier-General P. Gerardot) was itself attached to the French 1st Army. The United States 9th Air Force (Lieutenant-General Hoyt S. Vandenberg,) came under the overall command of General Bradley, and the British 2nd Tactical Air Force (Air-Marshal Sir Arthur Coningham) efficiently seconded Field-Marshal Montgomery's operations. On the German side there was nothing which could resist this formidable mass of flying artillery.

On November 12, 1944, 28 R.A.F. Lancasters attacked the great battleship *Tirpitz* in Tromsö with 12,000-lb "Tallboy" bombs and sank her at her anchorage. What was now left of the surface forces of the Kriegsmarine was being expended in the Baltic in attempts to help the army. As for the U-boats, which had lost 242 of their number during 1944, their successes in the North Atlantic between June 6, 1944 and May 8, 1945, were limited to the sinking of 31 merchant ships, displacing

altogether only 178,000 tons. This was virtually nothing at all.

Complete surprise

At 0500 hours on February 8, 1,400 guns of the Canadian 1st Army blasted the German 84th Division, which had dug itself in along a seven-mile front between the Maas and the Waal close to the Dutch-German frontier. At 1030 hours, the British XXX Corps, which Montgomery had put under the command of General Crerar, moved in to the attack with five divisions (the British 51st, 53rd, and 15th and the Canadian 2nd and 3rd) in the first wave and the 43rd Division and the Guards Armoured Division in reserve. In all, according to the commander of the corps, Lieutenant-General Horrocks, there were 200,000 men and 35,000 vehicles.

The German position was heavily mined, and included a flooded area on the right and the thick Reichswald forest on the left. Moreover, the day before the attack, a thaw had softened the ground. Neither Hitler, at O.K.W., nor Colonel-General Blaskowitz, commanding Army Group "H", had been willing to accept the idea that Montgomery would choose such a sector in which to attack. Yet

Introduced in 1945 the Pershing saw only limited service, although in one instance a single M.26 destroyed a Tiger and two Pzkw Mk IV tanks in rapid succession.

General Schlemm, commanding the 1st Parachute Army, had warned them of this possibility. At the end of the day the 84th Division had lost 1,300 prisoners and was close to breaking-point.

Meanwhile the American 9th Army had been ordered to unleash Operation "Grenade" on February 10. This would cross the Roer and advance to the Rhine at Düsseldorf. Now came the flooding caused by the destruction of the Eifel dams, which held up the American 9th Army completely for 12 days and slowed down the British XXX Corps. The latter's units were also hopelessly mixed up. These delays allowed Schlemm to send his 7th and 6th Parachute, 15th *Panzergrenadier,* and then 116th Panzer Divisions to the rescue one after the other. And as Colonel C. P. Stacey, the official Canadian Army historian, notes, the Germans, at the edge of the abyss, had lost none of their morale:

"In this, the twilight of their gods, the defenders of the Reich displayed the recklessness of fanaticism and the courage of despair. In the contests west of the Rhine, in particular, they fought with special ferocity and resolution, rendering the battles in the Reichswald and Hochwald forests grimly memorable in the annals of this war."

On February 13, the Canadian 1st Army had mopped up the Reichswald and the little town of Kleve, and had reached Gennep, where it was reinforced across the Maas by the British 52nd Division and 11th Armoured Division. Schlemm threw two divisions of infantry into the battle as well as the famous Panzer-*"Lehr"* Division, and so the intervention of Lieutenant-General G. G. Simonds's Canadian II Corps at the side of the British XXX Corps did not have the decisive effect that Crerar expected. The 11th day of the offensive saw the attackers marking time on the Goch–Kalkar line about 15 miles from their jumping-off point.

But, just like the British 2nd Army in Normandy, the Canadian 1st Army had

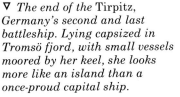

▽ *The end of the* Tirpitz, *Germany's second and last battleship. Lying capsized in Tromsö fjord, with small vessels moored by her keel, she looks more like an island than a once-proud capital ship.*

attracted the larger part of the enemy's forces, while the flood water in the Roer valley was going down. The weather also turned finer, and Montgomery fixed February 23 for the launching of Operation "Grenade". In his order of the day to the men of the 21st Army Group, Montgomery assured them that this was to be the beginning of the last round against Germany. The Third Reich was ready for the knock-out blow, which would be delivered from several directions.

Then, as an opening move, the Anglo-American Strategic Air Force launched 10,000 bombers and fighter escorts and made the heaviest attack of the war on the Third Reich's communications network.

More than 200 targets featured on the programme of this attack, which went under the name of Operation "Clarion". Some of these objectives were bombed from only 4,500 feet because enemy anti-aircraft action was almost totally ineffective since Hitler had stripped it

to supply the Eastern Front. The results of this bombing on February 22 were still noticeable when Colonel-General Jodl came to bring General Eisenhower the surrender of the Third Reich.

The following day, at 0245 hours, the artillery of the United States 9th Army opened fire on German positions on the Roer. The 15th Army (General von Zangen) which defended them, formed the right of Army Group "B" (Field-Marshal Model). Though it defended itself well, his 353rd Division was still thrown out of the ruins of Julich by the American XIX Corps (Major-General Raymond S. Maclain). Meanwhile, in the Linnich sector, XIII Corps (Major-General Alvan C. Gillem) had established a bridgehead a mile and a half deep. VII Corps (Lieutenant-General John L. Collins) of the American 1st Army, had also taken part in the attack and, by the end of the day, had mopped up Duren.

Hitler, Rundstedt, and Model used every last resource to tackle this new crisis looming on the horizon. Schlemm was stripped of the reinforcements which had just been despatched to him, and to these were added the 9th and 11th Panzer Divisions and the 3rd *Panzergrenadier* Division. These forces were instructed to hit the enemy's north-easterly push in its flank.

All the same, by February 27, the Allied breakthrough was complete near Erkelenz, and two days later, XIII Corps swept through the conurbation of Rheydt –Mönchengladbach. At the same time, to the right of the 9th Army, XVI Corps (Major-General J. B. Anderson) hurtled towards Roermond and Venlo behind the 1st Parachute Army, while on the right, XIX Corps was approaching Neuss.

In these circumstances Schlemm was ordered to retreat to the right bank of the Rhine, and he must be given all credit for carrying out this delicate and dangerous mission with remarkable skill. Rearguard skirmishes at Rheinberg, Sonsbeck, and Xanten gave him the time to get the bulk of his forces across and to complete the planned demolitions without fault. On March 6, the United States 9th Army and the Canadian 1st Army linked up opposite Wesel.

This joint Operation "Veritable/Grenade" cost the 18 German divisions engaged 53,000 prisoners. But Crerar alone had suffered 15,634 dead, wounded, and missing, of whom 5,304 were Canadian troops.

△ *The "Masters of the World" return home.*

The British Hawker Tempest V Series 1 fighter and fighter-bomber

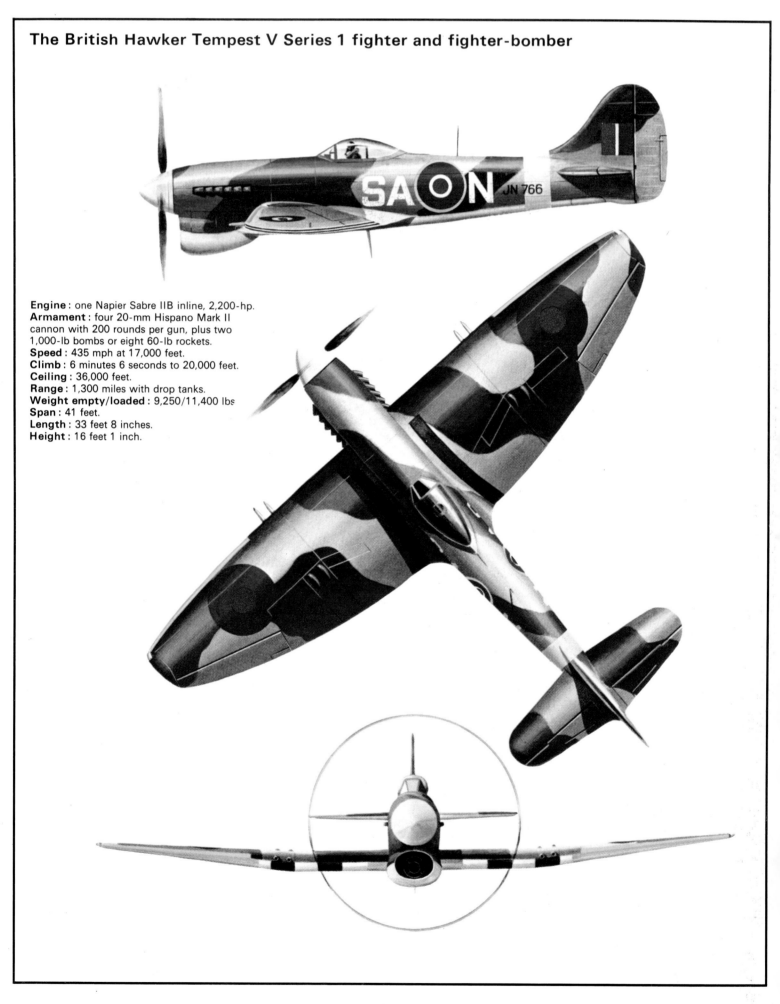

Engine : one Napier Sabre IIB inline, 2,200-hp.
Armament : four 20-mm Hispano Mark II
cannon with 200 rounds per gun, plus two
1,000-lb bombs or eight 60-lb rockets.
Speed : 435 mph at 17,000 feet.
Climb : 6 minutes 6 seconds to 20,000 feet.
Ceiling : 36,000 feet.
Range : 1,300 miles with drop tanks.
Weight empty/loaded : 9,250/11,400 lbs
Span : 41 feet.
Length : 33 feet 8 inches.
Height : 16 feet 1 inch.

Crossing the Rhine

On March 6, 1945, the leading division of the American VII Corps reached the city of Cologne. Now the Allies were lining the Rhine between Cologne and Nijmegen, more than 100 miles downstream, where the river, if the stream slows down, widens to reach a breadth as great as 250 or 300 yards, and all the bridges had been destroyed. Forcing the Rhine north of the Ruhr, according to Montgomery's formula, would result in a delay of two weeks and necessitate considerable reinforcements for the 21st Army Group. And here can be seen Eisenhower's farsightedness in keeping to his plan of operations of December 31, 1944: to defeat the enemy west of the Rhine. For, if he had kept Bradley marking time then, Hitler could have detached the forces necessary to check Montgomery on the Rhine below Cologne.

This did not happen, for, on March 6, Army Group "B" was fighting the American 1st Army on its right and the 3rd on its centre. Its 5th *Panzerarmee* (Colonel-General Harpe) was now well and truly outflanked and overrun on both wings. According to the original plan, the American 1st Army was to provide the left flank of Operation "Grenade". With this in view, General Bradley had increased its size to three corps (14 divisions). But it was not foreseen that the 3rd Army would take part in the attack and it was only by a rather surreptitious move that, during the second week of January, Patton had pushed his forces as far as the Moselle in Luxembourg, the Sûre, and the Our near the *Westwall,* covering himself at S.H.A.E.F. by claiming that his moves were "offensive defence", when his aggression had no other aim but that of reaching the Rhine at Koblenz.

The defeat of the German 15th Army opened a breach in Field-Marshal Model's line which General Hodges and his 1st Army did not delay in exploiting. Having occupied Cologne, VII Corps set off for Bonn on March 7. III Corps (Major-General J. Millikin), which was advancing on the right of VII Corps, had orders to take the crossings over the Ahr. This task was entrusted to the 9th Armoured Division (Major-General John W. Leonard).

Towards the end of the morning of March 7, Brigadier-General William M. Hoge, leading Combat Command "B" of the 9th Armoured Division, was informed that the Ludendorff Bridge near Remagen was still intact. He decided not to follow his orders (which had specified Sinzig as his target) to the letter and resolved there and then to chance his luck and seize the bridge. A little before 1600 hours, 2nd Lieutenant Karl Timmermann ventured on to the bridge, followed by the Burrows section. Seeing them, the German guard tried to set off the demolition charges, but in vain. Under American fire, Sergeant Faust, another hero of this episode, then lit the fuse. But the effect of the explosion was insignificant, and, a few minutes later, Sergeant Alex Drabik was the first American fighting man to step on the right bank of the Rhine. Behind him, Lieutenant Hugh B. Mott, a combat engineer, and three sappers tore the charges from the girders and threw the explosives into the river.

"The enemy had reached Kreuzberg and as far as a bridge near Remagen which, it appears, was encumbered with fugitives. They crossed the bridge and succeeded in forming a bridgehead on the eastern bank of the river. Counter-attack early this morning. The 11th Panzer Division will be brought from Bonn. But petrol is in short supply."

The O.K.W. war diary records this national catastrophe in these unemotional words. Therefore it gives no account of Hitler's rage, which was terrible. Major Scheler and three others were declared responsible, on Hitler's orders, for the success of the Allied surprise attack, court-martialled, and shot.

Twenty-four hours after this surprise, there were already 8,000 Americans in the bridgehead. By March 17, four divisions (9th, 78th, 99th, and 9th Armoured) were dug in. On the same day the bridge collapsed. Hitler had concentrated the fire of a battery of 17-cm guns on it, as well as ordering aircraft and V-2 attacks, and even attempts by Kriegsmarine human torpedoes and frogmen. But, protected by booms and nets, 1st Army engineers had already built another bridge and both banks of the Rhine were bristling with anti-aircraft guns.

Having transferred III Corps (three divisions) to the 1st Army, Patton remained in command of VIII, XII, and XX Corps, which had 12 divisions, three of which were armoured. The crossing of the Our and the Sûre, on the Saint Vith–Echternach line, was no little matter because

△ *The nemesis of Germany's civilian bombing campaigns early in the war: the avenging angel of the British and American strategic bombing forces.*

the rivers were in flood. The forcing of *Westwall* was also very tough. In XII Corps there was one division which had to reduce 120 concrete casemates. This it did with self-propelled 155-mm guns, pounding the embrasures from a range of only 300 yards.

In spite of everything, by the end of February VIII and XII Corps were on the Kyll, having advanced about 20 miles into German territory. XX Corps had taken Saarburg and advanced as far as the apex of the triangle formed by the Mosel and the Saar at their confluence a little above Trier. Up till then the German 7th Army (General Brandenberger), which faced Patton, had defended itself tenaciously, but this very tenacity explains why, on March 1, having exhausted its supplies, it literally collapsed. On that day, wrote Patton:

"At 14.15, Walker [commander of XX Corps] called up to say the 10th Armoured Division was in Trier and had captured a bridge over the Moselle intact. The capture of this bridge was due to the heroic act of Lieutenant Colonel J. J. Richardson, deceased. He was riding in the leading vehicle of his battalion of armoured infantry when he saw the wires leading to the demolition charges at the far end of the bridge. Jumping out of the vehicle, he raced across the bridge under heavy fire and cut the wires. The acid test of battle brings out the pure metal."

On March 3, the forcing of the Kyll at Kyllburg by the 5th Division, under Major-General S. LeRoy Irwin, enabled Major-General Manton Eddy, commanding XII Corps, to detach his 4th Division. Under the command of Major-General Hugh J. Gaffey, this division made a raid of mad audacity, covering 26 miles on March 4 alone and reaching Daun in the evening. Two days later, it reached the Rhine above Koblenz. On its left, the 11th Armoured Division (Major-General Holmes E. Dager), advancing ahead of VII Corps, established first contact with the American 1st Army on March 11, near Brohl.

On March 8, the O.K.W. war diary noted that LIII Corps had been steamrollered and that any co-ordinated conduct of operations was henceforth impossible. The truth of this is illustrated by the capture of General von Rothkirch und Panthen, in command of LIII Corps. Bradley recounts the story thus:

"So rapid was the dissolution that even the senior German commanders lost

△ △ *The last stand . . .*
△ *. . . and the last* Heil.

touch with their crumbling front. One day a German corps commander drove into a field of listless soldiers and asked why they were not fighting the Allies. Not until an American MP clasped him on the shoulder and invited him to join the throng, did the general learn that he had stumbled into a PW concentration."

Altogether, the second phase of the battle for the Rhineland, called Operation "Lumberjack", had brought the 12th Army Group 51,000 prisoners. It had also given it the priceless bridgehead at Remagen, which the German 15th Army was unable to destroy, since the four Panzer divisions which Model had given

the energetic Lieutenant-General Bayerlein for this purpose did not total more
than 5,000 men, 60 tanks, and 30 guns.
On the other side of the battlefield, the
Americans spread out in all directions.
So great and thorough was their push
that, on March 22, they were on the right
bank of the Rhine in a bridgehead 25 miles
long and ten miles deep.

No retreat

As explained earlier, because of the forces
and *matériel* requested by Montgomery
in order to lead his army group across the
Rhine to the north of the Ruhr,
Eisenhower had at first limited his operation to the left bank of the Mosel. However, Hitler's obstinate decision to keep
his Army Group "G" inside the salient
limited by Haguenau, Saarbrücken,
Cochem (north of the Mosel), and
Koblenz, would convince him that the
best thing to do was to strike a third blow
at the enemy on the west of the Rhine,
which meant that the 3rd Army and the
6th Army Group would be able to take
part.

Colonel-General Hausser, commanding Army Group "G", had just been given

△ *A German soldier lies dead
on the bank of the Rhine, the
Third Reich's "uncrossable"
natural defence in the West.*

An American artillery column streams past the wreckage of a German convoy blasted by the Allies' heavy guns.

the 7th Army, recently taken over by General Obstfelder, and which was at present heavily engaged against Patton.

Hausser still had the 1st Army (General Foertsch), which was occupying the Moder front and the Siegfried Line or *Westwall* as far as the approaches to Forbach. The 19th Army, having evacuated the Colmar pocket, now came directly under the command of O.K.W. But at this time all these units totalled only 13 divisions, most of them badly worn, though some of them still gave a good account of themselves, for example the 2nd Mountain Division (Lieutenant-General Degen), and the 6th S.S. Mountain Division (Lieutenant-General Brenner).

Under these conditions, Hausser and his army commanders were of the opinion that they ought to put the Rhine, between the junctures of the Mosel and the Lauter,

behind them as soon as possible and be ready to abandon the Siegfried Line after having destroyed all its installations. But Hitler reacted indignantly to this suggestion of destroying a masterpiece of German military engineering to which he had contributed so much.

The Führer was mistaken about the value of this construction, however. Patton, who visited one of the fortresses taken by the 76th Division, points out its weak point with his usual perspicacity:

"It consisted of a three storey submerged barracks with toilets, shower baths, a hospital, laundry, kitchen, store rooms and every conceivable convenience plus an enormous telephone installation. Electricity and heat were produced by a pair of identical diesel engines with generators. Yet the whole offensive capacity of this installation consisted of two machine guns and a 60-mm mortar operating from steel cupolas which worked up and down by means of hydraulic lifts. The 60-mm mortar was peculiar in that it was operated by remote control. As in all cases, this particular pill box was taken by a dynamite charge against the back door. We found marks on the cupolas, which were ten inches thick, where our 90-mm shells fired at a range of two hundred yards, had simply bounced."

But neither Hitler nor his subordinates imagined that Patton would need only four or five days to shift the centre of gravity of his 3rd Army from Brohl and Koblenz on the Rhine to Mayen on the Nette and Cochem on the Mosel. On the left, VIII Corps, now reduced to two divisions, would keep watch on Koblenz. In the centre, XII Corps, increased to six divisions (5th, 76th, 89th, and 90th Infantry, and 4th and 11th Armoured), was given Bingen on the Rhine and Bad-Kreuznach on the Nahe as its first targets. On the right, XX Corps with four divisions (26th, 80th, and 94th Infantry and 10th Armoured) had orders to press on to Kaiserslautern behind the backs of the defenders of the *Westwall*, which would be attacked frontally by the American 7th Army. The latter, commanded by Lieutenant-General Alexander M. Patch, had 12 divisions, including the 3rd Algerian Division. As can be seen, the third act of the Battle of the Rhine, named "Undertone" was about to match 22 more or less intact Allied divisions against 13 worn-out German ones. Actually, since the end of January, the 7th Army had been waiting poised between Haguenau and Forbach.

As for the 3rd Army, its losses, between January 29 and March 12, amounted to only 21,581 officers, N.C.O.s, and men, of which 3,650 had been killed and 1,374 were missing, which gives a daily divisional average of eight killed or missing and 32 wounded. These figures would suggest that despite his nickname of "Blood and Guts", Patton was not at all prodigal with the lives of his men.

Triumphant advance

On the evening of March 14, XII Corps had already got most of its 5th and 90th Divisions over on the right bank of the Mosel at Treis, eight miles below Cochem. Eddy then wasted no time in unleashing his 4th and 11th Armoured Divisions.

To his right, XX Corps was attacking towards Saint Wendel, in the rear of the *Westwall*. At last, at dawn on March 15, H-hour came for the 7th Army. Its VI Corps (3rd Algerian, 36th, 42nd, and 103rd Divisions and 14th Armoured Division), went into the attack on the Moder front. Its 15th Division attacked the *Westwall,* its left towards Saarlautern, the French Sarrelouis, in contact with XX Corps.

By March 16, the 4th Armoured Division had advanced 32 miles in 48 hours. As it crossed the Nahe, near Bad-Kreuznach, it clashed violently with the 2nd Panzer Division (Major-General von Lauchert). But Patton was aware of the audacity of Gaffey, his ex-chief-of-staff, and had not let him fight it out alone. Opportunely reinforced, the 4th Armoured Division defeated the desperate counter-attack and moved forward again. By March 19, it had arrived seven miles west of Worms and 12 miles south-west of Mainz. On the same day, XX Corps, to which the 7th Army had given the 12th Armoured Division, under Major-General R. R. Allen, pushed its armoured spearheads as far as 15 miles from Kaiserslautern. Since the crossing of the Mosel, the 3rd Army had lost, including accidents, only 800 men, while it had taken 12,000 prisoners.

Forty-eight hours later, in XII Corps, the 90th Division, which had lost two commanders in Normandy, was busy mopping up Mainz, the 4th Armoured Division was occupying Worms, and the 11th was pushing on to the south of the city.

In XX Corps, Major-General Walton H. Walker had thrown his 12th Armoured Division into Ludwigshafen and was pushing his 10th towards Landau. Just as the difficult terrain of the Eifel had been no impediment, that of the Hunsruck, which is just as bad, had not been able to hold back the *élan* of the 3rd Army, supported flexibly and efficiently by Major-General Otto P. Weyland's XIX Tactical Air Command of the 9th Air Force.

Facing the German 1st Army, the American 7th Army had had a considerably more difficult task. There is some evidence of this in a note made by Pierre Lyautey who, as liaison officer, was with the 3rd Algerian Division (General

△ *General Sir Miles Dempsey, commander of the British 2nd Army, on an inspection tour of his front line units.*

△ *An American quadruple .5-inch A.A. mounting on a half-track chassis on watch against German aircraft near the Château de Vianden in Luxembourg.*

Guillaume), when it attacked across the Moder.

"March 15: Artillery preparation. The planned 2,000 shells light up the scene. Attack by the 4th Tunisians. Skirmishes. The leading company runs, at seven in the morning, from ruin to ruin, lonely wall to lonely wall, reaches the railway, dives into the underground passage and jumps up into the mangled and dismantled gasworks. Violent reaction from German artillery, mortar, and machine guns. Impossible to move out. The whole sector is alive with fire. The company shelters in the gas-works. First one tank explodes, then another. Beyond the church, the scene is one of a major offensive: stretcher-bearers, stretchers, limping men walking around with white cards, a smell of blood, stifling heat. The last cows of Oberhoffen-Bénarès are in their death agony among the rubble."

It took four days for Major-General Edward H. Brooks, commanding VI Corps, to take back from the Germans the ground lost in lower Alsace as a result of Operation *"Nordwind"*. Then he closed in on the *Westwall* between the Rhine and the Vosges.

Both General de Gaulle and General de Lattre had no intention, however, of allowing the French Army to be restricted to a purely defensive function on the left bank of the Rhine. They wanted to see it play a part in the invasion of the Third Reich. While awaiting a definite decision from S.H.A.E.F., General de Gaulle writes, "General Devers, a good ally and a good friend, sympathised with de Lattre's wishes".

That is why, on March 18, General de Monsabert received command of a task force comprising the 3rd Algerian Division and two-thirds of the 5th Armoured Division; aiming for Speyer, it would give the French 1st Army a front over the Rhine in Germany.

The three infantry divisions of the United States VI Corps took three days and lost 2,200 men to overcome that part of the *Westwall* allotted to them as objective, but using its infantry and engineers

in turn, Brooks finally pierced the defences between Wissembourg and Pirmasens. As for Monsabert, he had difficulty in front of the Bienwald. Nevertheless, his tanks were around Maximiliansau opposite Karlsruhe by the evening of March 24.

Patch had taken Landau the day before, so the Battle of the Palatinate, the third act of the Battle of the Rhine, was drawing to its end.

The battle had been conducted to Eisenhower's complete satisfaction. Between February 8 and March 24, the enemy had lost 280,000 prisoners, the remains of five German armies which had crossed back over the Rhine between the German-Dutch and Franco-German frontiers. Army Group "B" had suffered most. Patton alone could claim 140,112 prisoners, against the 53,000 taken by the 21st Army Group in Operation "Veritable/Grenade". Therefore Eisenhower had proved his superiority not only over Hitler's arms but also over Montgomery's arguments.

Furthermore, on the night of March 22/23, Patton also succeeded in crossing the Rhine as Bradley had recommended, profiting from the Germans' disorder. The banks there being suitable, Patton chose the stretch near Oppenheim, which

△ *The great prize. Men and vehicles of the American 1st Army pour across the Ludendorff railway bridge over the Rhine at Remagen to establish an invincible bridgehead on the right bank.*

A Sherman of the U.S. Army is ferried across a river on a section of pontoon bridge pushed by motor-boats.
▷ The Allied advance to the Rhine, and the establishment of the first bridgeheads at Remagen and Oppenheim.

was occupied by the 5th Division (Major-General S. LeRoy Irwin), half-way between Worms and Mainz.

Surprise crossing

At 2230 hours, 200 Piper L-4 Grasshoppers began to shuttle from one bank to the other. These small observation and artillery-spotting aircraft carried an armed infantryman instead of an observer. Once the first bridgehead had thus been formed, the 12 L.C.V.P.s (Landing Craft Vehicle/Personnel) of the "naval detachment" which Patton had trained to a high pitch of efficiency on the Moselle at Toul, entered the river while his bridging crews, from which he had refused to be separated (lest he not get them back) when he had driven hard from the Sarre to the Ardennes, began to work at once under the command of Brigadier-General Conklin, the 3rd Army's chief engineer.

At dawn on March 23, the 5th Division had already placed six infantry battalions, about 4,000 or 5,000 men, on the right bank of the Rhine, at the cost of only eight killed and 20 wounded. The Germans were so surprised that when Patton made his report to Bradley, he asked him not to publicise the news, so as to keep the Germans in the dark while they expected him at the approaches to Mainz. As an all-American soldier, he was happy to have stolen a march over "Monty" by forcing the Rhine before him and without making any demands on anybody.

As a result, 48 hours later, five divisions of the 3rd Army had crossed the Rhine at Oppenheim, stretched along the valley of the Main: XII Corps towards Aschaffenburg, and XX Corps towards Hanau.

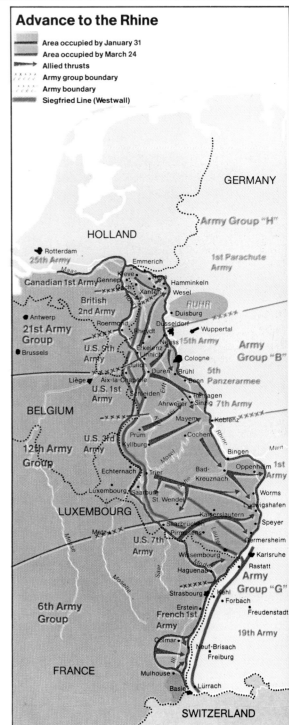

Advance to the Rhine

- Area occupied by January 31
- Area occupied by March 24
- Allied thrusts
- Army group boundary
- Army boundary
- Siegfried Line (Westwall)

CHAPTER 142
The End in Italy
by Lt.-Col. Alan Shepperd

△ *Sherman tank of the U.S. 1st Armoured Division moves up towards Lucca before the campaign to break the Gothic Line.*

Originally known as the Apennine Position, the Gothic Line ran across the mountains, coast to coast, for 200 miles, from near La Spezia on the Gulf of Genoa to Pesaro on the Adriatic. It was longer than the line through Cassino, and the mountain barrier reached across the peninsula to within a short distance of Route 16, which followed the coast-line through the narrow plain to Rimini. Orders for the line to be reconnoitred and fortified had in fact been given by Jodl almost a month before the evacuation of Sicily, but more recently the work had been interrupted by the pressing demands for *matériel* and labour for building the defences of the Gustav and Hitler Lines.

At the time of the capture of Rome, Alexander estimated that Kesselring would have only the equivalent of ten divisions to man the Apennine positions, but Hitler's immediate reaction to the threat of an Allied advance into northern Italy had completely changed the situation. Kesselring was now able to gain much-needed time for the Organisation Todt to complete most of the defences that had been so carefully planned.

At the very height of the fighting in Normandy, Hitler dispatched no fewer than seven divisions, withdrawn from Denmark, Holland, Hungary, and even the Russian front, to reinforce Army Group "C" in Italy. Finally O.K.W. sent a battalion of Tiger tanks from

France and the whole of three divisions, forming in Germany, to fill up the ranks of the infantry divisions that had been virtually annihilated in the Liri valley.

Although Alexander had been warned as early as May 22, 1944, that he must be prepared to provide seven divisions for a landing in the south of France, it was not until July 5, when the battle for Arezzo was in the balance and the Polish II Corps was still short of Ancona, that he was told that his pleas to be allowed to keep his force intact, for a thrust into northern Italy and beyond, had finally been turned down.

The task that Alexander was now given was:

1. to cross the Apennines to the line of the River Po; and
2. to cross the river and seize the line Venice – Padua – Verona – Brescia. After this he would receive further instructions.

In spite of the loss of so many divisions, including the French Expeditionary Corps with all its mountain troops, the Allied offensive must continue.

The long summer days were running out and the chance of any large scale penetration into the Po valley before winter set in now appeared most unlikely. But in Normandy the Battle of Caen was

about to start—it was imperative that the pressure by the Allies in Italy should be maintained, even increased.

So long as there had been hopes of a rapid advance, the bridges over the Po had been spared by the Allied bombers. On July 12 the Tactical Air Force went to work and in three days cut all 23 of the rail and road bridges over the river. The battle for the Gothic Line had begun.

Superb defences

In the mountains the German engineers had already constructed a series of strongpoints astride the routes leading to the Po valley at Borgo a Mozzano, Porretta, the Vernio pass north of Prato, and the Futa and Il Giogo passes north of Florence. From here the line ran south-east, again with every route blocked, from Casaglia to below Bagno and the Mandrioli pass, before turning eastwards to drop down to the valley of the Foglia and Pesaro on the Adriatic. Here, in the narrow coastal plain, was Route 16, the only road that the Allies could take which did not mean a climb across the great mountain barrier. This corridor, however, between the foothills and the sea, was cut across by numerous rivers; and the succession of ridges, which similarly were at right angles to the line of advance, was admirably suited for defence. Moreover, the rivers were liable to sudden flooding and rain quickly turned the heavy soil into a sea

△ *German infantry move down through the Dolomites from Austria towards the front.*

▽ *American motor transport in typical Italian terrain. The problems faced by the attackers in such country were particularly difficult: firstly the logistic difficulties of moving up men and supplies, and then the tactical disadvantage of having to attack uphill.*

of mud. The fortifications in this sector had been skilfully prepared, with anti-tank ditches, extensive minefields, and the usual deep bunkers. In June and July, while Kesselring's rearguards were slowly falling back through Tuscany, Todt engineers, with thousands of conscripted Italian labourers, were frantically engaged in constructing a ten mile deep belt of obstacles along the whole line, and in the mountains a series of positions to link up with the main strongholds, so as to form a continuous front. A report on the defences that had been completed when the battle started listed 2,376 machine gun nests, 479 anti-tank gun, mortar, and assault gun positions, 120,000 yards of wire entanglement, and many miles of anti-tank ditches. Only four out of the 30 7.5-cm Panther gun turrets ordered by O.K.W., however, were in position.

The balance of forces in the opening stages of the forthcoming battle pitted 26 German divisions, including six Panzer and *Panzergrenadier* divisions, and some six Italian divisions, against 20 Allied divisions, which included four armoured divisions. For the Germans the battle would be fought solely on the ground, as the Luftwaffe in Italy was reduced to 170 aircraft, the majority of which were obsolete. The Allies, with some 75 complete squadrons in the Tactical Air Force alone, enjoyed complete air superiority. This advantage, however, would soon be reduced as the weather deteriorated. Meanwhile Kesselring could neither "see over the hill", nor strike out at his enemy's rear communications. In spite of this and a weakness in both artillery and armour, he viewed his task of beating off the coming offensive with growing confidence, especially after an inspection of the defences on his eastern flank.

Throughout the whole campaign the Germans had overestimated the Allied capability to carry out amphibious operations against their rear and Kesselring, sensitive to the preparations for "Dragoon" (as "Anvil" was now named), feared a landing on the Ligurian coast or even in the Gulf of Venice. Consequently he allocated no fewer than six divisions to coastal defence. A further weakening of his forces resulted from the active resistance, backed by the Communists, of Italian workers in the industrial areas to Mussolini's puppet government. In effect civil war had broken out, and in spite of the arrival of two German-trained Italian divisions the partisans were also beginning to show their true strength in attacks on military depots and lines of communication. Thus there remained only 19 divisions to hold the Gothic Line itself. On the right was the 14th Army, with XIV Panzer Corps allocated to the long mountain stretch from the coast to Empoli, and I Parachute Corps to hold the shorter and more critical central section facing Florence, both with three divisions. In reserve were the inexperienced 20th Luftwaffe Field Division and the 29th *Panzergrenadier* Division, north of Florence. East of Pontassieve was the 10th Army, with LI Mountain Corps (five divisions) holding the spine of the Apennine range as far as Sansepolcro and LXXVI Panzer Corps in the foothills and coastal plain, again with five divisions, of which two were echeloned back watching the coast. The newly arrived 98th Division was in army reserve around Bologna. This again emphasised Kesselring's preoccupation with the central section of the mountain barrier, which was only 50 miles deep at this point, in spite of his prediction that the attack would be made on the Adriatic flank. Meanwhile the front line remained on the line of the Arno.

Revised plans

Alexander's initial plan was to press an early attack, with both armies side by side, into the mountains on the axis Florence–Bologna. Indeed the cover plan, with fake wireless traffic and soldiers arriving in the Adriatic sector wearing Canadian I Corps flashes, had already started. But this was before Clark's 5th Army was reduced to a single corps and the total strength of both armies to 20 divisions. Moreover there was no chance of any reinforcements other than the U.S. 92nd (Negro) Division in September and a Brazilian division by the end of October. So there could be no diversionary operations and no reserve to maintain the impetus of the advance. In spite of this, General Harding, Alexander's chief-of-staff, recommended the plan should stand. Lieutenant-General Sir Oliver Leese, the 8th Army commander, whose troops would have to bear the brunt of the fighting, felt there was a far better chance of breaking through on the Adriatic sector, where his superiority in tanks and guns could be employed to greater effect.

Furthermore General Clark would have greater freedom to make his own dis-

△ *Lieutenant-Colonel J. Sokol, of the Polish 3rd Carpathian Infantry Division, inspects U.S. artillery positions. The division formed part of the Polish II Corps that took Pesaro.*

▽ *Canadian armour crosses the Sieve, which flows into the Arno at Pontassieve, ten miles east of Florence.*

▷ An anti-tank mine clearing platoon of the U.S. 85th Division prepares to clear the approaches to a Bailey bridge being built by the 255th Combat Engineers of the U.S. IV Corps across a gorge on Route 64, south of Bologna.
△ ▷ U.S. infantry south of Bologna.
▽ ▷ American forces in the Piazza del Campo in Siena.
▽ Knocked-out motor transport in Italy.

positions. This plan suited one of Alexander's favourite strategies, the "two-handed punch", in that by striking at both Ravenna and Bologna the enemy's reserves would be split. At a secret meeting in Orvieto on August 4, 1944 between the two commanders, with only Harding present, the matter was decided by Alexander in favour of Leese's alternative proposal. As practically the whole of the 8th Army had to be moved across the mountains to the east coast, D-day was put back to August 25. The cover plan was put into reverse, with 5th Army being told to make "ostentatious preparations" for an attack against the centre of the mountain positions. In the greatest secrecy the regrouping of both armies was started immediately.

The transfer to north of Ancona of the bulk of the 8th Army–two complete corps headquarters, some eight divisions, and a mass of corps troops, with over 80,000 vehicles–was achieved in 15 days. This was a remarkable feat as there were only two roads over the mountains, and both had been systematically demolished by the Germans during their retreat. In many places the roads had to be entirely rebuilt and no fewer than 40 Bailey bridges were constructed by the Royal Engineers before the roads could be reopened. Even so the roads were largely one-way, and the movement tables were further complicated by the need to operate the tank transporters on a continuous shuttle service as a result of the short time available for the concentration of the tank brigades.

Meanwhile the British XIII Corps, of three divisions under Lieutenant-General Sidney Kirkman, joined the U.S. 5th Army, so as to be ready alongside U.S. II Corps to deliver the second blow of "the two-handed punch" towards Bologna. The remaining two U.S. divisions, joined by the 6th South African Armoured Division and a mixed force of American and British anti-aircraft and other support units, hastily trained as infantry, formed Major-General Crittenberger's U.S. IV Corps. This had the task of holding the remainder of the 5th Army front. On the inner flank, acting as a link between the two armies, was X Corps, with the 10th Indian Division, a tank brigade, and several "dismounted" armoured car regiments. Every other available man of the 8th Army was committed to the main assault on the right flank.

Leese's plan was to break into the

Gothic Line defences on a narrow front, with the Polish II Corps directed on Pesaro (before going into reserve), and the Canadians making straight for Rimini. The main attack would be through the hills further inland towards Route 9 by Lieutenant-General Sir Charles Keightley's V Corps, with the British 4th, 46th, and 56th, and 1st Armoured Divisions, and 4th Indian Division. The latter was briefed for the pursuit, and would attack alongside the Canadian 5th Armoured Division as soon as the breakthrough was achieved.

The offensive falters

Initially all went well. When the Allied advance started the Germans were engaged in carrying out a series of reliefs in the coastal area, which involved the pulling back of a division from forward positions on the Metauro. Kesselring indeed assumed that the attack on August 25 was no more than a follow-up of this withdrawal. Vietinghoff himself was on leave and only got back late on August 28. The next day the Allied infantry reached the Foglia and Kesselring, who had been taken completely by surprise, at last ordered up reinforcements. But it was too late to stop the penetration of the carefully prepared Gothic Line positions. On August 31 the 46th Division held the formidable bastion of Monte-gridolfo and the following night Gurkhas of the 4th Indian Division, using only grenades and kukris, captured the strongly fortified town of Tavoleto. In the plain,

the Canadians had suffered heavily crossing the river but by dawn on September 3 had a bridgehead across the Conca alongside Route 16. Meanwhile both the 26th Panzer and 98th Divisions had reached the battle area and already suffered heavily.

The way to a breakthrough by V Corps lay in the capture of two hill features, the Coriano and Gemmano Ridges, situated just where the plain begins to widen out. These afforded the Germans excellent observation and fine positions. The task of breaking through was given to the 46th and 56th Divisions. Meanwhile, the British 1st Armoured Division, with some 300 tanks, had already started (on August 31) to move forward in accordance with the original plan. The approach march over narrow and often precipitous tracks, which got progressively worse, proved a nightmare. On one stage "along razor-edged mountain ridges" to reach the Foglia, which was crossed on September 3, drivers of the heavier vehicles had to reverse to get round every corner and some spent 50 hours at the wheel. The tank route proved even more hazardous, and 20 tanks were lost before reaching the assembly area. The driving conditions were extremely exhausting and as the column ground its way forward in low gear many tanks ran out of petrol, while those at the rear of the column were engulfed in dense clouds of choking white dust.

At this critical moment the German 162nd Division and Kesselring's last mobile reserve, the experienced 29th *Panzergrenadier* Division (from Bologna) began to arrive. The renewed attacks

The American M24 Chaffee light tank

Weight: 18 tons.
Crew: 5.
Armament: one 75-mm M6 gun with 48 rounds, and one .5-inch Browning M2 and two .3-inch Browning M1919A4 machine guns with 420 and 4,125 rounds respectively.
Armour: hull front and sides 25-mm, lower sides and rear 19-mm, decking 13-mm, and belly 6.5-mm; turret front and mantlet 38-mm, sides 25-mm, and roof 13-mm.
Engines: two Cadillac Model 44T24 inlines, 110-hp each.
Speed: 30 mph.
Range: 100 miles.
Length: 18 feet.
Width: 9 feet 8 inches.
Height: 8 feet $1\frac{1}{2}$ inches.

by V Corps were broken up and held. Into the confused and unresolved struggle the armoured divisions were ordered forward late on September 4. There had been no breakthrough; the fleeting opportunity, if it had ever existed, had passed. The advance of the armoured brigades was met with a storm of shot and shell and an unbroken defence which now included tanks and self-propelled guns. In their advance towards Coriano, the British armoured brigades lost 65 tanks and many more were still struggling to cross the start line as dusk came.

That night rain began to fall and more German reinforcements (from the 356th Division) reached the front. By September 6 the tracks had turned to mud and air strikes could no longer be guaranteed. Alexander now ordered a regrouping for a set-piece attack (on September 12) to clear the two vital ridges. Now was the time for Clark to launch his attack into the mountains.

Since early August Kesselring's front line troops had been kept short of supplies through the interdiction programme of the Allied air forces. With the Brenner pass frequently blocked, north Italy was virtually isolated from the rest of Europe. There was no direct railway traffic across the Po east of Piacenza and south of the river the railway lines down as far as the Arno had been cut in nearly 100 places. But in spite of every difficulty, sufficient supplies were kept moving forward. Each

night, pontoon bridges were built across the Po and then broken up and hidden by day; and ferries were operating at over 50 points on the river.

The Desert Air Force, which had supported the 8th Army so magnificently at a time when almost all the American air effort had been diverted to the "Dragoon" landing, now switched its whole effort to helping Clark's offensive to get under way. Clark's attack came as no surprise to General Joachim Lemelsen, whose 14th Army had already been milked of three divisions to reinforce Colonel-General Heinrich von Vietinghoff's 10th Army. The latter was now seriously short of infantry, and had been ordered to fall back to the prepared defences in

△ Local intelligence for an
American soldier.

the mountains. Even after the transfer
to his command of the 334th Division from
the adjacent LI Mountain Corps, Lemelsen had no reserve and with all his force
in the line, each division was on at least a
ten mile front. From his post on the
"touch-line", as it were, in the quiet and
inaccessible Ligurian coastal sector,
General von Senger und Etterlin
correctly forecast the outcome of this
impasse. He later wrote:

"The incessant prodding against [the
left wing of] our front across the Futa
pass was like jabbing a thiek cloth with
a sharp spear. The cloth would give way
like elastic, but under excessive strain it
would be penetrated by the spear."

The 5th Army attack was made by two
corps and on a narrow front east of the
Il Giogo pass, at the junction of the two
German armies, and initially fell on two
thinly stretched divisions. Holding the
Il Giogo pass was the 4th Parachute
Division, which had been made up with
very young soldiers with barely three
months' training. The pass itself was
nothing but a way over a ridge only about
2,900 feet high, but overlooked by some
of the highest peaks in the whole moun-

tain range.

Clark used Lieutenant-General
Geoffrey Keyes's II Corps of four divisions (U.S. 34th, 85th, 88th, and 91st)
as his spearhead against the Il Giogo
defences. On the tail of the German
withdrawal he launched his offensive on
September 13. Once again, Kesselring
misread the situation. In spite of the
efforts of two U.S. divisions, a considerable artillery concentration, and 2,000
sorties by medium and fighter-bombers,
the 4th Parachute Division more than
held its ground for the first four days.
Meanwhile Kirkman's XIII Corps was
attacking on the right flank of the Americans along the parallel routes towards
Faenza and Forlì. By September 14 the
8th Indian Division was over the watershed and the following day the British
1st Division took Monte Prefetto and,
turning to help its neighbours, attacked
the German parachute troops on Monte
Pratone. As the pressure mounted on
the 4th Parachute Division, the leading
American infantry began to make ground,
and between September 16 and 18 Monti
Altuzzo and Monticelli and the nearby
strongholds and peaks were captured.

△ A British officer surveys the final goal of the Italian campaign: the Alps and Austria.

Coriano ridge taken

Keyes' II Corps held a seven-mile stretch of the Gothic Line defences either side of the Il Giogo pass. At last Kesselring awoke to the danger of a breakthrough to Imola and from either flank rushed in an extra division to hold Firenzuola and the road down the Santerno valley. This was indeed a critical sector for the Germans, for it was one of the few areas on the northern slopes of the mountains where any quantity of artillery and transport could be deployed once over the watershed.

By September 27 Clark's infantry had fought its way forward to within ten miles of Route 9 at Imola, before being halted by fierce and co-ordinated counterattacks by no less than four German divisions. In attempting to recapture Monte Battaglia, Kesselring threw in units from many divisions, including some pulled out from the Adriatic front, against the U.S. 88th Division. The battle lasted for over a week before the exhausted German infantry was ordered to dig in. But with mounting casualties and deteriorating weather, Clark also called a halt and turned his attention to Route 65, which would lead him to Bologna.

On the 8th Army front the Canadians and V Corps resumed the offensive on the night of September 12 and drove the Germans off the Coriano and Gemmano ridges, but it took the Canadians three whole days of bitter and costly fighting to clear San Fortunato. On September 20, Rimini fell to the 3rd Greek Mountain Brigade, who fought well in this its first engagement, and the following day Allied patrols were across the Marecchia. Now, as Freyberg's 2nd New Zealand Division passed through on Route 16, the rivers were filling and near spate and the heavy soil of the Romagna was beginning to grip both men and vehicles as they struggled forward. The Romagna is an immense flat expanse of alluvial soil carried down by a dozen or so rivers and

The Italian FIAT G.55 ''Centauro'' fighter

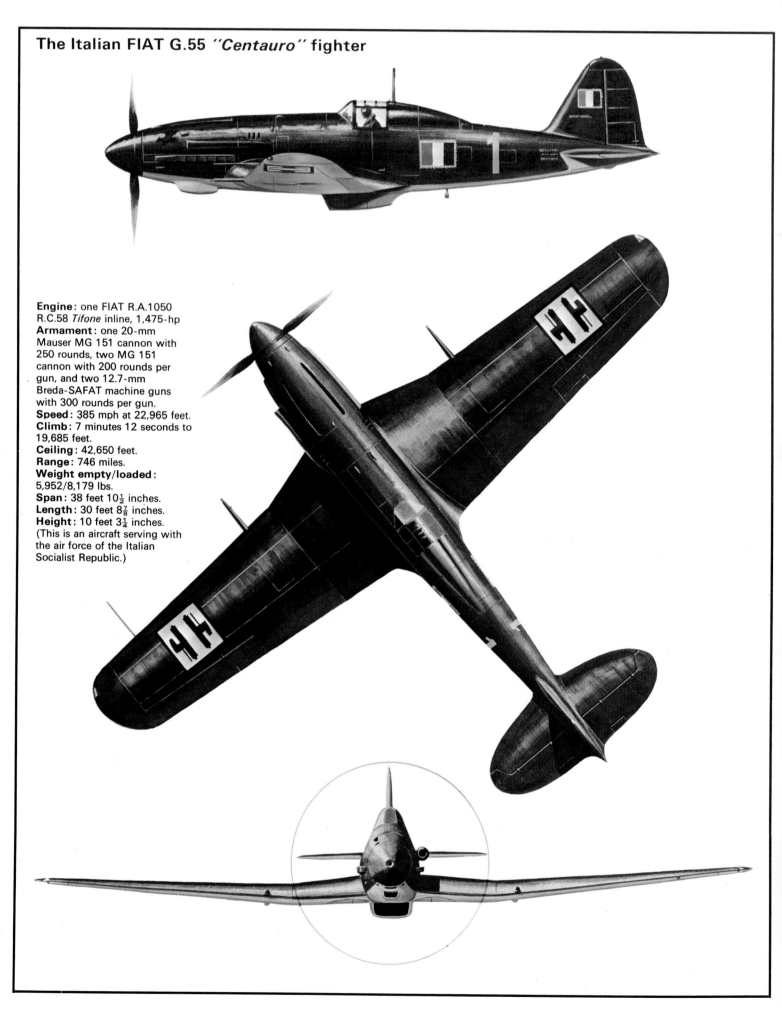

Engine: one FIAT R.A.1050 R.C.58 *Tifone* inline, 1,475-hp
Armament: one 20-mm Mauser MG 151 cannon with 250 rounds, two MG 151 cannon with 200 rounds per gun, and two 12.7-mm Breda-SAFAT machine guns with 300 rounds per gun.
Speed: 385 mph at 22,965 feet.
Climb: 7 minutes 12 seconds to 19,685 feet.
Ceiling: 42,650 feet.
Range: 746 miles.
Weight empty/loaded: 5,952/8,179 lbs.
Span: 38 feet $10\frac{1}{2}$ inches.
Length: 30 feet $8\frac{7}{8}$ inches.
Height: 10 feet $3\frac{1}{4}$ inches.
(This is an aircraft serving with the air force of the Italian Socialist Republic.)

innumerable smaller watercourses that discharge into the Adriatic. Reclaimed and cultivated over centuries, it is still essentially a swamp, criss-crossed by ditches and with the watercourses channelled between floodbanks that rise in places 40 feet above the plain. Moreover, the numerous stone-built farmhouses and hamlets, vineyards, and long rows of fruit trees afforded the defence ready-made strongpoints and cover. Inauspicious terrain indeed, with all the odds against a rapid advance. By the 29th only the leading elements of the New Zealand and 56th Divisions had reached the banks of the River Fiumicino and the Germans were still entrenched in the foothills south of Route 9. Torrential rain, however, brought all forward movement to a halt, sweeping away bridges and making fords impassable. But in the mountains X Corps still fought on and by October 8 was within ten miles of Cesena.

General Leese, who had been given command of the Allied Land Forces in South-East Asia, had now been succeeded by General Sir Richard McCreery. The new army commander, deciding to avoid the low ground, launched in succession the 10th Indian Division and the Poles through the mountains. And by October 21 Cesena had been taken and bridgeheads seized over the Savio. After resisting for four days the Germans voluntarily withdrew to the line of the Ronco.

Striking now towards Bologna, Clark's II Corps met growing resistance. Initially it had benefited from heavy air support, including strategic bombers, and the efforts of the 8th Army to break out along Route 9. It had been opposed by less than two divisions. By the time it reached the Livergano escarpment, however, it was faced by no less than five divisions (including the 16th S.S. Panzer Division), and elements from three other divisions. This was the work of von Senger, who was temporarily in command of the 10th Army owing to the illness of Lemelsen. Helped by a spell of fine weather, which gave the Allied air forces the chance to intervene, II Corps drove the Germans off the escarpment on October 14. But von Senger was bringing in more and more troops and had the defences of Bologna properly co-ordinated and well covered by artillery. Although the 88th Division captured Monte Grande on October 20, with the assistance of fighter-bombers and the expenditure of 8,600

△ *American troops in Monghidoro.*

Previous Page
▷ *Medical corpsmen of the U.S. 10th Mountain Division treat a wounded German prisoner.*

▽ *Bailey bridge at Vergato, named after the late president of the United States.*

rounds of gun ammunition, the Americans were beaten back from the little village of Vedriano on three successive nights by fierce counter-attacks.

Since September 10, in just over six weeks II Corps had lost 15,716 men, and over 5,000 of these casualties had been in the 88th Division. On October 25, Clark gave the order to dig in. He himself chose to share some of the discomforts of his men and proposed to sit the winter out in his caravan near the Futa pass, one of the highest parts of the Apennines.

On the other flank, the 8th Army's operations were similarly halted; the weather had broken completely and both sides were exhausted. Alexander wrote that "the rain, which was at that time spoiling Fifth Army's attack on Bologna, now reached a high pitch of intensity. On 26th October all bridges over the Savio, in our immediate rear, were swept away and our small bridge heads over the Ronco were eliminated and destroyed."

Since August the Germans had lost 8,000 prisoners, and LXXVII Panzer Corps alone had suffered over 14,500 battle casualties. Over a third of Kesselring's 92 infantry battalions were down to 200

men each and only ten mustered over 400. In the 8th Army, battle casualties since July totalled 19,975, and every infantry battalion had to be reorganised. Tank casualties were well over 400 and the 1st Armoured Division had to be disbanded.

Winter war

In north-west Europe all chances of a decisive victory over Nazi Germany in 1944 ended with the reverse at Arnhem and the delay in opening the port of Antwerp. A winter campaign was now inevitable. In Italy, Kesselring's Operation *"Herbstnebel"* (Autumn Fog), to shorten his line by withdrawing to the Alps, was peremptorily turned down by Hitler. Alexander's long-term proposal for an enveloping attack by landing in Yugoslavia could make no immediate contribution to Eisenhower's present predicament and indeed proved to be a pipe dream that for political reasons alone would never have been authorised. So it was the mixture as before, with Hitler still obsessed with the Balkans, Kesselring

continued on page 2092

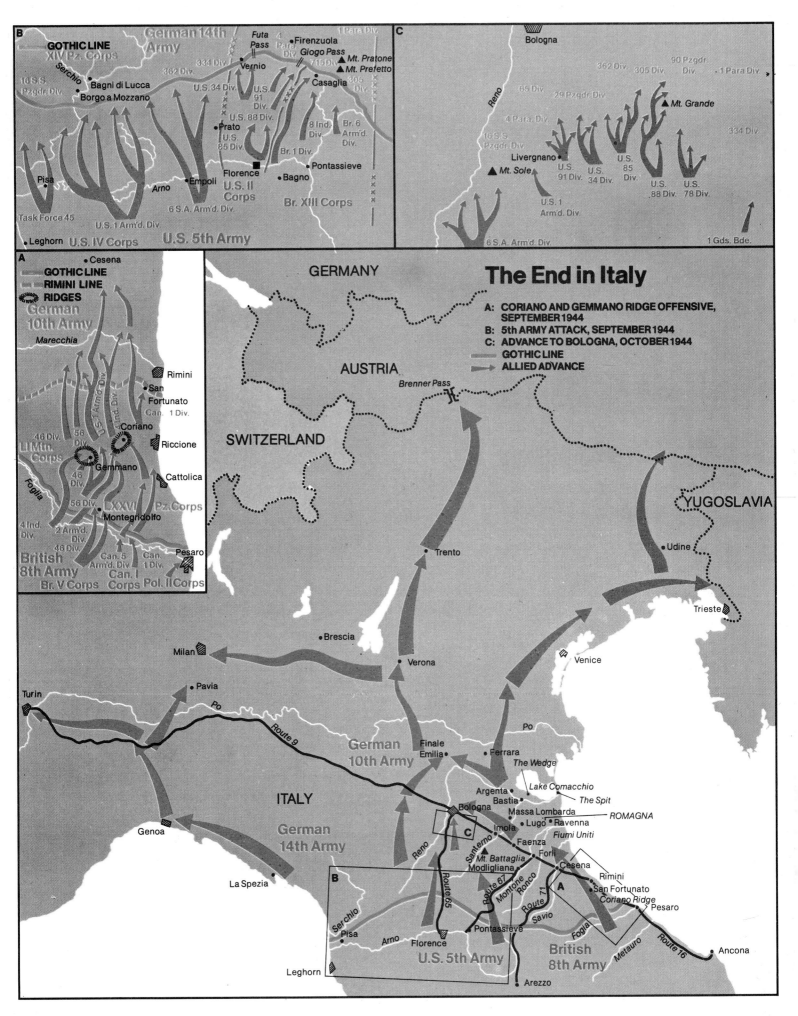

B

GOTHIC LINE
XIV Pz. Corps

German 14th Army

16 S.S. Pzgdr. Div.
Serchio
Bagni di Lucca
Borgo a Mozzano

362 Div.
334 Div.
Futa Pass
Vernio
U.S. 34 Div.
U.S. 91 Div.
4 Para. Div.
Firenzuola
Giogo Pass
715 Div.
▲ Mt. Pratone
▲ Mt. Prefetto
Casaglia
305 Div.
1 Para Div.

Pisa
Prato
U.S. 85 Div.
U.S. 88 Div.
Florence
8 Ind. Div.
Br. 6 Arm'd. Div.
Br. 1 Div.

Task Force 45
Arno
Empoli
6 S.A. Arm'd. Div.
Pontassieve
Bagno

Leghorn
U.S. 1 Arm'd. Div.
U.S. IV Corps
U.S. II Corps
U.S. 5th Army
Br. XIII Corps

C

Bologna
90 Pzgdr. Div.
1 Para Div.
362 Div.
305 Div.
334 Div.
Reno
66 Div.
29 Pzgdr. Div.
▲ Mt. Grande
4 Para. Div.
16 S.S. Pzgdr. Div.
Livergnano
▲ Mt. Sole
U.S. 91 Div.
U.S. 34 Div.
U.S. 85 Div.
U.S. 88 Div.
U.S. 78 Div.
U.S. 1 Arm'd. Div.
6 S.A. Arm'd. Div.
1 Gds. Bde.

A

Cesena
GOTHIC LINE
RIMINI LINE
RIDGES
German 10th Army
Marecchia
Rimini
San Fortunato
Can. 1 Div.
U.S. 1 Arm'd. Div.
Coriano
46 Div.
56 Div.
Riccione
LI Mtn. Corps
46 Div.
Gemmano
Cattolica
Fogila
56 Div.
LXXVI
Montegridolfo
Pz. Corps
4 Ind. Div.
2 Arm'd. Div.
46 Div.
Pesaro
British 8th Army
Can. 5 Arm'd. Div.
Can. 1 Div.
Can. I Corps
Pol. II Corps
Br. V Corps

The End in Italy

A: CORIANO AND GEMMANO RIDGE OFFENSIVE, SEPTEMBER 1944
B: 5th ARMY ATTACK, SEPTEMBER 1944
C: ADVANCE TO BOLOGNA, OCTOBER 1944
GOTHIC LINE
ALLIED ADVANCE

GERMANY

AUSTRIA

SWITZERLAND

Brenner Pass

YUGOSLAVIA

Trento

Udine

Brescia

Trieste

Milan

Verona

Venice

Turin

Pavia

Po

Route 9

Po

Finale Emilia

Ferrara

The Wedge

German 10th Army

Lake Comacchio

The Spit

Genoa

ITALY

German 14th Army

Argenta
Bastia
Massa Lombarda
Lugo
Ravenna
ROMAGNA

Bologna
Imola
Faenza
Forlì
Fiumi Uniti

La Spezia

Reno

Santerno

▲ Mt. Battaglia
Modligliana

Cesena
Rimini
San Fortunato
Coriano Ridge
Pesaro

Serchio
Pisa

Arno

Route 65

Route 67

Montone
Ronco

Florence

Pontassieve

Savio

Fogila

Metauro

Route 71

Route 76

Ancona

Leghorn

Arezzo

U.S. 5th Army

British 8th Army

TITO

AND THE YUGOSLAV PARTISANS

On April 17, 1941, the Yugoslav Army capitulated to the Germans. Resistance to the Axis forces began early, but it was divided between Mihailović's royalists and Tito's Communists. Tito formed a nation-wide resistance group, known as the Partisans, and played a major rôle in freeing Yugoslavia of the German occupation forces.

Tito's long term aim was the Communist control of a united Yugoslavia. Communist policy at this time was directed from Russia, but the practical organisation was left to Tito. The party organisation he had set up just before the war, which covered all regions of Yugoslavia, had now been disrupted. In April and May, he summoned the Yugoslav Communist Party Central Committee to meetings to decide on a plan of campaign. Orders went out to Communists in all parts of the country to collect secret stockpiles of weapons. The call for the revolt of the Yugoslav peoples did not come until July 4, however, after the Germans had attacked Russia, and this led to an intensive campaign of attacks all over the country. Tito had sent trained men out to the country, usually to the regions where they were born, to lead the uprisings.

The task of organising and co-

◁ *Tito, head of the Yugoslav partisan movement, with an aide in the mountains of northern Yugoslavia in 1945.*

▽ *Partisans prepare to blow the bridge at Nikšić, 40 miles east of Dubrovnik.*

▽ *Men of a Croatian Proletarian Brigade in May 1942.*
▷ *German infantry crouch behind a* leichter Panzerspähwagen Sd.Kfz 222 *armoured car in action against Bosnian partisans.*
▽ ▷ *There was no sexual discrimination among the partisans: this girl was a front line soldier wounded in the field after killing 20 Germans.*

ordinating the dispersed groups of partisans was difficult and dangerous, calling for a high degree of ability. Tito proved himself equal to it.

Clandestine operations were to be maintained in enemy-occupied towns, while a guerrilla war of movement was waged against the Germans in the countryside, with the aim of tying down as many enemy troops as possible over as wide an area as possible. The Germans could not hope to control the whole of the countryside, and Tito instructed his forces to avoid direct clashes with a superior enemy, and, if necessary, to retreat before the Germans.

Tito's efforts were extremely

successful, and the Germans were driven out of much of Serbia by mid-September. Partisan activity appealed to the national spirit, and to the love of freedom of many who were not Communists. Support for the revolts also increased after General Keitel ordered the execution of 50-100 Communists in reprisal for the death of any German soldier.

Tito's attention was diverted from the enemy when he tried and failed to reach a compromise with Mihailović, the leader of the other important resistance group, the Četniks. In the struggle between the two men to gain control of the complete resistance movement, open clashes occurred. This dis-

△ *Appalling terrain over which to fight, but it was the Yugoslavs' country and they knew how to use it in their struggle against the Germans. Here a German soldier watches a Stuka bombardment of a suspected partisan stronghold.*
▷ *Partisans unload supplies flown into Nikšić airfield by the British from Italy.*
▷ ▷ *Wounded partisans being evacuated to the mountains to recuperate.*

sension allowed the Germans to move in again. They launched their first attack in western Serbia in September 1941, and by December, most of Serbia was under Axis control.

At this time, enlistment to the partisans was on a voluntary basis and detachments had been local units fighting to defend their own home regions. Tito now needed a stable, trained army and

strike force to execute the war of movement. Accordingly, the 1st Proletarian Shock Brigade was formed in December 1941, and the 2nd during March the following year. By the end of November 1942, Tito's army had 28 brigades, each with 3-4,000 men and women. This People's Liberation Army was used increasingly for offensive action, and had its own training school, organisations for women and youths, and also a naval detachment. Each brigade had a political commissar as well as a commanding officer. Although the brigades were short of ammunition and uniforms, the partisans were very disciplined. All their supplies were paid for, and a high moral standard governed relations between men and women partisans.

Not until late 1943 did the Allies send him aid, and before that, Tito and the partisans had to fight off five German offensives. From the outset, the enemy embarked on a policy of deliberate extermination of the wounded and the sick as a weapon against the fighting morale of the rebel bands. This was contrary to the tradition of care of the wounded implicit in the code of Balkan guerrilla warfare. Tito's order was to save the wounded at all costs. As they were waging a war of mobility, the sick and the wounded had to accompany the army on the move.

By May 1944, Tito had the full support of the Allies, and the Germans were in full retreat by the end of August. In March 1945, Tito set up a provisional government with himself as Prime Minister.

continued from page 2084

over-sensitive of his coastal flank on the Adriatic, but ordered to fight where he stood, and Alexander with dwindling resources committed to a continuation of the battle of attrition against the grain of the country and in the most adverse climatic conditions. Furthermore, the bad weather was seriously limiting the use of Allied air power, at a time when the Allies were facing a world-wide shortage of certain types of artillery ammunition as a result of the extraordinarily sanguine and premature decision to set back production.

The fighting continued until early January, with the Allies aiming to reach Ravenna and break the line of the Santerno before reviewing the thrust to Bologna. In the north "Ponterforce",

consisting of Canadian and British armoured units and named after its commander, co-operating with "Popski's Private Army" of desert fame, reached the banks of the Fiumi Uniti and Ravenna itself fell to I Canadian Corps. Soon the Canadians reached the southern tip of Lake Comacchio, but it was only after a fierce and costly battle that they were able to force the Germans back behind the line of the Senio. Astride Route 9, attacking westwards, V Corps captured Faenza, and in the foothills south of the road the Poles fought forward to the upper reaches of the Senio. At this point the 5th Army was stood-to at 48 hours' notice on December 22 to resume the attack.

But the weather again broke and by a quirk of fate Mussolini, despised by friend and foe alike, and seeking a "spectacular" success for his newly formed divisions, made a last throw in a losing game. These two divisions, the "Monte Rosa" and the "Italia" Bersaglieri Divisions, led by the German 148th Division, now launched a counter-attack on the extreme left flank of the 5th Army. This advance towards the vital port of Leghorn came on the very day that virtually the whole of the 5th Army was concentrated and poised ready to attack Bologna. Only the 92nd (Negro) Division, posted around Bagni di Lucca, was in position to meet the attack down the wild and romantic valley of the Serchio. The arrival of 8th Indian Division on December 25 was only just in time to stop a complete breakthrough, as the leading German units overran the two main defence lines before being held and driven back by the Indians. Meanwhile this threat to the main supply base had caused two more of the 5th Army's divisions to be switched from the main battle area, and with heavy snow falling in the mountains, Alexander gave the order for both armies to pass to the defensive.

Command shuffles

During the winter months there were changes in command on both sides. On the death of Sir John Dill, head of the British mission to Washington, Maitland Wilson was sent in his place and Alexander became Supreme Allied Commander Mediterranean, with promotion to Field-Marshal, backdated to the capture

of Rome. Clark now commanded the 15th Army Group, and Truscott was recalled from France to take over the 5th Army. On the German side Lemelsen still commanded the 14th Army and General Traugott Herr, whose corps had held the early attacks on the Adriatic flank, the 10th Army in what was to prove the critical eastern sector. Kesselring left in the middle of March to become O.B. West and Vietinghoff, hurriedly recalled from the Baltic, took his place with unequivocal orders from Hitler to hold every yard of ground. This further example of the Führer's inept "rigid defence" doctrine proved disastrous, as Vietinghoff entered the ring for the final round of the campaign like a boxer with his bootlaces tied together!

In conditions of heavy snow and frost, the struggle on both sides was now against the forces of nature, and the Allied supply routes could only be kept open by the daily and unremitting efforts of thousands of civilians and all but those units in the most forward positions. While the Germans hoarded their meagre supplies of petrol and both sides built up stocks of ammunition, the Allied units at last began to receive some of the specialised equipment they had for so long been denied; "Kangaroos", the Sherman tanks converted to carry infantry; D.D.s, the amphibious tanks that had swum ashore onto the Normandy beaches; and "Fantails", tracked landing vehicles for shallow waters, of which 400 were promised for use on Lake Comacchio and the nearby flooded areas. At the same time the armoured regiments were re-equipped with up-gunned Sherman and Churchill tanks, Tank-dozers, and "Crocodile" flame-throwing tanks, many of which were fitted with "Platypus" tracks to compete with the soft ground of the Romagna. Throughout the remaining winter months the "teeth" arms were busy training with new assault equipment, such as bridge-laying tanks and flame throwers. The experience of the British 78th Division, back after refitting in the Middle East, is a typical example of the hard work put into preparing for the spring offensive.

"Training began almost at once—exercises for testing communications, in river crossings, in street fighting and, above all in co-operation with armour. 2 Armoured Brigade . . . was affiliated to the Division for these exercises . . . it was the first time in Italy that 78 Division

△ ◁ *In the British V Corps' rear area: men of the 8th Army get a chance to have a closer (and safer!) look at the armoured vehicles used by the Germans. Note the hoarding for the exhibition, featuring Jon's immortal "Two Types".*
▽ ◁ *British Churchill tanks in action in the artillery support rôle.*
△ *German prisoners in Italy.*

△ S.S. Obergruppenführer *Karl Wolff, military governor of northern Italy and Germany's liaison man with Mussolini.*
▷ *American liberation forces enter the city of Milan, led by an armoured car of the Italian Communist partisans.*
▽ *Vergato, south of Bologna: an M24 Chaffee of the 81st Reconnaissance Squadron of the U.S. 1st Armoured Division rolls confidently into the ruins.*

had lived, trained, and held the line with the armour with which it was later to carry out full-scale operations: this was the genesis of the splendid team work between tanks and infantry soon to be shown in the final battle.''

Before handing over, Kesselring kept his troops hard at work building defences on every river-line right back to the Reno and indeed on the line of the Po itself. Although milked of forces for the other fronts, his two armies still contained some of the very best German divisions. These were now well up to strength and fully rested, as for instance the two divisions of I Parachute Corps, commanded by the redoubtable General Richard Heidrich, which between them mustered 30,000 men. The active front, however, much of which was on difficult ground not of his own choosing, was 130 miles long, and his supply lines were constantly being attacked from the air and by partisans. To cover his front he

allocated 19 German divisions (including the 26th Panzer, and 29th and 90th *Panzergrenadier*). Five more German infantry divisions, plus four Italian divisions and a Cossack division, were held back to watch the frontiers and, in particular, to guard against a landing in the Gulf of Venice. Here, had he but known, sand-bars precluded large-scale amphibious operations.

The relative strength of the 15th Army Group was now lower than ever before. Three divisions had been rushed to intervene in the civil war in Greece and I Canadian Corps had left for Holland in February. There remained only 17 divisions, including the newly arrived American 10th Mountain Division. But Alexander held an ace–overwhelming strength in the air. With the combined bomber offensive drawing to a close, more and more heavy bomber squadrons were released to support the coming offensive and by April were pounding away at the

German supply routes. By D-day every railway line north of the Po had been cut in many places. Nor had the two tactical air forces been idle. On February 6, 364 sorties were flown against the Brenner pass and targets in the Venetian plain, while in March the German supply dumps, so carefully built-up during the winter, were systematically attacked. Above the battlefield, in clearing skies, the Allies' planes roamed at will and when the offensive opened, a total of 4,000 aircraft was available to intervene directly in the land battle.

The last lap

Alexander's plan was again for a double-fisted attack, but with a bold and care-fully set-up change of direction by the 8th Army at the very moment when the 5th Army was to deliver the second blow. Once again the Germans were to be mis-led into expecting a major landing (south of Venice) and realism was brought to this cover plan by the joint Commando/ 56th Division operations to clear the "spit" and "wedge", on the near shore, and the islands of Lake Comacchio, which in fact were vital to the real flanking thrust inland. Meanwhile the whole of the 8th Army, except for a skeleton force in the mountains, was secretly concen-trated to the north of Route 9. On 9 April, V Corps (8th Indian and 2nd New Zealand Divisions) and the Polish II Corps would open the offensive across the River Senio astride Lugo, with the object of seizing bridgeheads over the Santerno and ex-ploiting beyond. At this point the 5th Army would attack towards Bologna, while the 56th Division would cross Lake Comacchio in "Fantails" and the 78th Division would debouch from the San-terno bridgeheads and strike north-wards to Bastia. This change of axis by the 8th Army aimed at breaking the "hinge" of the whole German position at Argenta and cutting their lines of withdrawal eastwards.

Shortly after mid-day on April 9, the Allied air forces went to work with the medium bombers and close support squad-rons attacking command posts, gun posi-tions, and strongpoints on the Senio and beyond, while in an hour and a half the heavy bombers, using a line of smoke shells in the sky as a bomb line, saturated the German defences on the immediate

The end of the road for Hitler's armies in Italy.
△ Prisoners taken by the U.S. IV Corps await transfer to a prisoner-of-war camp and, in the long run, repatriation to Germany.

front of the two assault corps with 125,000 fragmentation bombs. This deluge of bombs was immediately followed by four hours of concentrated gun and mortar fire, alternating with low-level fighter-bomber attacks. At 1900 hours as the last shells burst on the forward defences, the fighter-bombers swept over in a dummy attack to keep the enemy's heads down until the infantry crossed the river. Within minutes the first flame-throwers were in action and "the whole front seemed to burst into lanes of fire". Overnight there was bitter fighting before the western flood banks were breached and bridges laid for the armour and anti-tank guns to cross. The next day over 1,600 Allied heavy bombers renewed their attack, and on the third day of the offensive the New Zealanders were across the Santerno at Massa Lombarda. The German 98th and 362nd Divisions had lost

over 2,000 prisoners and their forward battalions had been virtually destroyed.

Meanwhile the battle for the Argenta Gap had started. The 78th Division, having crossed the Santerno, was advancing rapidly, led by a special striking force (the Irish Brigade and 2nd Armoured Brigade) of all arms, part of which was entirely mounted on tracked vehicles, and which became known as the "Kangaroo Army". The approaches to Bastia, however, were covered by thousands of mines and the Germans fought to the last round, while in crossing Lake Comacchio, the 58th Division suffered heavy casualties. But slowly the pincer attacks closed on Argenta itself and McCreery's reserve divisions began to move up.

Now was the time for Truscott to launch his two corps, but poor flying conditions delayed the attack until April 14. Over the next four days the Allied air forces

continued on page 2100

The American Douglas A-20G Havoc attack bomber

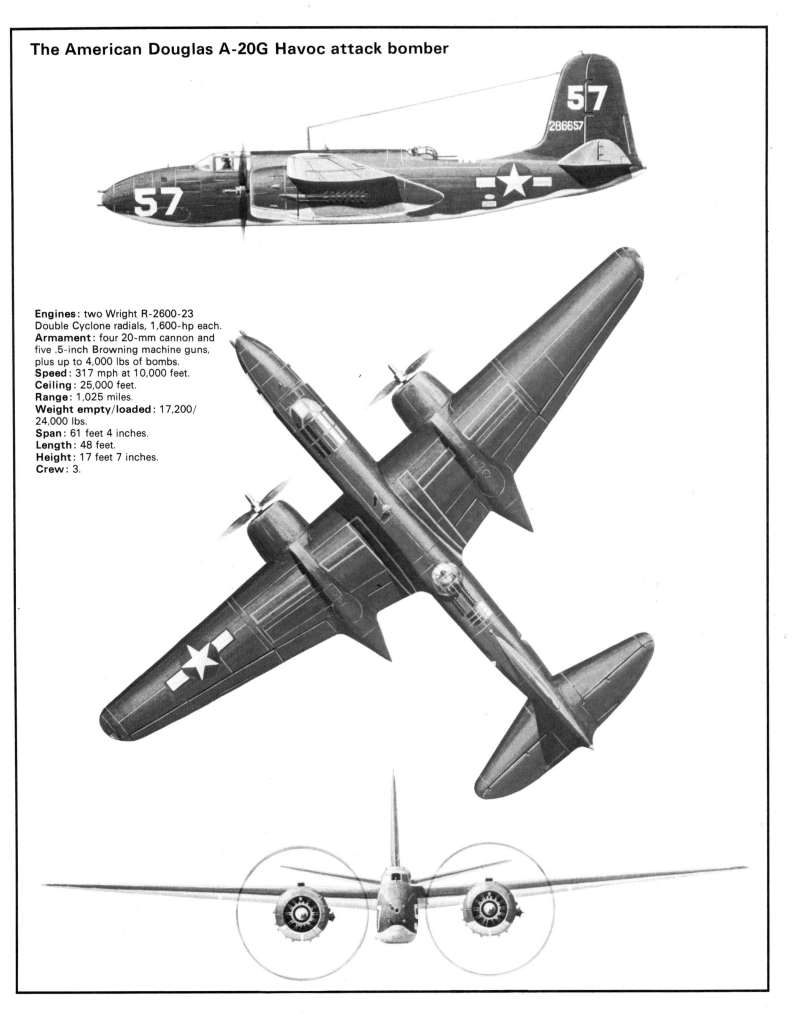

Engines: two Wright R-2600-23
Double Cyclone radials, 1,600-hp each.
Armament: four 20-mm cannon and
five .5-inch Browning machine guns,
plus up to 4,000 lbs of bombs.
Speed: 317 mph at 10,000 feet.
Ceiling: 25,000 feet.
Range: 1,025 miles.
Weight empty/loaded: 17,200/
24,000 lbs.
Span: 61 feet 4 inches.
Length: 48 feet.
Height: 17 feet 7 inches.
Crew: 3.

THE DEATH OF MUSSOLINI

After his rescue from the Gran Sasso by Otto Skorzeny on September 12, 1943, Mussolini met Hitler. Together the two leaders decided on the establishment of a new Fascist republic in what was left of Italy, and Mussolini's new government met at La Rocca on September 27. The German leader had no intention, however, of letting Mussolini's government actually run the country and refused to answer letters on the subject. The Fascist régime did manage to try some of those responsible for the July 1943 coup that ousted Mussolini. One of those found guilty and executed was Ciano. Opposition to the régime was growing, however, and in the middle of 1944 it was estimated that over 80,000 partisans were operating against the Fascists and Nazis.

With the final Allied victory imminent, Mussolini left for Como, where he was joined by his mistress, Clara Petacci.

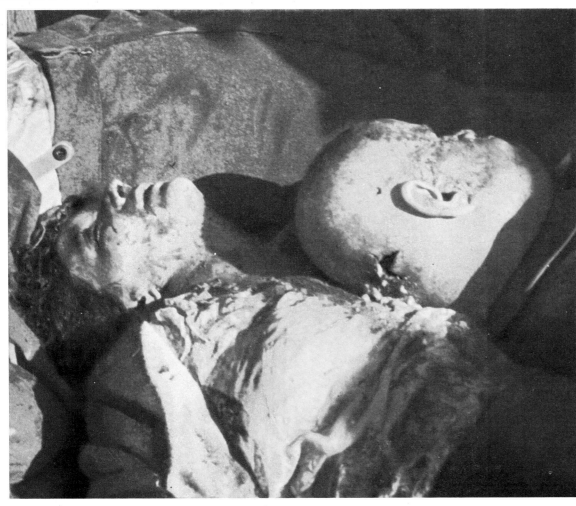

◁ ◁ *Mussolini's last days: the Duce inspects Fascist militia in Milan. There is little of his earlier swagger left in the "Caesar of the new Roman Empire".*

▽ ◁ *Arrested by Italian partisans on April 26, Mussolini and Clara Petacci were shot down without ceremony on the 28th in the small town of Dongo, near Como. The bodies of Mussolini, Petacci, and other Fascist leaders were then taken to Milan and dumped in the Piazza Loretto, where this photograph was taken.*

◁ *The mutilated bodies of Benito Mussolini and Clara Petacci.*

▽ *After lying in the street for several hours, the bodies were hung from the framework of a garage for the edification of the crowd. Mussolini is third from left and Petacci fourth.*

continued from page 2096

▷ *Lieutenant-General Frido von Senger und Etterlin discusses the terms for the surrender of the German forces in Italy with Major-General Gruenther in Caserta.*
▽ *The scene outside Milan Cathedral after the liberation of the city.*

flew over 4,000 sorties in support and in the first 30 minutes of the attack on Monte Sole and the nearby Monte Rumici, 75,000 shells fell on the German mountain strongpoints. In three days' fighting the U.S. II Corps was held down and advanced less than two miles. West of Route 64, however, the 10th Mountain Division captured Montepastore and for two days the U.S. 1st Armoured Division and the 90th *Panzergrenadier* Division, Vietinghoff's last reserve, fought it out in the valley of the Samoggia. Suddenly the end was within sight. Around Argenta the 29th *Panzergrenadier* Division and the remnants of a number of other divisions kept up a bitter struggle to prevent a breakthrough by the 6th Armoured Division, but by April 20 V Corps' leading columns were within 15 miles of Ferrara, advancing on a broad front. Along Route 9 the New Zealanders and Poles had fought three German divisions to a standstill and at dawn on April 21 a Polish brigade entered Bologna unopposed. The previous day a company of the U.S. 86th Mountain Infantry was across Route 9, west of the city, and now Truscott's II Corps, with the 6th South African Armoured Division, swept past on Route 64. On April 23 the leading tanks made contact with a squadron of 16th/5th Lancers, 15 miles west of Ferrara.

On April 20, Vietinghoff, in defiance of Hitler's demands, ordered a withdrawal to the Po, but the fate of his armies was already sealed. What was left of his shattered units was trapped against the Po, where every bridge was down or blocked by packed columns of burning vehicles. Von Senger was amongst those who succeeded in crossing. "At dawn on the 23rd we found a ferry at Bergantino; of the thirty-six Po ferries in the zone of Fourteenth Army, only four were still serviceable. Because of the incessant fighter-bomber attacks it was useless to cross in daylight."

When the Allied armoured columns crossed 36 hours later, they left behind them "a scene of extraordinary desolation and fearful carnage. There was no longer any coherent resistance, and along the river lay the ruins of a German army." In the first 14 days of the offensive the German casualties were around 67,000, of whom 35,000 had been taken prisoner. Allied casualties were a little over 16,500. On May 2 the remaining German and Italian troops of Army Group "C", nearly a million men, surrendered.

CHAPTER 143
Across the Rhine

On March 8, 1945, Field-Marshal Kesselring was ordered to leave the Italian theatre of operations immediately and go to an audience with the *Führer*. The following afternoon, Hitler told him that as a result of the unfortunate situation at Remagen, he had decided to make him Commander-in-Chief in the West. In his account of the meeting, Kesselring writes:

"Without attaching any blame to Rundstedt, Hitler justified his action with the argument that a younger and more flexible leader, with greater experience of fighting the Western powers, and still possessing the troops' full confidence, could perhaps make himself master of the situation in the West. He was aware of the inherent difficulties of assuming command at such a juncture, but there

▽ *British forces cross the great natural obstacle. Men of the Dorsetshire Regiment get under way in their Buffalo.*

▲ Trucks fitted with special jigs move pontoons up towards the west bank of the Rhine in preparation for the American 9th Army's crossing.

was no alternative but for me to make this sacrifice in spite of the poor state of my health. He had full confidence in me and expected me to do all that was humanly possible."

Such was the conclusion of the general review of the situation that Hitler had spent several hours discussing with Kesselring, first alone, later in the company of Keitel and Jodl. On the whole, Hitler was optimistic about the future. One might have suspected him of trying to mislead Kesselring as to the true situation were it not for his own unique capacity for self-deception. In any event, he appeared satisfied with the course of events on the Eastern Front.

Hitler certainly thought that a collapse in the East would be the end of the war, but he had provided for this eventuality and added, according to Kesselring's notes taken immediately after the audience: "our main military effort is directed to the East. He [Hitler] envisages the decisive battle there, with complete confidence. And he expects the enemy's main attack to be launched at Berlin."

For this reason the 9th Army, which was charged with the defence of the city, had been given priority consideration. Under the command of General T. Busse, it had:

1. adequate infantry strength, together with Panzer and anti-tank forces;
2. standard artillery strength and more than adequate anti-aircraft defences, deployed in considerable depth under the best artillery commanders available;
3. excellent positions, with the best of defences, especially water barriers, on both sides of the main battle line; and
4. in its rear the strongest position of all, Berlin, with its fortified perimeter and whole defensive organisation.

So there were grounds for assurance that the Berlin front would not be broken; similarly with Army Group "Centre", on the borders of Silesia and Czechoslovakia, which had gained notable successes. Its commander, Schörner, assured Hitler that "with reinforcements and sufficient supplies, he would repel all enemy attacks launched at him".

As regards the situation on the Western Front, the heavy losses sustained by the British, Americans, and French over months of heavy fighting were a factor that should be taken into account. Furthermore, in Hitler's opinion, "the Allies could not dismiss the natural obstacles covering the German Army's positions. The Allied bridgehead at Remagen was the danger point and it was urgent it should be mopped up; but there too Hitler was confident."

In these conditions, Kesselring's task was to hold on long enough for the Eastern Front armies to be brought up to strength, so that O.K.W. could then despatch the necessary reinforcements to the armies in the West. Within a short while, the deficiencies of the Luftwaffe, held to blame for the failures of recent months, would be forgotten and Grand-Admiral Dönitz's new submarines would have turned the tables in the Battle of the Atlantic, bringing much needed relief to the defence of the Third Reich.

Kesselring caught off balance

Thus armed with encouragement, Kesselring received his chief-of-staff's report in the night of March 9-10 at the H.Q. at Ziegenberg just vacated by Rundstedt. General Westphal had been his chief-of-

The Canadian Ram Kangaroo armoured personnel carrier

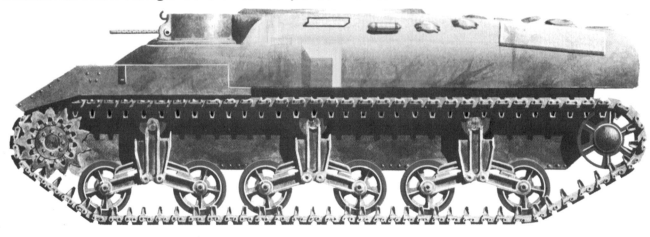

Weight: 26 tons.
Crew: 2.
Load: 12 infantrymen.
Armament: one .3-inch Browning machine gun.
Armour: front 45-mm, nose, sides, rear, and decking 38-mm, and belly 25-mm.
Engine: one Wright Continental R-975 radial, 400-hp.
Speed: 25 mph.
Range: 145 miles.
Length: 19 feet.
Width: 9 feet 6 inches.
Height: 6 feet 1 inch.

staff during his time as supreme commander in Italy, and Kesselring had complete confidence in him.

The new commander must have been considerably shocked by the unembroidered account of the situation that he received. With 55 battle-worn divisions giving him, on average, a coverage of 63 fighting men for each mile of the front, it was his task to hold 85 full strength Allied divisions, which also enjoyed all the benefits of undisputed air superiority.

On March 11, at the H.Q. of LIII Corps, Kesselring met Field-Marshal Model and General von Zangen, commanding the 15th Army, which had been given the job of wiping out the Remagen bridgehead. All were agreed that this objective could not be attained unless there was considerable speeding up in the supply of substantial reinforcements, and above all of ammunition, and this filled Kesselring with apprehension. The morale of Army Group "H" gave him some comfort, however, especially since the enemy attack across the lower Rhine was taking time in getting under way. On the other hand, the position of Army Group "G", without any mobile reserves worthy of the name, seemed fraught with risk.

Hence Kesselring was not so much caught unawares as off guard by Operation "Undertone", the American offensive south of the Moselle, which he learnt had been launched when he returned from this rapid tour of inspection. The series of attacks by the American generals came as a disagreeable revelation to the Germans; Kesselring wrote:

"What clearly emerged was the rapid succession of operations (showing that the Allies had abandoned their Italian campaign strategy) as well as the competency of command and the almost reckless engagement of armoured units in terrain that was quite unsuited for the use of heavy tanks. On the basis of my experience in Italy in similar terrain, I was not expecting the American armoured forces to achieve rapid success, in spite of the fact that the reduced strength of tired German troops gave undoubted advantage to the enemy operation."

△ *Men of the Cheshire Regiment prepare to board the Landing Vehicles Tracked that will ferry them over the Rhine in the afternoon of March 24. At 2200 hours the previous night, the 1st Commando Brigade had made an assault landing on the east bank and secured the bridgehead into which the Cheshire Regiment moved as reinforcements.*
Overleaf: *White phosphorus shells from the U.S. 3rd Army's artillery rain down on the slopes above a small Rhenish town.*

In the face of this violent American thrust, O.B. West appealed to O.K.W. for authorisation to withdraw the German 1st and 7th Armies to the right bank of the Rhine; typically, Hitler procrastinated until it was too late to accept this eminently reasonable course. And the only reinforcement destined for the Western Front was a single division, which was not even combat-worthy as it had spent some considerable time in Denmark on garrison duties. To cap this, Kesselring was informed of the surprise attack at Oppenheim, while the 1st Parachute Army brought news that north of the Ruhr, smokescreens maintained over several hours showed that Montgomery was putting the final touches to his careful preparations.

To surrender or not?

It was in these circumstances that Kesselring was contacted by *Obergruppen-führer* Karl Wolff of the *Waffen*-S.S., whom he had known in the capacity of "Plenipotentiary for the Wehrmacht in the rear of the Italian Front". For the past few weeks, this officer had been engaged, via Major Waibel of Swiss Army Intelligence, in negotiation with Allen Dulles, head of the American Secret Services in Berne, about terms for the capitulation of the German forces fighting in Italy. On March 23, Kesselring, who knew what Wolff was up to, saw him in his office in Ziegenberg, where Wolff suggested directly that the German armies in the West should be associated with this bid for surrender.

Kesselring refused, in spite of the succession of telephone calls informing him of the rapid progress made by the Americans, who had broken out of the Oppenheim bridgehead. According to Wolff's report to Dulles, Kesselring's opposition was based on both moral and practical arguments:

"He was defending soil and he was bound to continue even if he died himself in the fighting. He said he personally owed everything to the Führer, his rank, his appointment, his decorations. To this he added that he hardly knew the generals commanding the corps and divisions under him. Moreover, he had a couple of well-armed S.S. divisions behind him which he was certain would take action against him if he undertook anything

Field-Marshal Albrecht von Kesselring was born in Bavaria in 1885. He served as a staff officer in the artillery throughout World War I and the 1920's, and in 1933 he was transferred to the air force. He commanded the Luftwaffe in the German invasion of Poland and Belgium, and ordered the bombing of the B.E.F. as it evacuated Dunkirk. He conducted the extremely successful bombing raids on R.A.F. bases in southern England in 1940 and in July of that year he was made a Field-Marshal. In 1941 he was appointed C.-in-C., South, sharing with Rommel the command of the North African campaign and taking over during Rommel's absence and later during the retreat from Tunisia. In 1943 he was C.-in-C. in Italy, conducting a brilliant campaign despite the indifference of his superiors to his constant pleas for air reinforcements. For over a year he held out against the Allied advance, with a superbly conceived line of defences behind Cassino. In 1945 he succeeded the cream of Hitler's generals on the Western Front in a desperate attempt to check the Allied advance, but in March he had to surrender the southern half of the German forces to the Allies. He was sentenced to death by a British military court for executing Italian hostages, but in 1947 his sentence was commuted to life imprisonment and in 1952 he was released on the grounds of ill health. He died in 1960.

▷ American paratroops dig in under the trees of a German orchard after the airborne landings just to the east of the Allied bridgeheads over the Rhine. The Germans, who had expected landings much further behind their lines, were caught entirely on the wrong foot by the Allied use of airborne troops in a tactical rather than a strategic rôle.

▽ The parachute drops begin in the Wesel area. This photograph was taken by Sergeant Fred W. Quandt of San Francisco, California, from a B-17 camera plane. The B-17 was shot down a few minutes later – the first aircraft casualty of the operation.

The British General Aircraft Hamilcar I glider

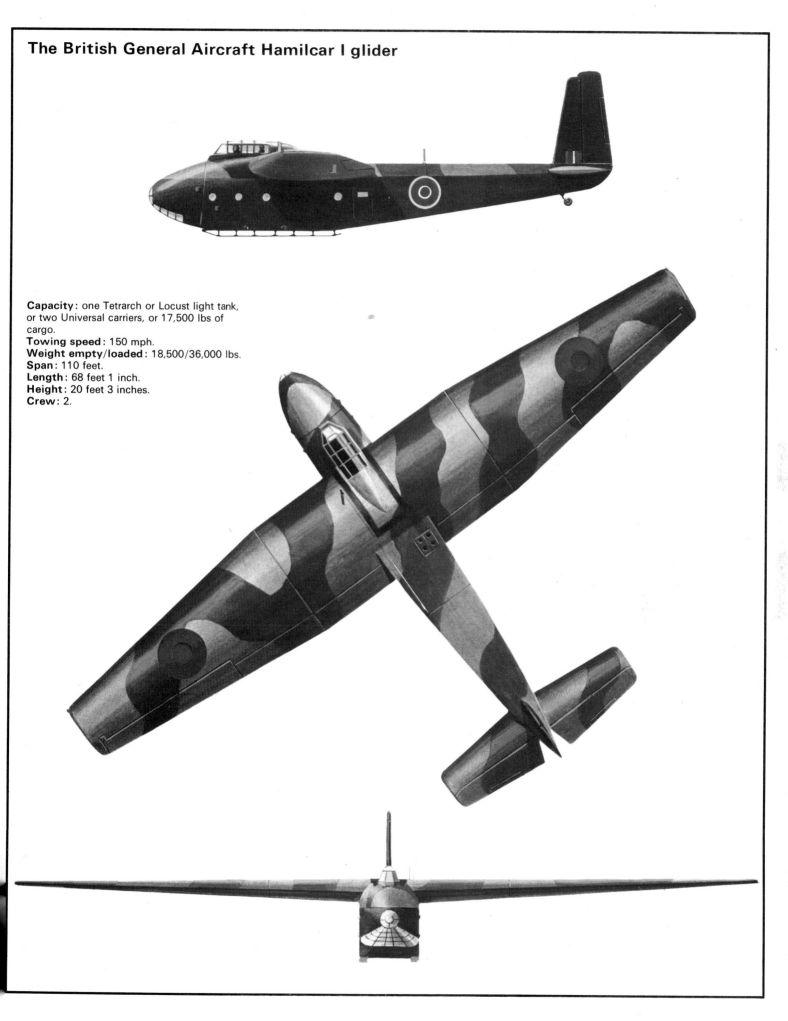

Capacity: one Tetrarch or Locust light tank, or two Universal carriers, or 17,500 lbs of cargo.
Towing speed: 150 mph.
Weight empty/loaded: 18,500/36,000 lbs.
Span: 110 feet.
Length: 68 feet 1 inch.
Height: 20 feet 3 inches.
Crew: 2.

A German N.C.O. illustrates how to fire a Panzerfaust 30m anti-tank rocket projector. There were four Panzerfaust models, all working the same way: the rocket was contained in a tube held under the arm or over the shoulder. When fired, the rocket motor drove the weapon out of the tube and on towards the target. Just as the weapon left the tube, a cap at the latter's rear was pushed off, allowing the exhaust to fan out to the rear. The warhead of the rocket was a hollow-charge device containing 3 pounds 7½ ounces of explosive, capable of penetrating 200 mm of armour sloped at 30 degrees. It was an extremely efficient weapon, with a punch equal to that of the dual-purpose 8.8-cm gun.

⊳ German prisoners are escorted through the town of Hamminkeln by their captors, men of the British 6th Airborne Division.

▽ ⊳ German civilians and prisoners hug the ground in the courtyard of a captured farmhouse in an effort to protect themselves from retaliatory German artillery fire.

against the Führer's orders."

Nevertheless Kesselring had no objection to a German capitulation in Italy, and the *Obergruppenführer* was quite free to convey to the former's successor, Colonel-General von Vietinghoff, that O.B. West entirely approved the project as outlined to him.

Scorched earth policy

Whatever one may think of the ethical considerations behind Kesselring's refusal, he understandably felt no scruples in giving his support to Albert Speer, Reich Minister for Armaments and War Production, who was doing all he could to sabotage the execution of the "scorched earth" order promulgated by Hitler on March 19, 1945.

In setting out its motives, the monstrous *Führerbefehl* used the following line of argument:

"The fight for the existence of our people obliges us to make total use, even within the Reich, of whatever means may weaken the fighting power of the enemy and prevent him from pursuing his advance. Any means capable, directly or indirectly, of inflicting lasting damage on the offensive strength of the enemy must be resorted to. It is erroneous to think that by leaving them intact or with only superficial damage, we may more profitably resume exploitation of our communication and transport systems and our industrial or productive installations when we reconquer our invaded territory. When the enemy comes to retreat, he will have no consideration for the population, and will leave only scorched earth behind him.

"For this reason I command:

1. that within the Reich the communications and military transport systems, and the industrial and productive installations, which the enemy may use immediately or within a limited period for the prosecution of the war, be destroyed."

Article 2 of the same decree divided powers for this purpose between the military chiefs and the civil administrators; and Article 3, ordering the immediate transmission of the order to army commanders, declared invalid any directive which sought to nullify it.

So Hitler joined Morgenthau, whereas even Churchill and Roosevelt had re-

jected the inhuman and demented notion of "pastoralising" the German people. Albert Speer, however, devoted his entire energies to opposing the implementation of this insane order: verbally on March 18; and in writing in two letters, the second of which, dated March 29, is preserved among the appendices that Percy Ernst Schramm adds as a supplement to his masterly edition of the O.K.W. war diary.

"From what you have told me this evening [March 18] the following emerges clearly and unequivocally, unless I have misunderstood you: if we are to lose the war, the German people are to be lost as well. This destiny is unavoidable. This being so, it is not necessary to secure the basic conditions to enable our people to ensure their own survival even in the most primitive form. Rather, on the contrary, we should ourselves destroy them. For they will have proved themselves the weaker, and the future will belong exclusively to the people of the east, who will have shown themselves the stronger. Furthermore, only the unworthy will survive since the best and bravest will have fallen." Here revealed was the ugly bedrock of Hitler's totally nihilistic nature.

Speer's opposition

Speer did not limit his opposition merely to pious utterances. He put the enormous weight of influence he had as dictator of industrial production to the task of avoiding implementation of the "scorched earth" order.

In this covert activity he received positive support from Kesselring; as a result, in its retreat from the Rhine to the Elbe and beyond, the German Army restricted itself to forms of destruction which are common in such cases to all the armies in the world. Two circumstances favoured Speer in carrying out his policy: the headlong nature of the Allied advance after March 31 and, in the German camp, the explosives crisis, further exacerbated by the disorganisation of transport.

At the end of 1966, on his release from Spandau prison, to which he had been sent by the Nuremberg trial, Albert Speer was greeted by manifestations of sympathy. This was interpreted by some as the sign they had been seeking since

1945 of a recrudescence of Nazism in the Federal Republic. Such an interpretation seems quite unwarranted. Rather, it would seem that Speer's sympathisers wanted to show public recognition of the man who, in spite of Hitler and at the risk of his life, had chosen to safeguard the means of survival and recovery so that one day another Germany might live.

Montgomery prepares to cross the Rhine

On March 23, at 1530 hours, under a clear sky and with a favourable weather forecast, Montgomery launched Operation "Plunder/Varsity" and addressed the American, British, and Canadian troops under his command with an order of the day which concluded with these words: "6. 21 ARMY GROUP WILL NOW

The American Landing Vehicle Tracked (L.V.T.) 2 Buffalo

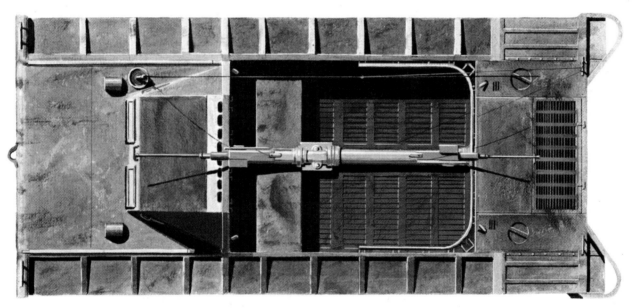

Weight: $14\frac{3}{4}$ tons.
Crew: 2 to 7.
Armament: one .5-inch M2 and one .3-inch M1919A4 machine gun.
Engine: one Continental W670-9A radial, 250-hp.
Speed: 20 mph on land and $7\frac{1}{2}$ mph in water.
Range: 150 miles on land and 100 miles in water.
Length: 26 feet 2 inches.
Width: 10 feet 8 inches.
Height: 8 feet $2\frac{1}{2}$ inches.

CROSS THE RHINE

The enemy possibly thinks he is safe behind this great river obstacle. We all agree that it is a great obstacle; but we will show the enemy that he is far from safe behind it. This great Allied fighting machine, composed of integrated land and air forces, will deal with the problem in no uncertain manner.

7. And having crossed the Rhine, we will crack about in the plains of Northern Germany, chasing the enemy from pillar to post. The swifter and the more energetic our action, the sooner the war will be over, and that is what we all desire; to get on with the job and finish off the German war as soon as possible.

8. Over the Rhine, then, let us go. And good hunting to you all on the other side.

9. May 'The Lord mighty in battle' give us the victory in this our latest undertaking, as He has done in all our battles since we landed in Normandy on D-Day."

The Rhine, which in 21st Army Group's sector is about 400 yards wide and has a current of about six feet per second, was the "great obstacle" of which Montgomery spoke. But the means given him to cross it were also great.

Under his command he had two armies, eight corps, and 27 divisions (17 infantry, eight armoured, and two airborne; or, in national terms, 13 American, 12 British, and two Canadian). To these should be added the equivalent of three divisions represented by five armoured brigades, a British commando brigade, and the Canadian 9th Infantry Brigade.

The British 2nd Army's attack, supplemented by the Canadian II Corps, was prepared for and supported by 1,300 pieces of artillery, with 600 guns fulfilling the same function for XVI Corps, which was to open the right bank of the Rhine for the American 9th Army. Such concentration of firepower necessitated the transport and dumping of 60,000 tons of ammunition. Massive area bombing by the Allied air forces extended the artillery action to German rail and road communications, isolating the battlefield. Between March 20 and 22, R.A.F. Bomber Command and the U.S. 8th and 9th Air Forces made 16,000 sorties over the area in question and dropped 49,500 tons of bombs (including 22,000-lb "Grand Slams").

△ *A battery of British 40-mm Bofors guns in action in the direct support rôle.*
Overleaf: *An American Landing Vehicle Tracked (L.V.T.) splashes into the Rhine under cover of a thick smokescreen.*

Special attacks were launched on airfields where the Luftwaffe's new jet aircraft were stationed.

To build bridges across the Rhine, 30,000 tons of engineering equipment and 59,000 engineers had to be transported to the area. But before the construction required by Operation "Plunder" could be used, divisions in the first line of attack had to be conveyed from one bank to the other by other means. This task was carried out by a detachment of the Royal Navy, which left Antwerp to reach its departure point by a series of Belgian, Dutch, and German canals. With Vice-Admiral Sir Harold M. Burrough in overall command, it comprised 45 landing craft (L.C.M.), plus a formation of the 12-ton amphibious tanks known by the British as Buffaloes and as Alligators by the Americans. Prepara-

tions on this scale were obviously observable by the enemy, but the final deployment of the Allied forces was concealed by the smokescreen which hid the left bank of the Rhine over a distance of 75 miles between dawn on March 21 and 1700 hours on March 23.

As is apparent, Montgomery had once more showed his immense capacity for organisation. In the course of the battle which followed, he would confirm his reputation as an exceptional tactician, by winning back for himself the advantage of surprise which he had lost as a result of such tremendous concentration of forces. And, it should be noted, there are few men who, like him, combine such attention to detail in preparation with such vigour of execution.

On the right bank of the Rhine, the 1st Parachute Army was deployed with its

right slightly upstream of Emmerich and its left in the region of Duisburg. It was thus defending a front of 45 miles with seven weak and, by now, worn-out divisions, but nonetheless, an adequate concentration for defence bearing in mind the natural obstacle of the broad river, had the divisions been at full complement. During the relative lull following March 11, they had dug themselves in well and the rapid construction of their defensive positions was entirely satisfactory to Kesselring. General Schlemm had played a considerable rôle here; Major Milton Shulman, of the Canadian 1st Army, had the opportunity of interrogating him later, and writes:

"His record, coupled with an orderly mind and a keen grasp of tactical problems, placed him amongst the more able generals available in the Wehrmacht."

Schlemm's only mobile reserves were the 116th Panzer and 15th *Panzergrenadier* Divisions, of XLVII Panzer Corps, which he had put in reserve behind his centre. At a higher command level, in Army Group "H", Colonel-General Blaskowitz was similarly short of men, and the meagre reserves found by Kesselring were spent in containing the twin thrust of the American 1st Army bursting out of the Remagen bridgehead, and the 3rd Army exploiting at record speed the bridgeheads it had won at Hanau and Aschaffenburg on the Main.

O.K.W. and O.B. West confidently expected an airborne landing. Accordingly, an entire anti-aircraft corps was put at the disposal of Blaskowitz, who deployed batteries all over the area between Munster and the right bank of the Rhine. But apparently to little effect:

The disillusionment of defeat on the face of a 16-year old captured by the Americans.
▷ *U.S. troops move off towards the front after crossing the Rhine.*

as on previous occasions the German soldier had to put up with implacable and practically unchallenged machine gun and cannon fire and bombing from Allied aircraft without seeing any fighters of his own in the sky.

The battle begins

At 1700 hours on March 23, the smoke-screen vanished and the entire artillery of the British 2nd Army and the American 9th Army opened fire on the enemy positions, maintaining their barrage of shells of all calibres until 0945 hours the following morning. This was, however, interspersed with pauses at times varying from sector to sector to allow the divisions launching the attack to feel out the enemy strength.

The main action devolved upon the British 2nd Army, in position north of the Lippe. On its left, XXX Corps had during the night got four battalions of the 51st Division (Major-General Thomas Rennie) across the Rhine; on its right, XII Corps had established its 15th Division (Major-General Colin Muir Barber) on the right bank of the river, opposite Xanten, while the 1st Commando Brigade went into action against the 180th Division in the ruins of Wesel. Further south, the American 9th Army, whose task was to cover the flank of the British attack, engaged its XVI Corps, whose 30th and 79th Divisions crossed the Rhine to either side of Rheinberg. According to Montgomery, German resistance was only sporadic, and certainly the two American divisions mentioned above suffered only 31 killed in the enterprise.

The offensive undertaken by the 21st Army Group was no surprise for Blasko-witz, who had even correctly estimated its main point of impact and line of advance. Accordingly–and with a degree of haste for which Kesselring reproached him–he judged it opportune to throw in his armoured reserves. The dawn saw furious counter-attacks which drew the following observation from Sir Brian Horrocks, then in command of XXX Corps:

"Reports were coming in of Germans surrendering in large numbers to the British and American forces on our flanks but there was no sign of any collapse on our front. In fact the 51st Highland Division reported that the enemy was fighting harder than at any time since Normandy. It says a lot for the morale of those German parachute and panzer troops that with chaos, dis-organisation and disillusionment all around them they should still be resisting so stubbornly."

In the course of the fighting between XXX Corps and the 15th *Panzergrenadier* Division, which brought into the line the paratroops from the German 6th and 7th Parachute Divisions, Major-General Rennie was killed, evidence enough of the enemy's determination.

Airborne landings

However, at 1000 hours the "event", in the Napoleonic sense of the word, took place. In the German camp, remembering the precedent of Arnhem, the Allies' airborne troops were expected to attack at the time that Montgomery's infantry was attempting to cross the Rhine, and to drop to the rear of the battlefield to effect a vertical encirclement of the 1st Parachute Army. But their attack came three hours after it had been anticipated, and the drop took place in the region of Ham-minkeln, barely five miles from the right bank of the river. Under the command of Lieutenant-General Matthew B. Ridgway, XVIII Airborne Corps comprised the British 6th Airborne (Major-General E. Bols) and the American 17th Airborne (Major-General William E. Miley) Divisions, their transport being undertaken by 1,572 planes and 1,326 gliders, under close escort from 889 fighters. The 6th Airborne Division took off from 11 airfields in the south-east of England, the American 17th from 17 that had just been built in the area bounded by Rheims, Orléans, Evreux, and Amiens. The effect of surprise was so great and the German *flak* so well neutralised by Allied artillery pounding from the left bank that losses on landing amounted to no more than 46 transport planes and three per cent of the glider force employed in this operation, known as "Varsity".

The British and Americans fell on the enemy battery positions and reduced a good many of them to silence, then thrust on across the Diersforterwald to meet XII Corps, whose advance was strongly supported by 580 heavy guns of the 2nd Army, responding to calls for fire cover with most admirable speed and precision.

At the end of the day, XVIII Airborne Corps made contact with the British XII Corps. Furthermore, thanks to units flown in by glider, XVIII Airborne Corps had taken intact a number of bridges over the IJssel which, flowing as it does parallel to the Rhine between Wesel and Emmerich, could have constituted an obstacle to the rapid exploitation of the day's successes. Moreover, the 84th Division was taken in rear and as good as annihilated, with the loss of most of the 3,789 prisoners counted by General Ridgway's Intelligence services.

Large bridgehead

As night fell, in the zone between Dinslaken and Rees, where resistance from German parachute troops had lost none of its spirit, the 21st Army Group had taken a bridgehead 30 miles wide on the right bank of the Rhine, running, in the British XII Corps' (Lieutenant-General Sir Neil Methuen Ritchie) sector to a depth of nearly eight miles; the Allied bridge builders were free to get to work without any threat of retaliation on the part of enemy artillery. Montgomery could feel all the more satisfaction with the way things had gone on March 24 as he had committed only four of his eight corps.

Eisenhower's excellent plan

From an observation post situated a mile or so south of Xanten, which commanded a good view over the vast Westphalian plain, Churchill, together with Brooke and Eisenhower, saw the British and American XVIII Airborne Corps' transport planes cross overhead and return, but missed the drop itself because of the mist. As the success of the operation became apparent, General Eisenhower reports that Field-Marshal Brooke turned to him and said:

"Thank God, Ike, you stuck by your plan. You were completely right, and I am sorry if my fear of dispersed effort added to your burdens. The German is now licked. It is merely a question of when he chooses to quit. Thank God, you stuck by your guns."

△ △ ◁ *American infantry embark on an L.C.V.(P.) to cross the Rhine.*

△ ◁ *Men of the U.S. 7th Army prepare to cross south of Worms in outboard engine-powered "Duck" craft.*

◁ *Chaffee light tanks of the U.S. 9th Army and their transport.*

△ *Troops of the 7th Army embark during the morning of March 26.*

▷ *A pensive moment just before the landings for infantry of the 7th Army.*

△ *Supplies for the 9th Army arrive by D.U.K.W. and jeep on the east bank of the Rhine.*

been rendered mobile, as well as all the units brought up from the rear to fill the gaps."

Collapse of the German 15th Army

On March 25 and 28, two further events of comparable scale and importance took place on the 12th Army Group's front: firstly, the collapse of the German 15th Army, whose task it was to contain the enemy within the Remagen bridgehead; and secondly, adding its effect to the clean breakthrough by the American 1st Army, the crossing of the Main at the Aschaffenburg and Hanau bridges by the American 3rd Army. This manoeuvre followed from a carefully prepared plan of General Bradley's after the launching of Operation "Lumberjack", which was given its final touches following the surprise assault on Remagen. He describes it as follows in *A Soldier's Story:*

"Now that Hodges had established the Remagen bridgehead to the south of Bonn, he was to trace that original pattern. First he would speed his tanks down the autobahn where it ran through Limburg on the road to Frankfurt. At Limburg he was to turn east up the Lahn Valley to Giessen. There he would join Patton's pincer coming up from the Main.

"The First and Third Armies would then advance abreast of one another in a parallel column with Hodges on the inside, Patton on his flank, up the broad Wetteran corridor toward a union with Simpson. Then while Hodges and Simpson locked themselves around the Ruhr preparatory to cleaning it out, Patton would face his Army to the east and be prepared to advance toward the oncoming Russians."

So it was, but according to Kesselring, the execution of Bradley's plan was considerably eased by Model's preconceived ideas of the enemy's intentions. The commander of Army Group "B" was obsessed with his right flank, fearing an attack down the eastern bank of the Rhine aimed at an assault on the Ruhr industrial complex from the south; and he was deaf to all telephone calls from his superior, remonstrating with him for leaving his centre thinly protected. This was a serious mistake.

Coming across this passage in *Crusade in Europe,* Lord Alanbrooke refers to an entry in his diary made at the close of that same March 24, claiming that Eisenhower's remarks resulted from a misunderstanding, and that he had not in fact "seen the light" that day near Xanten. He wrote in 1949:

"To the best of my memory I congratulated him heartily on his success and said that, as matters had turned out, his policy was now the correct one; that, with the German in his defeated condition, no dangers now existed in a dispersal of effort."

Thus Brooke corrects the remark attributed to him (on this occasion) by Eisenhower. Obviously there is a difference between the two versions. Nevertheless, it does not necessarily follow that Eisenhower was mistaken in defending his strategic plans, unless it can be shown that the German armies would have fallen into the state of ruin and confusion noted by Brooke that March 25 evening had not Operations "Lumberjack" and "Undertone" taken place.

Kesselring settles that question with greater authority than we can possibly lay claim to when he writes:

"Just as Remagen became the tomb of Army Group 'B', the Oppenheim bridgehead seemed destined to become that of Army Group 'G'. There too, the initial pocket became a deep chasm, and devoured all the strength of the other parts of the front, that somehow or other had

The Ruhr pocket

On March 25, the American 1st Army began its fresh offensive by smashing LXXIV Corps in the region of Breitscheid. Hodges immediately unleashed his 3rd, 7th, and 9th Armoured Divisions, which reached Giessen and Marburg on the 28th, 53 and 66 miles respectively from the Rhine at Neuwied. On the same day, in the 3rd Army, VIII Corps complèted the mopping up of Frankfurt and made contact with Hodges's right in the region of Wiesbaden, thus trapping the enemy elements left on the right bank of the Rhine between the Lahn and the Main. But most strikingly, Patton's 4th, 6th, and 11th Armoured Divisions, in formation ahead of XII and XX Corps, had moved from the Main valley into that of the Fulda, making in the direction of Kassel. Thus Hodges, whose task was to reach the eastern outlets of the Ruhr

basin, found himself provided with cover, just as Bradley intended, against a counter-attack striking from the Harz mountains.

On the day after the surprise breakthrough at Oppenheim, Kesselring, according to his own account, had wondered "whether it was not best to accept the army groups' proposals and withdraw the entire front from the Rhine. I finally refrained from doing so, because the only result would have been to retreat in disorder. Our troops were heavily laden, barely mobile, in large part battle-weary, and encumbered by units in the rear which were still in a state of disorder. The enemy had all-round superiority, especially in mobility and in the air. If nothing occurred to check or slow his advance, our retreating columns would be overtaken and smashed. This type of combat would have become an end in itself—no longer a means employed to an end—the end being to gain time. Every day on the Rhine, on the contrary, was a day

△ *American armour rumbles through the streets of Mönchengladbach in the Ruhr industrial area.*

△ *Sherman tanks roll into the ruins of Munster on April 3.*

gained, signifying a strengthening of the front, even if it were only to enable points in the rear to be mopped up or stray troops to be rounded up."

Quite clearly, at the point reached in the German camp on March 28, Kesselring's conclusions were still more justified.

This was all the more true as the sappers of the 21st Army Group had by March 26 opened seven 40-ton bridges to traffic, and the American 9th Army and British 2nd Army came down both banks of the Lippe to overwhelm the 1st Parachute Army. Two days later, on the left bank of this river, Lieutenant-General Simpson had his 8th Armoured Division (Major-General J. M. Devine) in the region of

Haltern, more than 25 miles east of the Rhine. At the same time, Sir Miles Dempsey pushed the Guards Armoured Division (Major-General Allan Adair) down the Münster road, while his XXX and Canadian II Corps, on a line linking Borken – Bocholt – Isselburg – Emmerich, reached the Dutch frontier. The 1st Parachute Army was helplessly cut off, and its LXIII Corps and XLVII Panzer Corps (five divisions) were thrown back onto Army Group "B". And Montgomery poured his armoured units resolutely into the breach.

On April 2, 1945, as the day closed, the inevitable happened. The American 3rd Armoured Division, driving ahead of

region of the Ruhr". To reduce it, General Bradley formed a new 15th Army, under the command of Lieutenant-General Leonard T. Gerow, with a strength of five corps, including the newly-formed XXII and XXIII Corps, in all 18 divisions taken from the 1st and 9th Armies.

The encirclement of the Ruhr meant not only the rapid destruction of Army Group "B", but more importantly, the end of all organised resistance on the part of the Wehrmacht between Würzburg on the Main and Minden on the Weser. Between the inside of the wings of Army Groups "G" and "H", a breach of more than 180 miles was opened. It was too late for the unfortunate Kesselring to cherish the notion of repositioning his armies on a line along the courses of the Weser, Werra, Main, Altmuhl, and Lech, as favoured by 18th Century strategists.

Eisenhower gives up the idea of Berlin . . .

To stop this breach, O.K.W. still had, in the Harz mountains, the 11th Army, comprising five divisions under the command of General Wenck, and a 12th Army being formed on the right bank of the Elbe. But clearly the way to Berlin lay open to the 12th Army Group and on April 4 S.H.A.E.F. transferred it to the American 9th Army, to the great satisfaction of General Simpson, its commander, and even more so of General Bradley, who saw the forces under his command now rise to four armies (11 corps of 48 divisions, 14 of them armoured, with some 3,600 tanks). But Eisenhower had no intention of giving Bradley the German capital as an objective. The question had already been considered by him among other options open to him after the encirclement of the Ruhr, and he had decided against going for Berlin for strategic and logistic reasons – in particular the lengthening of his lines of communication that this would entail, and the obstacle of the Elbe, something short of 200 miles from the Rhine and 125 from Berlin.

As a result of this decision, Eisenhower set himself the following objectives:
1. to make contact without delay with the Soviet forces moving west, and thus make it impossible for the enemy to try to regroup;

VII Corps (1st Army), met up at Lippstatt with the 8th Armoured Division coming from Haltern. In the course of this fighting, Major-General Rose, commanding the 3rd Armoured Division in its finest foray, was killed. Now Army Group "B" was encircled, with the exception of LXVII Corps, which had been attached to Army Group "B" following the breakthrough at Breitscheid.

Including the ruins of the 1st Parachute Army mentioned above, there were the 5th *Panzerarmee* and the 15th Army, of seven corps or 19 divisions (three of them Panzer, and the 3rd *Panzergrenadier* Division) caught in a trap that Hitler was quick to qualify as "the fortified

△ *Ulm Cathedral, surprisingly undamaged amidst the debris of the rest of the city.*

2. to hurl the 21st Army Group to the north-east, its right wing keeping its objective steadily fixed on Lübeck, to cut off the Wehrmacht forces occupying Norway and Denmark; and
3. for the 12th and 6th Army Groups, Eisenhower writes:

"Equally important was the desirability of penetrating and destroying the so-called 'National Redoubt'. For many weeks we had been receiving reports that the Nazi intention, in extremity, was to withdraw the cream of the S.S., Gestapo, and other organisations fanatically devoted to Hitler, into the mountains of southern Bavaria, western Austria, and northern Italy. There they expected to block the tortuous mountain passes and to hold out indefinitely against the Allies. Such a stronghold could always be reduced by eventual starvation if in no other way. But if the German was permitted to establish the redoubt he might possibly force us to engage in a long-drawn-out guerrilla type of warfare, or a costly siege. Thus he could keep alive his desperate hope that through disagreement among the Allies he might yet be able to secure terms more favourable than those of unconditional surrender. The evidence was clear that the Nazi intended to make the attempt and I decided to give him no opportunity to carry it out."

So, with the Elbe reached in the vicinity of Magdeburg, it was understood that Bradley would make his main line of advance along a line Erfurt–Leipzig–Dresden, with a secondary thrust on Regensburg and Linz. Contact would be made with the Russians in Saxony, and at the same time a march would be stolen on Army Group "G" in its task of occupying the redoubt. However logical this line of argument was from a strategic point of view, it rested on a hypothesis which was shown to be false after Germany's capitulation: the "national redoubt" concept was no more than a figment of the imagination of those who fed it to S.H.A.E.F.'s Intelligence services.

▽ *A huge column of German prisoners wends its way back towards the American rear along one of the* Autobahns *constructed by the Nazis to move troops and equipment swiftly— but with a different aim in mind.*

Stalin approves warmly . . .

In any event, on March 24, in accordance with a decision taken at the Yalta Conference, Eisenhower communicated his plan, summarised above, to Stalin who approved it most warmly. In the terms of a telegram cited in Churchill's memoirs but absent from *Crusade in Europe*, Stalin assured Eisenhower that his plan "entirely coincides with the plan of the Soviet High Command . . . Berlin has lost its former strategic importance. The Soviet High Command therefore plans to allot secondary forces in the direction of Berlin." Knowing as we do that at the very moment these lines were dictated, Stalin was concentrating five tank armies and 25,000 guns (expending 25,600 tons of shell) on an allegedly secondary objective, one sees what was in the wind.

. . . but Churchill objects violently

The plan elaborated by S.H.A.E.F. found its strongest opponent in Churchill. Embodying as he did the ancient traditions which had inspired British diplomacy since the reign of Henry VIII, he held as a maxim that "as a war waged by a coalition draws to its end political aspects have a mounting importance."

So it seemed obvious to him that since the military collapse of the Third Reich was a matter of only a few weeks, the time had come for the two great Anglo-Saxon powers quietly to dismiss purely strategic considerations and consider political issues while there was still time. And in this field he was forced to admit that Stalin and Molotov viewed the Yalta agreement about Poland as no more than a scrap of paper.

Likewise, on March 2, Vishinsky, Soviet Deputy Minister of Foreign Affairs, in the course of a scene of abominable violence, had imposed a government chosen by the Kremlin on King Michael of Rumania. The ten per cent minority voice that Churchill had reserved in that country had fallen to all but nothing, and things were worse still in Bulgaria.

Hence Churchill thought that future operations conducted by S.H.A.E.F. should take account of political as well as military considerations, and these he enumerated and summarised as follows:

"*First,* that Soviet Russia had become a mortal danger to the free world.
Secondly, that a new front must be immediately created against her onward sweep.
Thirdly, that this front in Europe should

The American M22 Locust air-transportable light tank

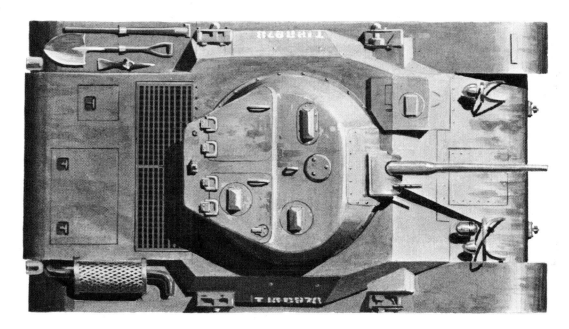

Weight: 7.4 tons.
Crew: 3.
Armament: one 37-mm M6 gun with 50 rounds and one .3-inch Browning machine gun with 2,500 rounds.
Armour: hull lower front 25-mm, upper front, lower sides, rear, and belly 13-mm, upper sides and decking 9-mm; turret 25-mm.
Engine: one Lycoming O-435T inline, 162-hp.
Speed: 40 mph on roads and 30 mph cross-country.
Range: 135 miles on roads.
Length: 12 feet 11 inches.
Width: 7 feet $4\frac{1}{2}$ inches.
Height: 4 feet 1 inch.

Lt.-Gen. Sir Miles Dempsey was born in 1896 and first came to prominence at the head of XIII Corps in the Sicilian and Italian campaigns. Before the Normandy landings he was promoted to command the 2nd Army, which he then led up to the end of the war, winning a considerable reputation for committing his men to major actions only when he was convinced that success was almost certain.

Lt.-Gen. Henry Crerar was born in 1888 and served with the Canadian artillery in World War I. From 1935 to 1938 he was Director of Military Operations and Intelligence. He was Chief-of-Staff of the Canadian Army in 1940. He commanded the Canadian I Corps and later the 1st Army in Europe.

be as far east as possible.

Fourthly, that Berlin was the prime and true objective of the Anglo-American armies.

Fifthly, that the liberation of Czechoslovakia and the entry into Prague of American troops was of high consequence.

Sixthly, that Vienna, and indeed Austria, must be regulated by the Western Powers, at least upon an equality with the Russian Soviets.

Seventhly, that Marshal Tito's aggressive pretensions against Italy must be curbed.

Finally, and above all, that a settlement must be reached on all major issues between the West and the East *before the armies of democracy melted,* or the Western Allies yielded any part of the German territories they had conquered, or, as it could soon be written, liberated from totalitarian tyranny."

Eisenhower's plan therefore displeased him all the more because in communicating his intentions to Stalin, the Supreme Allied Commander appeared to have exceeded the commonly accepted limits of competence of a military chief; a somewhat dubious argument since Stalin had concentrated in himself the functions of head of government and generalissimo of the Soviet armed forces, in which capacity the communication had been addressed to him. With the approval of the British Chief-of-Staffs Committee and of Montgomery, the Prime Minister endeavoured to persuade Eisenhower to go back on his decision, and on April 1 an appeal was made to President Roosevelt, Field-Marshal Brooke making a similar appeal to General Marshall.

Eisenhower cabled Marshall:

"I am the first to admit that a war is waged in pursuance of political aims, and if the Combined Chiefs-of-Staff should decide that the Allied effort to take Berlin outweighs purely military considerations in this theatre, I should cheerfully readjust my plans and my thinking so as to carry out such an operation."

However, the future zonal boundaries had already been formally agreed between Russia, Britain and America, and there was little political point in occupying territory which would have to be evacuated.

In his appeal to the American President, Churchill based his case for the occupation of Berlin on the following hypothesis:

"The Russian armies will no doubt overrun all Austria and enter Vienna.

If they also take Berlin will not their impression that they have been the overwhelming contributor to our common victory be unduly imprinted in their minds, and may this not lead them into a mood which will raise grave and formidable difficulties in the future?"

Eisenhower refuses to countermand his orders

On the next day Eisenhower received a telegram from the American Joint Chiefs-of-Staff, telling him that despite the objections of the British chiefs, they supported him entirely, and that, in particular, the communication of his future plans to Stalin seemed to them "to be a necessity dictated by operations". Marshall concluded with the following point to his allies:

"To deliberately turn away from the exploitation of the enemy's weakness does not appear sound. The single objective should be quick and complete victory. While recognising there are factors not of direct concern to S.C.A.E.F., the U.S. chiefs consider his strategic concept is sound and should receive full support. He should continue to communicate freely with the Commander-in-Chief of the Soviet Army."

△ ◁ *M26 Pershing tanks of the American 9th Army's 2nd Armoured Division pass the wrecked town hall of Magdeburg.*
△ *An American M36 90-mm Motor Gun Carriage crosses the Rhine to reinforce the Allied troops clawing their way into Germany.*
◁ *American infantrymen prepare to break into a house.*

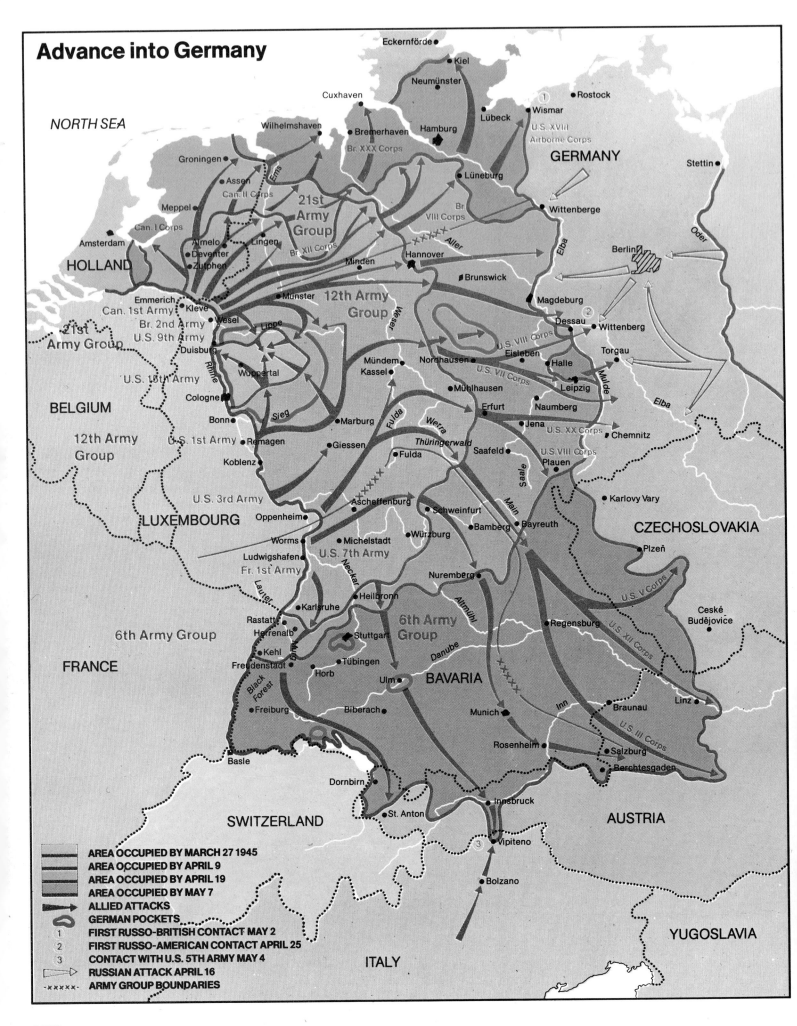

Advance into Germany

NORTH SEA

GERMANY

HOLLAND

BELGIUM

LUXEMBOURG

FRANCE

SWITZERLAND

ITALY

AUSTRIA

CZECHOSLOVAKIA

YUGOSLAVIA

BAVARIA

Eckernförde
Kiel
Neumünster
Rostock
Cuxhaven
Wismar
Lübeck
U.S. XVIII
Airborne Corps
Stettin
Wilhelmshaven
Bremerhaven
Hamburg
Groningen
Br. XXX Corps
Lüneburg
Assen
Ems
Meppel
Can. II Corps
21st
Army
Group
Wittenberge
Almelo
Lingen
Br
VIII Corps
Amsterdam
Can. I Corps
Deventer
Zutphen
Br. XII Corps
Minden
Hannover
Aller
Elba
Berlin
Emmerich
Kleve
Münster
12th Army
Group
Brunswick
Magdeburg
Can. 1st Army
Wesel
Br. 2nd Army
Lippe
Weser
Dessau
Wittenberg
U.S. 9th Army
Duisburg
U.S. VIII Corps
Torgau
21st
Army Group
Rhine
Wuppertal
Mündem
Kassel
Nordhausen
Eisleben
Halle
Mulde
U.S. 18th Army
Cologne
Sieg
Erfurt
Naumberg
Leipzig
Elba
BELGIUM
Bonn
Marburg
Fulda
Mühlhausen
U.S. VII Corps
12th Army
Group
Remagen
Giessen
Werra
Jena
U.S. XX Corps
Chemnitz
U.S. 1st Army
Koblenz
Fulda
Thüringerwald
Saafeld
U.S. VIII Corps
Karlovy Vary
Ascheffenburg
Schweinfurt
Plauen
U.S. 3rd Army
Oppenheim
Saale
Würzburg
Bamberg
Bayreuth
Plzeň
Worms
Michelstadt
Main
Ludwigshafen
U.S. 7th Army
Nuremberg
Fr. 1st Army
Neckar
Ceské
Budějovice
Lauter
Karlsruhe
Heilbronn
6th Army
Group
Regensburg
U.S. V Corps
Rastatt
Altmühl
U.S. XII Corps
Herrenalb
Stuttgart
6th Army Group
Kehl
Tübingen
Danube
Linz
Freudenstadt
Horb
Ulm
Black
Forest
Biberach
Munich
Inn
Braunau
Freiburg
Rosenheim
Salzburg
Berchtesgaden
U.S. III Corps
Basle
Dornbirn
Innsbruck
AUSTRIA
SWITZERLAND
St. Anton
Vipiteno
Bolzano
ITALY

AREA OCCUPIED BY MARCH 27 1945
AREA OCCUPIED BY APRIL 9
AREA OCCUPIED BY APRIL 19
AREA OCCUPIED BY MAY 7
ALLIED ATTACKS
GERMAN POCKETS
① FIRST RUSSO-BRITISH CONTACT MAY 2
② FIRST RUSSO-AMERICAN CONTACT APRIL 25
③ CONTACT WITH U.S. 5TH ARMY MAY 4
RUSSIAN ATTACK APRIL 16
-×××× ARMY GROUP BOUNDARIES

CHAPTER 144

GERMANY: The trap closes

One of General Bradley's tasks was to reduce the "fortified area of the Ruhr" where, on Hitler's orders, Field-Marshal Model had shut himself in. Given the job of carrying out the operation, the American 15th Army attacked southwards across the Ruhr and westwards across the Sieg.

By April 12, Lieutenant-General Gerow had occupied the entire coal basin in which, despite the *Führerbefehl* of March 19, the Germans had done nothing to add to the destruction wrought by British and American bombing. Two days later, the pocket had been cut in two from north to south. In these conditions, Colonel-

General Harpe, commanding the 5th *Panzerarmee*, recognising the fact that his chief had disappeared, ordered Army Group "B" to cease fighting. Capitulation delivered 325,000 prisoners (including 29 generals) into Allied hands. A vain search was instituted for Field-Marshal Walther Model, and it was learnt only four months later that he had committed suicide on April 21, lest he be handed over to the Russians after his surrender, and had been buried in a forest near Wuppertal.

Without waiting for the outcome here, the American 9th, 1st, and 3rd Armies exploited their advance to the full. Resis-

▽ *American infantry press on into Germany past an enormous concrete air raid shelter in Aachen. Parked in the lee of the building is a Sherman tank.*

tance grew weaker every day, and the average daily haul of prisoners rose from 10,600 between February 22 and March 31 to 29,000 for the week April 2 to 9, and reached 50,000 in the middle of the month. Evidently, the *Landser* (German "Tommy") was at the end of his tether, in spite of the growing wave of drumhead courts martial and summary executions. In the heart of the Reich, the multiplication of divisions went on almost to the final day, but whether they belonged to the Wehrmacht or to the *Waffen*-S.S., these new divisions, *Volksgrenadier* for the most part, revealed the paucity of their training as soon as they came under fire.

The *Volkssturm,* which was intended to fill the gaps in defence, was a pitiful ragbag of middle-aged men and adolescents, armed and equipped with any weapon that came to hand. Witness the battalion leader, taken prisoner by the Canadian Army, who confided to Major Shulman:

"'I had 400 men in my battalion,' he said, 'and we were ordered to go into the line in our civilian clothes. I told the local Party Leader that I could not accept the responsibility of leading men into battle without uniforms. Just before commitment the unit was given 180 Danish rifles, but there was no ammunition. We also had four machine-guns and 100 anti-tank bazookas (Panzerfaust). None of the men had received any training in firing a machine-gun, and they were all afraid of handling the anti-tank weapon. Although my men were quite ready to help their country, they refused to go into battle without uniforms and without training. What can a Volkssturm man do with a rifle without ammunition! The men went home. That was the only thing they could do.'"

In these conditions, allowing for sporadic but short-lived retaliation here and

▽ *An American 9th Army infantryman shelters behind a blasted tree as a road mine is exploded. Note the Sherman flail tank on the right, waiting to go into action. The sloping box at its rear contains chalk dust to mark the path cleared.*
▷ *American soldiers examine a Messerschmitt Me 262 fighter-bomber found in the outskirts of a wood. Note the 20-mm cannon shells in the foreground.*
▽▷ *Two soldiers with their families surrender to the British.*

The American Republic P-47M Thunderbolt fighter

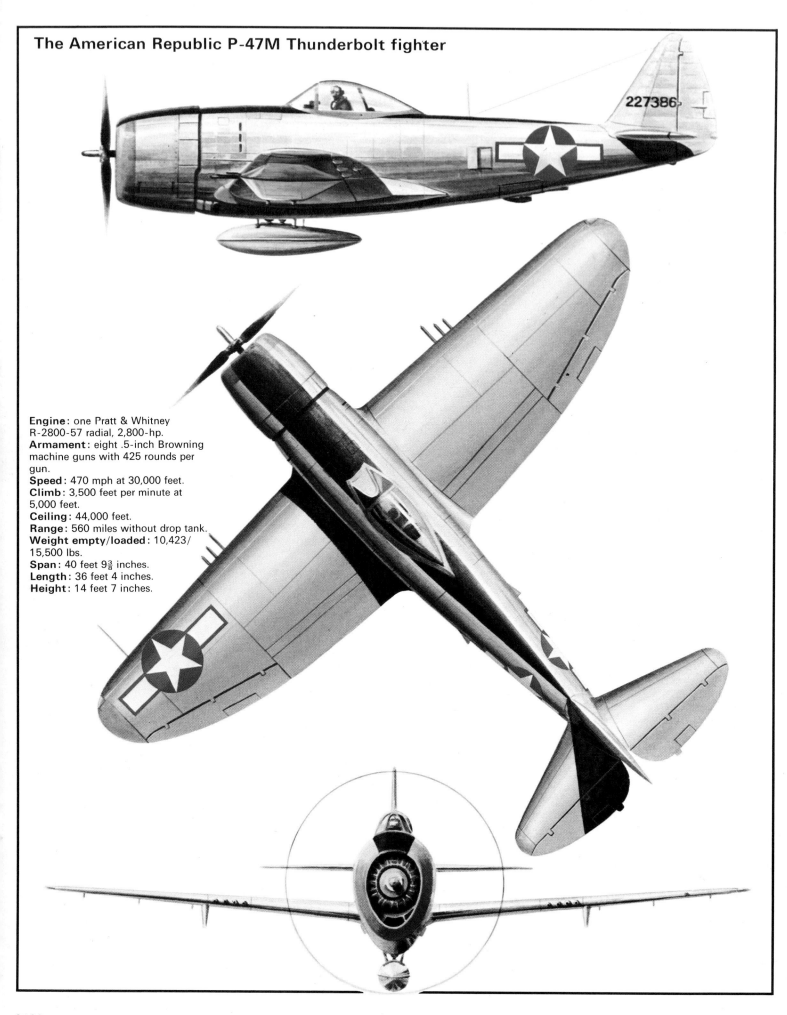

227386

Engine: one Pratt & Whitney R-2800-57 radial, 2,800-hp.
Armament: eight .5-inch Browning machine guns with 425 rounds per gun.
Speed: 470 mph at 30,000 feet.
Climb: 3,500 feet per minute at 5,000 feet.
Ceiling: 44,000 feet.
Range: 560 miles without drop tank.
Weight empty/loaded: 10,423/ 15,500 lbs.
Span: 40 feet 9¾ inches.
Length: 36 feet 4 inches.
Height: 14 feet 7 inches.

there from a few units that still retained some semblance of order and strength, the advance of the 12th Army Group across Germany gathered speed and took on more and more the character of a route march, facilitated by the *Autobahn* system, which in by-passing the towns removed inevitable bottlenecks. As a result, American losses dropped to insignificant figures. In the 3rd Army, according to Patton's record, for three corps of 12, then 14, divisions, between March 22 and May 8, 1945, they amounted to 2,160 killed, 8,143 wounded, and 644 missing, under 11,000 in all, compared with nearly 15,000 evacuated because of sickness and accidental injury.

On the left of the 12th Army Group, the American 9th Army, straddling the *Autobahn* from Cologne to Frankfurt-am-Oder to the south of Berlin, thrust towards Hannover, which it took on April 10, and three days later reached Wolmirstedt on the left bank of the Elbe, 85 miles further east. With the capture of Barby, slightly upstream of Magdeburg, it established a first bridgehead on the right bank of the river, thus putting its 83rd Division (Major-General R. C. Macon) some 75 miles from the New Chancellery. But then it turned instead towards Dessau and made contact there with the 6th Armoured Division (Major-General G. W. Read), which was moving ahead of the 1st Army.

The 1st Army had crossed the Weser at Münden and driven across Thuringia on a line linking Göttingen, Nordhausen, and Eisleben, covering nearly 80 miles between April 8 and 12. As has been mentioned above, it was its left flank that made contact with the 9th Army's right. This pincer movement cut off the retreat of the German 11th Army, which had stayed in the Harz mountains as ordered. To clear a way through for withdrawal, O.K.W. sent the *"Clausewitz"* Panzer Division to the rescue. It attacked at the junction between the 21st and 12th Army Groups and inflicted some damage on the 9th Army. But having got 35 to 40 miles from its point of departure, in the region of Braunschweig, it too was enveloped and annihilated. The same fate struck the 11th Army, falling almost to a man into Allied hands.

In the centre of the 1st Army, VIII Corps, after reaching the Elbe, managed to establish a bridgehead at Wittenberg, while to its right, VII Corps took Halle and Leipzig on April 14. The capture

of Leipzig was a combined effort with the 9th Armoured Division, from the 3rd Army. In accordance with his instructions, General Hodges waited for some days on the Mulde, and it was only on April 26 at Torgau that he met up with Colonel-General Zhadov, commanding the Soviet 5th Guards Army. In the course of this rapid advance the 1st Army came across 300 tons of *Wilhelmstrasse* archives deposited in various places in the Harz. At Nordhausen, it occupied the vast underground factories where most of the V-1 and V-2 missiles were manufactured.

On March 30 the impetuous Patton was on the Werra and the Fulda. On April 12, the 3rd Army, changing its direction from north-east to east, crossed the Saale at Naumburg, Jena, and Saalfeld, having broken the last serious resistance offered by the enemy at Mühlhausen in Thuringia. And on April 7 the 3rd Army took the 400,000th prisoner since its campaign opened. On the 21st following, XX Corps reached Saxony and the vicinity of Chemnitz, VIII Corps reached a point beyond Plauen, while XII Corps, changing course from east to south-east, had got well beyond Bayreuth in Bavaria. This was the last exploit by Manton S. Eddy

△ *Germany* in extremis: *bombed mercilessly, short of food, and without motor transport as a result of the fuel shortage. This is Darmstadt, which fell to the 26th Division of the U.S. 3rd Army.*
Overleaf top: *An unfortunate reminder of better days in shattered Rheydt–"What have you done for Germany today?"*
Overleaf bottom: *German civilians and their protection against stray bullets.*
Page 2135: *An American motor transport column, headed by a jeep, wends its way into Germany.*

who suffered a heart attack and had to hand over his corps to Major-General Stafford LeRoy Irwin. If the 1st Army had captured the *Wilhelmstrasse* archives, the 3rd discovered the last reserves of the *Reichsbank,* composed of gold bars worth 500,000,000 francs, small quantities of French, Belgian, and Norwegian currency and 3,000,000,000 marks in notes.

An ultimate regrouping by Bradley switched VIII Corps from Patton's command to Hodges's, and the progressive collapse of Army Group "B" permitted III and V Corps to be switched to the 3rd Army. Thus strengthened, it was given the assignment of supporting the activities of the 7th Army in Bavaria and upper Austria; specifically, to prevent the enemy establishing himself in the "national redoubt" zone, which General Strong, head of S.H.A.E.F. Intelligence, in a memorandum dated March 11, depicted as follows:

"Here, defended both by nature and by the most efficient secret weapons yet invented, the powers that have hitherto guided Germany will survive to reorganise her resurrection; here armaments will be manufactured in bombproof factories, food and equipment will be stored in vast underground caverns and a specially selected corps of young men will be trained in guerrilla warfare, so that a whole underground army can be fitted and directed to liberate Germany from the occupying forces."

Patton advanced with all speed, and on the day of the surrender he had pushed his XII Corps to a point ten miles below Linz on the Austrian Danube, and his III Corps, whose command had been taken over by Major-General James A. Van Fleet, as far as Rosenheim at the foot of the Bavarian Alps. On May 2, his 13th Armoured Division (Major-General Millikin) crossed the Inn at Braunau, birthplace of Adolf Hitler, who had just committed suicide in his bunker in the Berlin Chancellery.

Patton would have liked to complete his triumph by maintaining the drive of V (Major-General Clarence R. Huebner) and XII Corps as far as Prague. But on May 6, Eisenhower sent him categorical instructions via Bradley not to go beyond the Ceské Budejovice – Plzen – Karlovy Vary line in Czechoslovakia which he had reached. By this action, the Supreme Allied Commander, who had consulted Marshal Antonov, Stalin's Chief-of-Staff,

on the matter, yielded to the objections such an operation raised in the Soviet camp. In any event, the American 3rd Army met the spearhead of the 3rd Ukrainian Front, which had come up the Danube from Vienna, at Linz.

Montgomery drives for Lübeck

Montgomery's main task now was to push through to Lübeck and cut off the German forces occupying Norway and Denmark. He put the more energy and dispatch into the task knowing that its accomplishment would bring supplementary benefits:

"With the Rhine behind us we drove hard for the Baltic. My object was to get there in time to be able to offer a firm front to the Russian endeavours to get up into Denmark, and thus control the entrance to the Baltic."

For this purpose, he disposed of the British 2nd Army and the Canadian 1st Army, comprising five corps of 16 divisions (six of them armoured). Before him in Holland he found the German 25th Army, of which General von Blumentritt had just assumed command, and the debris of the 1st Parachute Army. This debilitated force had been put under the overall command of Field-Marshal Busch, who had been placed at the head of a Northern Defence Zone, to include the Netherlands, north-west Germany, Denmark, and Norway. Weakness in numbers and *matériel* was, however, to some extent offset by the fact that tracts of

▽ *Stuttgart Cathedral, heavily damaged but still standing amidst the ruins of the rest of the city on March 31, 1945.*

bog and the otherwise marshy nature of the ground kept the tanks to the main roads.

Having captured Münster, the key to Westphalia, General Dempsey, commanding the British 2nd Army, pushed forward his XXX Corps in the direction of Bremen, XII Corps towards Hamburg, and VIII Corps towards Lübeck.

On the right, VIII Corps (Lieutenant-General Sir Evelyn H. Barker) was momentarily delayed by the "Clausewitz" Panzer Division's counter-attack which, as has been mentioned above, was aimed at the point of contact of the 21st and 12th Army Groups. Nonetheless, VIII Corps reached the Elbe opposite Lauenburg on April 19. Here, Montgomery, anxious to move with all possible speed, requested support from Eisenhower and was given the U.S. XVIII Airborne Corps (8th Division, 5th and 7th Armoured Divisions, and the U.S. 82nd Airborne and British 6th Airborne Divisions). On April 29-30, British and Americans under cover provided by the first R.A.F. jet fighters, Gloster Meteors, forced the Elbe. On May 2, 11th Armoured Division (Major-General Roberts), which was the spearhead of the British VIII Corps, occupied Lübeck and the 6th Airborne Division entered Wismar, 28 miles further east, six hours ahead of Marshal Rokossovsky's leading patrols.

Hamburg and Bremen taken

XII Corps (Lieutenant-General Ritchie) had to sustain one last challenge on April 6 when crossing the Aller, a tributary on the right bank of the Weser. Afterwards, it took advantage of the bridgehead won on the Elbe by VIII Corps and closed in on Hamburg. On

▽ *Infantry of the 3rd Algerian Division cross the Lauter during their advance towards southern Germany and Austria.*

2138

May 2, Lieutenant-General Wolz surrendered the ruins of the great Hanseatic port. Two days later, the 7th Armoured Division (Major-General Lyne) captured intact a bridge over the Kiel Canal at Eckernförde. Ritchie, who was within 35 miles of the town of Flensburg, where Grand-Admiral Dönitz had recently taken over the responsibilities of head of state, had brilliantly avenged the defeat inflicted on him at Tobruk.

In their drive on Bremen, Sir Brian Horrocks and his XXX Corps were held up by a great deal of destruction, and met with altogether fiercer resistance. Before Lingen, what was left of the 7th Parachute Division carried through a hand-to-hand counter-attack with frenetic *"Heil Hitler"* battle cries.

The 2nd *Kriegsmarine* Division showed the same aggressive spirit in defence, and it needed a pincer movement staged by three divisions to bring about the fall of Bremen on April 26. A few hours before the cease-fire, the Guards Armoured Division occupied Cuxhaven at the mouth of the Elbe.

△ *An historic occasion: General Courtney Hodges, commander of the American 1st Army, greets Colonel-General A. S. Zhadov, commander of the Soviet 5th Guards Army, outside Togau on the Elbe on April 25. The Eastern and Western Allies had at last linked up, and Germany had been cut in two.*
◁ *The Möhne dam as the Americans found it in May 1945, rebuilt since the celebrated "dambuster" raid.*

Canadians in Holland

On April 1, General Crerar, commanding the Canadian 1st Army, recovered his II Corps, reinforced by the British 49th Division, thus bringing his divisions up to six. His mission was twofold: to drive between the Weser and the Zuiderzee with the British XXX Corps in the general direction of Wilhelmshaven and Emden; and to liberate the Dutch provinces still occupied by the enemy. The Canadian II Corps (Lieutenant-General Simonds), which had taken part in the crossing of the Rhine, fulfilled the first of these missions. On April 6, it liberated Zutphen and Almelo, and four days later Groningen and Leeuwarden. In this fine action, it was greatly helped by Dutch resistance while the French 2nd and 3rd Parachute Regiments dropped in the area of Assem and Meppel to open a way for it over the Orange Canal. On German territory, however, General Straube's II Parachute Corps put up a desperate fight, and Crerar had to call on Montgomery for help from the Polish 1st Armoured Division, the Canadian 5th Armoured Division, and the British 3rd Division. With this shot of new blood, the Canadian II Corps accelerated its advance and on May

△ An incongruous slogan in a town overrun by the Allies: "One People, one Reich, one Leader!"

wounded, and missing.

Last German high command change

While Field-Marshal Busch had been entrusted with the command of a "Northern Defence Zone", Kesselring was called upon to lead a "Southern Defence Zone" which included the German forces fighting between the Main and the Swiss frontier. So during the final phase of the campaign he found himself facing General Devers, whose 6th Army Group numbered 20 divisions on March 30, 1945, and 22 (13 American and nine French) the following May 8.

More French advances

The task of Lieutenant-General Patch and the American 7th Army was to cross the Rhine upstream of the 3rd Army, then having gained enough ground to the east, turn down towards Munich and make an assault on the "national redoubt", where, according to Eisenhower's Intelligence, Hitler would seek ultimate refuge. But there was no such mission in store for the French 1st Army which, in the initial plans, was ordered to send a corps over the Rhine, following the Americans, to operate in Württemberg, and later a division which would start off from Neuf-Brisach and occupy Baden-Baden.

Neither General de Gaulle nor General de Lattre accepted this view of their intended mission. On March 4, de Gaulle remarked to de Lattre on "reasons of national importance that required his army to advance beyond the Rhine"; and de Lattre expounded the plan he had conceived to this end, which involved moving round the Black Forest via Stuttgart.

While de Gaulle worked on Eisenhower, de Lattre convinced General Devers of his point of view. The operation as conceived by de Lattre required possession of a section of the left bank of the Rhine below Lauterbourg; this was provided by the dexterity with which General de Monsabert managed to extend his II Corps from Lauterbourg to Speyer in the course of Operation "Undertone".

5, 1945, General Maczek's Polish 1st Armoured Division was within nine miles of Wilhelmshaven, and the Canadian 5th Armoured Division on the outskirts of Emden.

The Canadian I Corps (Lieutenant-General C. Foulkes) took Arnhem by an outflanking movement and three days later reached the Zuiderzee at Harderwijk. The Germans responded to this attack by opening the sea-dykes, and Crerar, who was concerned to spare the Dutch countryside the ravages of flooding, agreed to a cease-fire with General von Blumentritt, stipulating in exchange that British and American aircraft be given free passage to provide the Dutch population with food and medical supplies. This dual operation cost the Canadian 1st Army 367 officers and 5,147 N.C.O.s and other ranks killed,

Patch moves south-east

On March 26, XV Corps of the American 7th Army managed without much trouble to cross the Rhine at Gernsheim below Worms. Patch exploited this success by taking Michelstadt then, turning south, he took Mannheim and Heidelberg on March 30. On April 5, having moved up the Neckar as far as Heilbronn, he captured Würzburg in the Main valley. With his left as spearhead, he hurled his forces in the direction Schweinfurt–Bamberg–Nuremberg and on April 19, after some violent fighting, ended all resistance in Munich. With its right wing in contact with the French 1st Army in the Stuttgart area, and the left in touch with the American 3rd, the 7th Army moved in a south-easterly direction. On April 25, it crossed the Danube on an 80 mile front, capturing on the way what was left of XIII Corps with its commanding officer, Lieutenant-General Count d'Oriola.

Berchtesgaden taken

From that moment German resistance in Bavaria collapsed. On May 2, the American XV Corps occupied Munich. Two days later, the French 2nd Armoured Division, once more free for assignment with the Royan pocket liquidated, scaled the slopes of the Obersalzberg and occupied the Berghof, from which *Reichsmarschall* Hermann Göring had just fled. On the same day, the American 3rd Division, which had sped through Innsbruck, crossed the Brenner Pass and met up with the 88th Division of the American 5th Army at Vipiteno. On May 5, General Schulz, last commander of Army Group "G", avoiding capture by the French, surrendered at General Jacob L. Devers's H.Q.

On March 29, General de Gaulle telegraphed de Lattre: "It is essential that you cross the Rhine even if the Americans are against you doing so and even if you cross in boats. It is a matter of the highest national interest. Karlsruhe and Stuttgart are expecting you even if they don't want you."

When he received this message, de Lattre was on his way back from General Devers's H.Q. with the task of sending one

corps, of at least three divisions (one of them armoured), across the Rhine to take Karlsruhe, Pforzheim, and Stuttgart. De Lattre had done all in his power to wring this order out of the army group commander. Pierre Lyautey remarks, on seeing him in the H.Q. of the Algerian 3rd Division on March 17, that he was in the process of conceiving "a great German campaign", which would be "full of Napoleonic dash and fury".

In any event, the 1st Army had ceded most of its bridging equipment to the 7th Army to compensate it for similar equipment made over to the 21st Army Group; in addition, in the afternoon of March 30, the French II Corps had barely completed the relief of the American VI Corps at Germersheim and Speyer. Nevertheless, Monsabert, who was down to about 50 motorised and unmotorised boats, was ordered to take two divisions across that very night.

The venture succeeded in conditions of apparently impossible improvisation, and in spite of resistance from the 47th *Volksgrenadier* Division, on March 31. By nightfall, the 3rd Algerian Division (General Guillaume), opposite Speyer, and the 2nd Moroccan Division (General Carpentier), opposite Germersheim, al-

△ *An armoured column of the American 3rd Army pushes over the border between Germany and Czechoslovakia. Patton, the army's commander, was typically impetuous in advancing far past his official stop line with "deep patrols".*

△ *A German tank factory, considerably damaged by U.S. heavy bombers and then overrun by American ground forces. Note the half-completed* Jagdpanther *tank destroyer on the left. Even though the Germans continued to step up the output of* matériel *right up to the end of the war, they did not have the fuel to make use of the weapons they already had.*

ready had five battalions in Baden-Baden. The next day, the two bridge-heads were connected and the French advanced as far as the Karlsruhe–Frankfurt *Autobahn,* over 12 miles from the right bank. As for the 5th Armoured Division (General de Vernejoul), it crossed the Rhine either by ferrying or with the co-operation of General Brooks, commanding the U.S. VI Corps, "the perfect companion in arms" in de Lattre's words, over the American bridge at Mannheim. Finally, on April 2, the 9th Colonial Division, now under the command of General Valluy, crossed the river in its turn at Leimersheim (six miles south of Germersheim). Two days later, the 1st Army had taken its first objective, Karlsruhe.

As the German 19th Army was resisting fiercely in the Neckar valley and in the hills above Rastatt, making a stand in a strongly fortified position which covered the Baden-Baden plain, de Lattre shifted the weight of his thrust to the centre. This gave him Pforzheim on April 8, and he then sent his 2nd Moroccan Division, 9th Colonial Division, and 5th Armoured Division deep into the relative wilderness of the Black Forest. On April 10, the fall of Herrenalbon, and the

crossing of the Murg allowed Valluy to by-pass Rastatt and open the Kehl bridge to General Béthouart's I Corps.

In the meantime, Monsabert had seized Freudenstadt, the key to the Black Forest, and Horb on the Neckar above Stuttgart, while the American VI Corps was moving up on the capital of Württemberg by way of Heilbronn. On April 20, pushing on from Tübingen, the 5th Armoured Division completed the encirclement of the city. All resistance ceased after 48 hours. The French took 28,000 prisoners, what was left of the four divisions of LXIV

Corps (Lieutenant-General Grimeiss).

The Stuttgart manoeuvre was the third act of this military tragedy, although by April 22, the fourth act, which saw the entrance of I Corps (4th Moroccan Division, 9th Colonial Division, 14th Division, and 1st Armoured Division), was well under way. Béthouart moved on Horb by way of Kehl and Oberkirch, where he turned south up the Neckar, reaching the Swiss frontier in the vicinity of Schaffhausen on the day Stuttgart fell. This led to the cutting off of XVIII S.S. Corps (General Keppler), which comprised four army divisions. These 40,000 Germans attempted to cut their way through the lines of the 4th Moroccan Mountain Division but they were taken in the rear by the 9th Colonial Division and on April 25 all résistance ceased.

The manoeuvre employed here by the 9th Colonial Division was the result of a request made by the Swiss High Command—as is told in the *History of the French 1st Army*—who were understandably not very enthusiastic about disarming and interning thousands of allegedly

△ *When the British arrived in Kiel they found the superb heavy cruiser* Admiral Hipper *there. She had spent the last months of her life supporting the army along the south coast of the Baltic Sea, but had then been heavily bombed in Kiel. She was scuttled in dock on May 3, 1945.*

The German *Flakpanzer* IV *"Wirbelwind"* (Whirlwind) self-propelled A.A. mounting

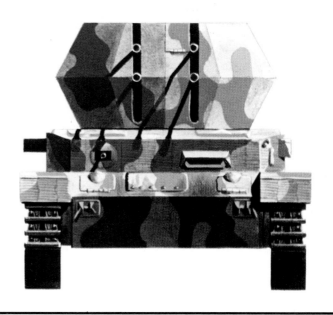

Weight: 25 tons.
Crew: 5.
Armament: one 2-cm *Flakvierling* 38
four-barrelled A.A. gun with 620 rounds.
Armour: hull front 85-mm, hull sides 30-mm, and
turret 15-mm.
Engine: one Maybach HL 120 TRM inline, 300-hp.
Speed: 25 mph on roads and 10 mph cross-country.
Range: 125 miles on roads and 80 miles cross-country.
Length: 18 feet 9½ inches.
Width: 9 feet 4¾ inches.
Height: 8 feet 9½ inches.

fanatical Germans. Although his plans were slightly put out by this development, de Lattre agreed:

"It is an obligation of another kind to give consideration to the permanent interests of Franco-Swiss friendship, especially when Switzerland, while keeping to its age old principle of neutrality, has always been faithful to this cause.

"The problem confronted me while Valluy was still about to attack the Kaiserstuhl and Lehr's combat command (5th Armoured Division) was still some hours away from Schaffhausen. But my hesitation was only momentary. I had no illusions as to the risks I ran but my inclination was on the side of Franco-Swiss comradeship. This inspired me to issue General Order No. 11 in the night April 20-21, ordering I Corps to 'maintain the drive of the right flank along the Rhine towards Basle, then Waldshut, with simultaneous action from Schaffhausen towards Waldshut so as to link up with the forces coming from Basle', hence ensuring the complete encirclement of the Black Forest and at the same time denying the S.S. divisions any opportunity to force the Swiss-German frontier."

In addition, the alacrity with which General Valluy tackled this new mission without the slightest warning deserves mention, Waldshut being not far short of 90 miles from the Kaiserstuhl via Lorrach.

The fifth and final act of the Rhine–Danube campaign involved the pincer movement carried out by Monsabert and Béthouart on Ulm, the one with the 5th Armoured Division and 2nd Moroccan Division (General de Linarès) to the north of the Danube, the other thrusting his 1st Armoured Division (General Sudre) south of the river along the line of Donaueschingen and Biberach. On April 24 at noon, the tricolour flew above the town which on October 21, 1805, had seen Mack surrender his sword to Napoleon. With the capture of Ulm a new pocket was established, and this yielded 30,000 prisoners.

On April 29, General de Lattre reformed I Corps, putting the 2nd Moroccan Division, the 4th Moroccan Mountain Division, and the 1st and 5th Armoured Divisions under its command, and giving it the task of destroying the German 24th Army, recently formed under General Schmidt with the object of preventing the French from gaining access into the Tyrol and Vorarlberg.

On the next day the 4th Moroccan Mountain Division (General de Hesdin) and the 5th Armoured Division, of which General Schlesser had just assumed command, captured Bregenz in Austria.

Once over the frontier, the French could count on the Austrian resistance to provide guides and information, leading in numerous instances to preventing planned demolition being carried out by the Wehrmacht. At Dornbirn the tanks of the 5th Armoured Division were bombarded with bouquets of lilac; at Bludenz, which was liberated on May 4, General Schlesser was made an honorary

citizen. Meanwhile, the 2nd Moroccan Division and the 1st Armoured Division were moving beyond Ulm up the valley of the Iller; from Oberstdorf General de Linarès's Moroccan troops scaled the snow-covered slopes of the Flexenpass (5,800 feet). Nightfall on May 6 found them at Saint Anton, on the road to the Arlberg, having made contact with the American 44th Division on their left.

On May 7, at 1340 hours, a cease-fire was declared in Austria, following Kesselring's capitulation to General Devers. During its five weeks' campaign, the French 1st Army had brought total destruction on eight German divisions and taken 180,000 prisoners. Among these was Field-Marshal Rommel's son, whom de Lattre, with other considerations than victory in mind, generously released.

▽ *Torpedoes that the Germans never had the chance to use. Although the menace of the conventional U-boat had been beaten by 1945, the Germans had high hopes of their new generation of fast Type XXI and XXIII boats. Post-war Allied evaluation of these new classes proved how dangerous such U-boats would have been.*

The British Supermarine Spitfire XIVE fighter and fighter-bomber

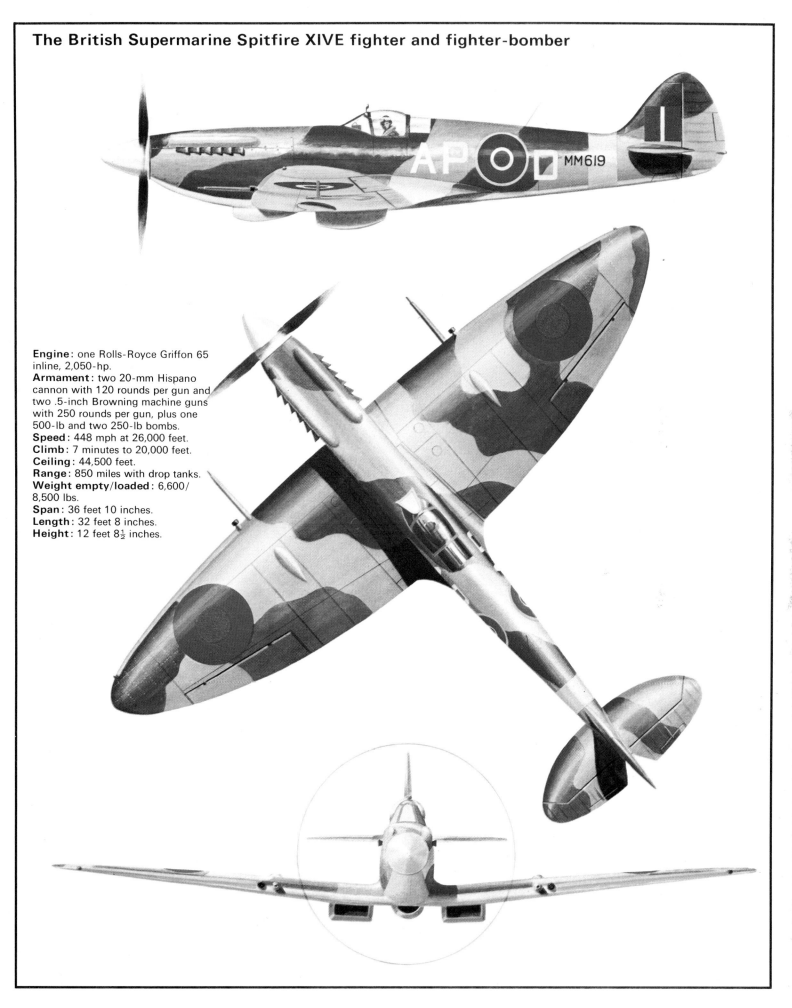

Engine: one Rolls-Royce Griffon 65 inline, 2,050-hp.
Armament: two 20-mm Hispano cannon with 120 rounds per gun and two .5-inch Browning machine guns with 250 rounds per gun, plus one 500-lb and two 250-lb bombs.
Speed: 448 mph at 26,000 feet.
Climb: 7 minutes to 20,000 feet.
Ceiling: 44,500 feet.
Range: 850 miles with drop tanks.
Weight empty/loaded: 6,600/ 8,500 lbs.
Span: 36 feet 10 inches.
Length: 32 feet 8 inches.
Height: 12 feet 8$\frac{1}{2}$ inches.

Prisoners of war: the lost armies

The mobile type of warfare of World War II often made it impossible for outnumbered land forces to be extricated, and left them no alternative to destruction but surrender. It was thus that millions of able-bodied soldiers, in addition to seriously wounded, were taken prisoner between 1939 and 1945.

The rights of prisoners-of-war were fully safeguarded by the Geneva Convention of 1929, a copy of which was displayed in every P.O.W. camp, or should have been. The protecting power, a neutral government appointed by a belligerent to look after its interests in enemy territory until the restoration of normal diplomatic relations, was entrusted with control of P.O.W. camps, and authorised to send delegates to visit camps and investigate complaints. The International Committee of the Red Cross also had the right to visit camps, and these visits soon became established as regular practice. Article 79 of the Convention entitled the International Committee to propose to the belligerent powers the organisation of a Central Information Agency for the reception, recording, and forwarding of information and replies to enquiries about prisoners-of-war. The Agency was established in September 1939.

But not all nations were signatories to the Convention. Japan had signed but not ratified it and was not, therefore, bound by its terms. The Japanese Government declared, however, shortly before entering the war in December 1941, that it would apply the provision *mutatis mutandis* to all prisoners-of-war, and, subject to reciprocity, non-combatant internees of enemy countries. The Red Cross Societies of the Allies and the International Committee were thus led to expect that they would be granted the same facilities to carry out their work as in other countries. But they were mistaken. The Committee's office in Tokyo was regarded with suspicion by the Japanese, and the work of the delegates was tolerated rather then permitted. Their mail was censored, delayed, and withheld. They had to obtain permits to visit camps and reasons were often found to cancel or delay visits. They were not notified of the existence of a great many camps and never obtained a complete list of prisoners.

1

2

3

1. German prisoners-of-war in a British camp. Extensive use was made in Britain during both World Wars of large country houses as prisoner-of-war camps. Many such houses were situated in remote rural areas, from which it would be relatively difficult to escape.

2. An early prisoner: a German airman captured in August 1940 during the Battle of Britain enjoys a drink provided by his captors, a warden, a policeman, and men of the Royal Army Service Corps.

3. Survivors from a U-boat sunk by British naval units await transport to a camp on the quayside.

2149

Russia applied the terms of The Hague Regulations of 1907 (which the Geneva Convention superseded), according to which each belligerent state set up an information bureau to answer enquiries. The transmission of a nominal roll was not stipulated nor any mention made of the Central Agency. The Soviet Union, in fact, shrouded its actions in mystery. Consequently, Germany received no information regarding troops captured by the Russians, and ceased to transmit lists of Russian prisoners, or to allow camp visits to them, although the state of Russian prisoners in Germany greatly concerned the International Committee. In Germany, the Committee's delegates visited camps for prisoners of all countries except Russia.

The enormous variety of camp conditions and of individual experiences makes difficult any wide generalisation regarding P.O.W.s. Conditions varied in different countries and, inside these countries, in different camps at different periods of the war, quite often according to the personality of the camp commandant. The local supplies of food, water, and medicine as well as local conditions of heat, cold, and dampness all had influence. In general it may be said that prisoner conditions in the Far East were more damaging to health than those in Europe.

Accommodation for P.O.W.s was limited and of varying quality. Allied troops captured in North Africa often waited months in transit camps, in very poor conditions, spending days in crowded trucks, and nights herded into wire pens. Many contracted dysentery, and were weakened by a lengthy period on short rations. Louse infestation was common, together with a shortage of water. More permanent P.O.W. camps in Italy and Germany were sometimes purpose-built stone barracks, or may previously have been a school or a castle. The camp at Eichstätt, *Oflag* VIIB, was previously a cavalry barracks, and that at Gavi, an old castle. Gavi was extremely damp and unpleasant in the winter. Here, officers slept eight or ten to a room 20 feet long by 12 feet wide, with one small window and one faint electric light. It was short of latrines and water. And there was no exercise space except the castle yard at restricted times. On the other hand, *Oflag* VIIB had fine grounds with garden, sports field, and two tennis

4. *German prisoners taken during the Commando raid on the Lofoten islands arrive at a prisoner-of-war camp in Scotland, watched by a private of the Gordon Highlanders.*
5. *A game of chess in the P.O.W. camp at Harpenden on February 1, 1945.*
6. *Entertainment in a British P.O.W. camp.*
7. *German P.O.W.s creating their own entertainment.*

4

courts for the use of prisoners.
There were also parole walks
in the Bavarian countryside, and
in winter an ice-skating rink was
prepared.

Some of the worst conditions
in Europe were at the camp
Oflag VIB at Dössel. In a desolate
and exposed area, it comprised a
number of old wooden huts with
leaking roofs and walls. There
were no proper paths and the
area became a slough of mud
when it rained. The huts were
rat-infested, and beds and bed-
ding were dirty and flea-ridden.
Between 16 and 52 officers were
quartered in rooms measuring
21 feet by 12 feet. Latrines here
discharged into three open cess-
pools which, in bad weather,
overflowed inside the camp.

Most prisoners experienced
something like this at some time
in their captivity. Many camps in

5

6

7

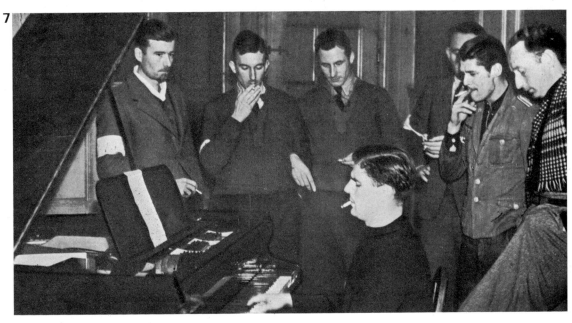

8

9

Europe were improved as time went on, and many of the improvements were due to the visits by neutrals.

Conditions did not improve in the Far East. Prisoners of the Japanese were imprisoned in various camps around Changi when they surrendered in early 1942. For the first few months, life was not intolerable, but conditions got worse as time went on. Five or six men were crammed in a one-man cell, rations were cut and drug supplies dwindled. The Japanese came to look on the prisoners only as a source of labour, and many of them were moved out of Changi to go to work in Borneo, where only a few

survived the notorious death march, to go to Thailand to build the railway, or to go to Japan to work in the mines.

Conditions were really appalling at the jungle camps for the railway workers. The Japanese had a deadline to meet, and were not worried when their prisoners died in their hundreds from overwork, undernourishment, cholera, or malaria. To the Japanese, there were plenty more prisoners. The P.O.W.s lived in bamboo huts at these jungle camps, and monsoon rains added further to their discomfort. All except the officers were accustomed to being beaten up by Japanese guards, and men were

10

8. *An interesting contrast in expressions between a German Luftwaffe officer P.O.W. and his British Intelligence Corps sergeant escort.*
9. *German P.O.W.s on agricultural work in England.*
10. *May 19, 1945: the war in Europe is over, but not for these German prisoners. After being collected at a reception camp, they are being marched off to the station in batches of 50, under armed guard.*
11. *In Russia, huge columns of Axis P.O.W.s were frequently paraded through towns behind the front to show off the success of Soviet arms. From there the road led to P.O.W. camps and the most appalling conditions.*
12. *Many thousands of German prisoners gathered together at a concentration point outside Moscow.*
13. *German prisoners receive their food ration in a Russian camp.*
14. *Soup distribution in a Russian camp.*

2153

16

15. *Four Germans abandon the "Crusade against Bolshevism"*
16. *The "masters of the East" humbled. Ahead lay many years in the Russian camps unless they recanted their belief in the Nazi doctrine and admitted the superiority of the Soviet way of life.*
17. *The long wait for transport to a camp.*
18. *The other side of the coin: Poles, the first P.O.W.s of the war, receive their rations from the Germans.*

15

sometimes beaten to death.

It is now well known how much the ill-treatment of P.O.W.s in the Far East owed to the Japanese tradition that a captive brought dishonour on himself and his family. In fact the traditions of the Imperial Japanese Army established a principle that the military honour of a soldier forbade his surrender to the enemy. The military regulations promulgated by the Japanese Minister of War in January 1942 reaffirmed the idea and made it enforceable. The Japanese training manual said "Those becoming prisoners-of-war will suffer the death penalty." Combat instructions advised troops to commit suicide rather than be captured. When a Japanese soldier left his family to join a combatant unit, a farewell ceremony was held in accordance with funeral rites; and after his departure, he was regarded as dead by his family unless he should return as a conqueror. Since notification of his capture would disgrace his family, few Japanese desired it.

In view of these considerations, the attitude of Japanese troops towards their captives was hardly likely to be other than one of contempt. Since prisoners were little better than dead men, their living conditions were of small importance. It was no wonder that the Japanese authorities took little interest in transmitting information concerning captives. Their neglect of wounded prisoners and their murder of some of them were the logical consequences of their military code. The beatings into unconsciousness, the mass punishments in the presence of an arch-offender before his more frightful

19

19. *British prisoners and some of their Italian guards in the camp at San Bernardino in the spring of 1945.*
20. *San Bernardino camp again, photographed by an Italian civilian.*
21. *Cheerful British prisoners from the sick-bay of Stalag 357, liberated by the British 7th Armoured Division on April 16, 1945. The Germans had managed to march off some 7,000 P.O.W.s, however, leaving only 350 British and a few Allied prisoners to be freed on the 16th.*
22. *British prisoners in Oflag 79, a camp for officers near Braunschweig (Brunswick).*
23. *San Bernardino camp.*

20

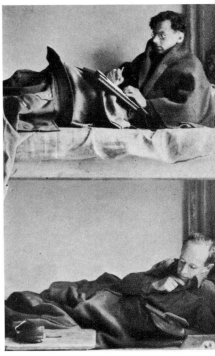

torture in private, the bayonet- **23** ting to death and the beheading of recaptured escapers, all become more explicable in terms of the severe discipline of the Japanese.

The Nazi Government was committed to being *korrekt* in its observance of the Geneva Convention, and did not physically mistreat prisoners as did the Japanese, although they did shackle some British P.O.W.s at *Stalag* VIIIB, at *Stalag* IXC, and at Hehenfels. This was a High Command order and was a reprisal for British ill-treatment of German prisoners at the time of the Dieppe raid and also during the commando raid on Sark. As time went by, however, conditions were relaxed for the shackled prisoners.

It was also Nazi policy to use their prisoners to the utmost and make them as little of a drain on the national economy as possible. Officers and N.C.O.s did not have to work, but as many troops as could be were pushed out into farm work, coal-mining, factory work, and any unskilled tasks that would free Germans for a more active part in the war effort. Work camps were called *Arbeitskommandos*. The majority of them were in industrial areas, and sometimes in the centre of a town. Although long hours may have been expected, treatment of P.O.W.s was often quite good.

Prisoners who remained inside P.O.W. camps soon organised their lives. In 1942 Changi camp organised itself into an establishment of battalions, regiments, brigades, and divisions, each with

24. *Allied prisoners wait to be let out of the cages as the U.S. 9th Army liberates the huge camp at Altengrabow on April 5, 1945. A local truce had been arranged to give the liberators safe passage to and from the camp, which was some 15 miles behind the German lines. The camp held about 18,000 prisoners, including 1,500 Americans and 800 British, plus contingents from the French, Dutch, and Belgian forces.*

25. *After the liberation of Oflag 79, with its 1,957 officers and 412 other ranks: Private Walter Shaddick, who had been a prisoner in both World Wars, shows other ex-prisoners the can in which he kept potato peelings for hard times.*

26. *A small celebration as Oflag 79 is liberated: Inter-Keystone correspondent F. Ramage shakes hands with Lieutenant W. Vanderson, a British official photographer who had been a prisoner for 1,027 days.*

27. *Altogether grimmer – the camp run by the Japanese in Rangoon. These are men freed from the camp when the British arrived in May 1945.*

28. *A British prisoner, reduced to a travesty of his former self by his ordeal in a Japanese camp.*

29. *Recognition for those who did not last until the liberation in 1945: an ex-prisoner paints crosses for some of the 800 who died in the Singapore camp.*

25

27

8

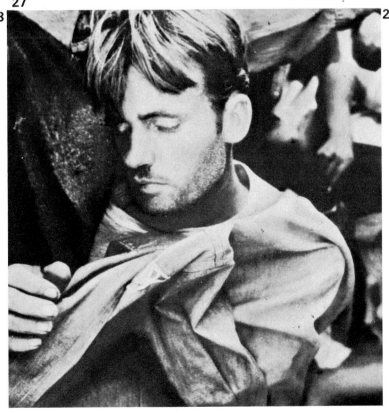

29

its own headquarters and formal staff. The digging of more bore-holes was organised to try to stem the dysentery outbreak, and the cook houses were adapted to meet the needs of such a vast influx of people. The Japanese gave food and money only to those who worked, so food was shared and each pay-day, workers made a contribution to a welfare fund which bought drugs and special foods for the sick.

The majority of P.O.W.s in camps in Europe had long periods during which conditions were bearable and when they made good use of their time. With amazing improvisation for which captivity was the stimulus, many were able to lead a vigorous and intellectual life. By summer 1942, for example, prisoners had got life at Lamsdorf pretty well organised. Enough supplies of Red Cross food, and private clothing and tobacco parcels arrived regularly. The medical supplies were adequate. Here, half a barrack was set aside as a church, the other half serving as the camp school. There were vegetable and flower gardens and facilities for football, cricket, and all-in wrestling.

All these other activities did not prevent much attention being devoted to escaping. There were many attempts, both from permanent and work camps. Men tried to walk out of camps disguised in German uniforms, or tried to leave hidden in some form of transport. There was much tunnelling activity. Many camps had escape organisations, with escape officers. Here, all escape activity was co-ordinated, with the officers taking turns to warn of the approach of the German guards. These "escape routes", permitted many men to reach Allied territory. A series of mass breakouts in 1944 culminated in that from *Stalag Luft* III in March 1944, when 76 P.O.W.s escaped through tunnels. Three reached England, a few got to Danzig, but the majority were recaptured. Fifty of these were shot in the back by the Gestapo.

Escape activity was different in the Far East. For white prisoners, there was the difficulty of conceal-ment in a city of Asiatics. Also, at Japanese camps, successful breakouts were followed by re-prisals on the rest of the inmates, and the knowledge of this did much to discourage attempts.

Medical treatment for P.O.W.s in Europe was not a great problem. The Red Cross was usually able to supply necessary medicines, and Allied prisoners were treated in German civil or military hospitals, or in special hospitals for P.O.W.s. There was no such treatment for prisoners in Japanese hands. No drugs reached them in usable quantities until the end of 1944, and under the appalling conditions already described, the medical teams had to rely on their own resources and initiative. Wood saws were used to amputate limbs, razor blades served as scalpels, and old pieces of clothing were the only available material for bandages.

30. *Prisoners in the camp in Singapore gather round to shake hands with their Australian liberators on September 18, 1945.*

CHAPTER 145
The Battle of Lake Balaton

△ *The first Russian officer to enter Vienna poses in front of his Lend-Lease Sherman tank.*

By May 1945, the German resistance had collapsed before the Red Army. The ring was closing round the New Chancellery in Berlin, and Vienna, the second capital of the Nazi Greater Germany, had been under Marshal Tolbukhin's control since April 13.

Between the Drava and the Carpathians, General Wöhler, commanding Army Group "South", had tried to break the Budapest blockade during the first fortnight of January. Although he had been reinforced by IV S.S. Panzer Corps, which had been withdrawn from East Prussia just before the Soviet attack on the Vistula, he failed in this attempt. The German 6th Army, which had just been transferred to General Balck's command, nevertheless managed to regain possession of the important military position of Székesfehérvár, but the effort exhausted its strength.

This setback sealed the fate of IX S.S. Mountain Corps, which, under the command of General Pfeffer-Wildenbruch, made up the Hungarian capital's garrison. On February 13, Buda castle, the defenders' last stronghold, fell to Marshal Malinovsky's troops (2nd Ukrainian Front), whilst the 3rd Ukrainian Front under Marshal Tolbukhin cleared Pest. The Russians claimed the Germans had lost 41,000 killed and 110,000 prisoners. The figures are certainly exaggerated, but nevertheless the 13th Panzer Division, the *"Feldherrnhalle"* Panzergrenadier Division, and the 33rd Hungarian S.S. Cavalry Division had been wiped out.

On March 6, the 6th *Panzerarmee*

△ Colonel-General Heinz
Guderian, architect of the
German Panzerwaffe, a very
competent field commander, and
lastly the O.K.H.
chief-of-staff. But as
chief-of-staff he had the
impossible task of trying to
moderate the Führer's
increasingly impossible military
plans, and on March 28, 1945,
he was replaced by
Colonel-General H. Krebs.
▷ Hitler's last futile offensive,
the battle of Lake Balaton.
▷▷ The Nazi party attacked
from within: an army officer
hanged for having negotiated
with the Russians in Vienna.

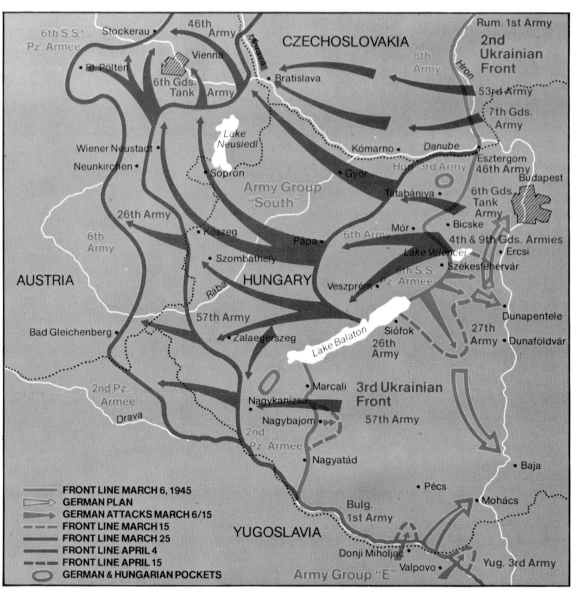

(Colonel-General Sepp Dietrich) went over to the offensive from the bastion of Székesfehérvár. Dietrich had left the Ardennes front on about January 25; it had taken six weeks for him to travel and take up his position. He might, on the other hand have reached the Oder front between February 5 and 10 if the plan that Guderian had vainly recommended to the Führer had been followed. The Führer in fact expected a miracle from this new offensive, indeed even the recapture of the Ploieşti oilfields.

The 3rd Ukrainian Front was to be smashed under the impact of a triple attack:

1. the left, the 6th *Panzerarmee*, consisting of eight Panzer (including the *"Leibstandarte Adolf Hitler", "Das Reich", "Hohenstaufen",* and *"Hitlerjugend"*), three infantry, and two cavalry divisions, was to deliver the main blow; it was to reach the Danube at Dunaföldvar and exploit its victory

towards the south, with its left close to the Danube, its right on Lake Balaton;

2. between Lake Balaton and the Drava, the 2nd *Panzerarmee* (General de Angelis: six divisions) would immobilise Tolbukhin by attacking towards Kaposzvár; and

3. on the right, Army Group "E" (Colonel-General Löhr), in Yugoslavia, would send a corps of three divisions across the Drava, and from Mohacs move to the Danube.

The offensive of March 6 therefore committed 22 German divisions, including 19 from Army Group "South", out of the 39 that General Wöhler had under his command at the time. But this tremendous effort was of no avail. On the Drava and south of Lake Balaton, the German attack collapsed after 48 hours. The outlook for the 6th *Panzerarmee* seemed better on the day the engagement started, as the Panzers, massed on a narrow front, succeeded in breaking through, but the poorly-trained infantry proved incapable of exploiting this brief success. Tolbukhin, on the other hand, had organised his forces in depth and countered with his self-propelled guns. In fact, on March 12, Dietrich was halted about 19 miles from his starting point, but about 16 miles from his Danube objective.

The Russian riposte

On March 16, Marshals Malinovsky and Tolbukhin in their turn went over to the attack from the junction point of their two Fronts. Malinovsky planned to drive the German 6th Army back to the Danube between Esztergom and Komárom, whilst Tolbukhin, driving north-west of Lakes Velencei and Balaton, intended to split at its base the salient made in the Soviet lines by the 6th *Panzerarmee*.

The 2nd Ukrainian Front's troops had the easier task and reached their first objective by March 21, cutting off four of the 6th Army's divisions.

Tolbukhin, on the other hand, met such firm resistance on March 16 and 17 from IV S.S. Panzer Corps, forming Balck's right, that the *Stavka* put the 6th Guards Tank Army at his disposal. However, because of Malinovsky's success, Wöhler took two Panzer divisions from the 6th *Panzerarmee* and set them against Malinovsky's forces. As the inequality between attack and defence became increasingly marked, Dietrich managed to evacuate the salient he had captured between March 6 and 12, and then on March 24 he brought his troops back through the bottleneck at Székesfehérvár. But what he saved from the trap was merely a hotchpotch of worn-out men with neither supplies nor equipment.

On March 27, the 6th Guards Tank Army was at Veszprém and Devecser, 35 and 48 miles from its starting point. On March 29, Tolbukhin crossed the Rába at Sárvár, and Malinovsky crossed it at Györ, where it meets the Danube. The Hungarian front had therefore collapsed; this was not surprising as Wöhler, who had no reserves, had had 11 Panzer divisions more or less destroyed between March 16 and 27.

On April 6 Hitler, consistent in his misjudgement, stripped Wöhler of command of Army Group "South" and gave it to Colonel-General Rendulic, whom he

The German *Sturmmörser* Tiger heavy assault vehicle

Weight: 70 tons.
Crew: 7.
Armament: one 38-cm *Raketenwerfer* 61 rocket projector with 12 projectiles and one 7.92-mm MG 34 machine gun.
Armour: hull nose and front plate 100-mm, rear 82-mm, upper sides 80-mm, lower sides 60-mm, and belly 26-mm; superstructure front 150-mm, sides and rear 84-mm, and roof 40-mm.
Engine: one Maybach HL 230 P45 inline, 700-hp.
Speed: 25 mph on roads and 15 mph cross-country.
Range: 87 miles on roads and 55 miles cross-country.
Length: 20 feet 8½ inches.
Width: 12 feet 3 inches.
Height: 11 feet 4 inches.

recalled from the Kurland pocket for the task.

Vienna falls

But Malinovsky had already driven between Lake Neusiedl and the Danube on April 2, and had forced the Leitha at Bruck, whilst Tolbukhin, who had captured the large industrial centre of Wiener Neustadt, launched one column along the Semmering road towards Graz and another towards Mödling and Vienna. The day he took over his command, Rendulic was informed that the advance guard of the 3rd Ukrainian Front was already in Klosterneuburg north of Vienna, and that the 2nd Ukrainian Front was already approaching it from the south. A week later, a cease-fire was signed in the famous Prater Park, but in addition to the ordeal of a week's street fighting, the wretched Viennese still had to suffer much brutality and shameless looting from their "liberators".

Tolbukhin, who boasted of the capture of 130,000 prisoners, 1,350 tanks, and 2,250 guns, went up the right bank of the Danube, but his main forces did not go further than Amstetten, a small town 75 miles west of Vienna. On May 4, his patrols in the outskirts of Linz met a reconnaissance unit of the U.S. 3rd Army, and on the same day made contact with the advance guard of the British 8th Army on the Graz road. After helping to clear Vienna, Malinovsky sent his armies on the left across the Danube in the direction of Moravia. At Mikulov they crossed the pre-Munich (1938) Austro-Czechoslovak frontier. On the left bank of the Danube, the right wing of the 2nd Ukrainian Front, including the Rumanian 1st and 4th Armies (Generals Atanasiu and Dascalesco), liberated Slovakia and then, converging towards the north-west, occupied Brno on April 24 and were close to Olomouc when hostilities ceased. Slovakia's administration was handed over to the representatives of the Czechoslovak government-in-exile under Eduard Beneš as the occupation proceeded. On

▽ *Russian T-34/85 medium tanks move through an Austrian village in the closing days of the war.*

General Guderian viewed the matter differently; urging Himmler to take soundings in Stockholm for surrender, he repeated several times: "It's not 11.55 now – it's 12.05!" In view of the open pessimism of his O.K.H. Chief-of-Staff, Hitler dismissed him on March 28 on grounds of ill health and appointed Colonel-General H. Krebs, who had been the German military attaché in Moscow on June 22, 1941, as his successor.

Army Group "Vistula" was charged with the defence of Berlin; Heinrich Himmler had just been replaced by Colonel-General Gotthard Heinrici, who rightly enjoyed the complete confidence of his staff and his troops. Cornelius Ryan's judgement seems quite correct: "A thoughtful, precise strategist, a deceptively mild-mannered commander, Heinrici was nevertheless a tough general of the old aristocratic school who had long ago learned to hold the line with the minimum of men and at the lowest possible cost."

Heinrici was in contact with Army Group "Centre" a little below Guben on the Neisse, and was in control of the Oder front between Fürstenberg and Stettin, but the 1st Belorussian Front on both sides of Küstrin already had a wide bridgehead on the left bank of the river.

The German 9th Army, under General Busse, had the special mission of barring the invader's path to Berlin. It was accordingly deployed between Guben and the Hohenzollern Canal connecting the Oder and the Havel:

1. V S.S. Mountain Corps (337th, 32nd "Freiwilligen" S.S. Grenadier, and 236th Divisions) under General Jeckeln;
2. Frankfurt garrison of one division;
3. XI S.S. Panzer Corps ("Müncheberg" Panzer, 712nd, 169th, and 9th Parachute Divisions) under General M. Kleinheisterkamp;
4. XCI Corps (309th "Berlin", 303rd "Döberitz", 606th, and 5th Jäger Division) under General Berlin.

This gave a total of 12 divisions on an 80 mile front. Busse, on the other hand, had kept the "Kurmark" Panzer Division in reserve on the Frankfurt axis and the 25th Panzer Division on the Küstrin axis.

The 3rd Panzerarmee was deployed between the Hohenzollern and Stettin canal; on a 95-mile front it had about ten divisions incorporated in XLVI Panzer Corps, XXXII Corps, and the 3rd Marine Division.

the other hand, Stalin seized Ruthenia in the lower Carpathian mountains; it had never even been a part of the Tsarist empire.

The defence of Berlin

On March 10, 1945, Hitler told Kesselring that he viewed the offensive Stalin was preparing to launch against Berlin with complete confidence. Colonel-

The British Cruiser Tank Mark VIII Cromwell VI

Weight: 27.5 tons.
Armament: one 95-mm Tank Howitzer
Mark I and two 7.92-mm Besa machine guns.
Armour: hull front 63-mm, glacis 30-mm,
nose 57-mm, sides 32-mm, decking 20-mm,
belly 8-mm, and rear 32-mm; turret front
76-mm, sides 63-mm, rear 57-mm, and
roof 20-mm.
Engine: one Rolls-Royce Meteor inline,
600-hp.
Speed: 38 mph.
Range: 173 miles on roads, 81 miles
cross-country.
Length: 20 feet 10 inches (hull).
Width: 10 feet.
Height: 8 feet 3 inches.

Heinrici kept his 18th *Panzergrenadier*, 11th *"Nordland"* S.S. *Freiwilligen Panzergrenadier*, and 23rd *"Nederland"* S.S. *Freiwilligen Panzergrenadier* Divisions, composed of Norwegian, Danish, Dutch, and Belgian volunteers.

Finally, O.K.H. kept control of XXXIX Panzer Corps, but as Hitler's intuition told him that the Russians' main attack would be directed not against Berlin, but along the Görlitz–Dresden–Prague axis, he handed over this corps to Field-Marshal Schörner and put LVI Panzer Corps, which was considerably weaker, in the rear of Army Group "Vistula".

Roosevelt dies

On April 12, Franklin Roosevelt's sudden death seemed to Hitler like a long awaited and providential miracle, comparable in every respect to the divine intervention which had eliminated the Tsarina Elizabeth and saved Frederick II, who had been on the point of taking poison at the worst moment of the Seven Years' War. Hitler thought he would not only defeat the Russians at the gates of Berlin, but that the English, American, and Soviet forces would become inextricably confused in Mecklenburg and Saxony, German guns would fire themselves, and he would remain master of the situation.

The Russians, according to the message sent to Eisenhower by Stalin, were using only "secondary forces" against Berlin in this last battle of the war on the Eastern Front. These "secondary forces" totalled at least three army groups or fronts, consisting of 20 armies, 41,000 mortars and guns, 6,300 tanks, and 8,400 planes in the attack, which started at 0400 hours on April 16. On the 1st Belorussian Front, which broadly speaking was facing the German 9th Army, Marshal Zhukov had ten armies: 3rd and 5th Shock Armies, 8th Guards Army (General V. I. Chuikov), 1st and 2nd Guards Tank Armies (Generals M. E. Katukov and S. I. Bogdanov), the 1st Polish Army (General S. G. Poplavsky), and the 61st, 47th, 8th, and 33rd Armies. He also had eight

▽ *Russian armour/infantry attack. Note the man at the left, carrying a mortar base plate.*

artillery divisions and General S. I. Rudenko's 16th Air Army. His task was to encircle and take Berlin.

On Zhukov's left, Marshal I. S. Konev's 1st Ukrainian Front contained seven armies: 3rd and 5th Guards Armies (Generals V. N. Gordov and A. S. Zhadov), 3rd and 4th Guards Tank Armies (Colonel-General P. S. Rybalko and General D. D. Lelyushenko) 2nd Polish Army (General K. Swierczewski), and 13th and 52nd Armies. He also had seven artillery divisions and Colonel-General K. A. Vershinin's 4th Air Army. After forcing the Neisse, Konev was to exploit his victory along the Bautzen–Dresden axis, but in case Zhukov's thrust slowed down, he was to be prepared to converge his mobile troops on Berlin and take part in the encirclement and assault on the city.

To the right of Zhukov, the 2nd Belorussian Front (Marshal K. K. Rokossovsky) had five armies (2nd Shock, and 19th, 65th, 70th, and 49th) with four tank or mechanised corps, and Colonel-General S. A. Krasovsky's 2nd Air Army. On April 20, Rokossovsky was to attack on the Schwedt–Neustrelitz axis, drive the 3rd *Panzerarmee* to the Baltic, and link up with Field-Marshal Montgomery's forces. Although Telpukhovsky as usual does not state the number of Soviet divisions taking part in this campaign, they may be assessed at 140 divisions or their equivalent. The Germans had 37 weakened divisions to take the first blow, including the 4th *Panzerarmee*, which faced the 1st Ukrainian Front on the Neisse. Another difficulty was caused by the fact that the defence was extremely short of fuel and munitions, and the German troops were seriously undertrained. Moreover, as Telpukhovsky points out, Soviet planes had complete air supremacy. Busse, for instance, only had 300 fighters, all desperately short of fuel, to oppose Zhukov's 16th Air Army.

The final appeal

As Zhukov and Konev started the attack, the German troops were handed out Adolf Hitler's last order of the day, which included the following passages:

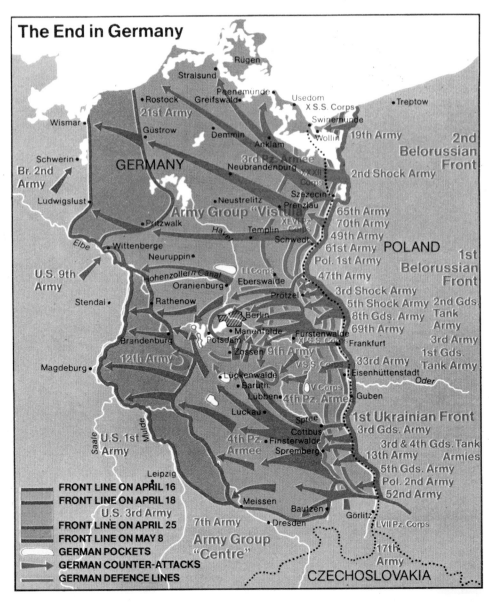

The End in Germany

Rügen
Stralsund
Rostock • Greifswald
Peenemünde •
Usedom
• Treptow
X S.S. Corps
Schwerin •
Swinemünde
Wismar
Güstrow
Demmin •
Anklam
Wollin
19th Army
2nd Belorussian Front
GERMANY
3rd Pz. Armee
Neubrandenburg
XXXII Corps
2nd Shock Army
Br. 2nd Army
Ludwigslust
Neustrelitz •
Szczecin
Pritzwalk •
Army Group "Vistula"
XLVII Corps
Prenzlau
65th Army
70th Army
Templin
49th Army
POLAND
Havel
Schwedt
61st Army
Elbe
Wittenberge
Pol. 1st Army
1st Belorussian Front
Neuruppin
U.S. 9th Army
Hohenzollern Canal
Eberswalde
47th Army
Oranienburg
3rd Shock Army
Stendal •
Rathenow
Prötzel
5th Shock Army
2nd Gds. Tank Army
Berlin
8th Gds. Army
Brandenburg
Mariendorf
Fürstenwalde
69th Army
Potsdam
XI S.S. Corps
Frankfurt
3rd Army
12th Army
Zossen
9th Army
1st Gds. Tank Army
Magdeburg •
V S.S. Corps
33rd Army
Luckenwalde •
Eisenhüttenstadt
Baruth •
Oder
Lübben
4th Pz. Armee
Guben
Luckau •
Spree
1st Ukrainian Front
4th Pz. Armee
Cottbus
3rd Gds. Army
Finsterwalde
3rd & 4th Gds. Tank Armies
Spremberg
13th Army
Saale
U.S. 1st Army
Mulde
5th Gds. Army
Pol. 2nd Army
Leipzig
52nd Army
Meissen •
Bautzen •
U.S. 3rd Army
Görlitz
7th Army
• Dresden
LVII Pz. Corps
Army Group "Centre"
17th Army
CZECHOSLOVAKIA

FRONT LINE ON APRIL 16
FRONT LINE ON APRIL 18
FRONT LINE ON APRIL 25
FRONT LINE ON MAY 8
GERMAN POCKETS
GERMAN COUNTER-ATTACKS
GERMAN DEFENCE LINES

△ *The Allies crush Germany.*
▷ *Russian armour on the move.*

"For the last time, the deadly Jewish-Bolshevik enemy has started a mass attack. He is trying to reduce Germany to rubble and to exterminate our people. Soldiers of the East! You are already fully aware now of the fate that threatens German women and children. Whilst men, children, and old people will be murdered, women and girls will be reduced to the rôle of barrack-room whores. The rest will be marched off to Siberia."

But the Führer had provided the means to put a stop to this terrible assault; everything was ready for meeting it, and the outcome now depended on the tenacity of the German soldiers. He therefore wrote: "If every soldier does his duty on the Eastern Front in the days and weeks to come, Asia's last attack will be broken, as surely as the Western enemy's invasion will in spite of everything finally fail.

"Berlin will remain German. Vienna will become German again and Europe will never be Russian!"

At the same time the Soviet leaders told their front-line troops: "The time has come to free our fathers, mothers, brothers, sisters, wives, and children still languishing under the Fascist yoke in Germany. The time has come to draw up the balance sheet of the abominable crimes perpetrated on our soil by the Hitlerite cannibals and to punish those responsible for these atrocities. The time has come to inflict the final defeat on the enemy and to draw this war to a victorious conclusion."

CHAPTER 146
Victory in Europe

Over the 30 miles of the Küstrin bridge-head, the attack started at 0400 hours, lit up by 143 searchlights. Five armies, including the 1st Guards Tank Army, took part in it, but this concentration did not favour the attack, which had only advanced between two and five miles by the end of the day. In the Frankfurt sector, Zhukov's successes were even more modest. Zhukov's crude frontal attacks were blocked by the German defences in depth. Nevertheless, on the first day, O.K.W. had to hand over LVI Panzer Corps (General Weidling) to Busse, who put it between XI S.S. and LI Corps.

On the Neisse, between Forst and Muskau, the troops of the 1st Ukrainian Front had had a better day. At 0655 hours the engineers had already thrown a bridge across this 130-foot wide obstacle so that at nightfall Konev had a bridgehead which was eight miles deep in places on a 16-mile front. The 4th *Panzerarmee* (General F.-H. Gräser) was more than

half shattered, which appeared to con-firm the soundness of Hitler's instinct in showing him that the enemy's main effort would bear on Dresden and not Berlin.

For three whole days attacks and coun-ter-attacks followed each other on the Oder's left bank to a depth of nine miles. German supplies brought up towards the line were stopped by the ceaseless attacks of countless Soviet fighter-bombers. But Zhukov had suffered heavy losses and Hitler was confident that at a daily rate of loss of 250 T-34's and JS-3's, the enemy offensive would finally become exhausted. But again Busse, to stop the gaps which were opening every day along his front, was in the position of a player forced to throw down his last chips onto the table: LVI Panzer Corps, 25th and 18th *Panzergrenadier*, *"Nordland"* and *"Nederland"* Panzer Divisions; and the defeat of the 4th *Panzerarmee,* which became more and more complete, threatened his communications.

△ *The culmination of Russia's enormous war effort: the Red flag flies over the ruins of Berlin. The Red Army's last offensive had been crowned by success – but only at a terrible cost.*

April 19: day of decision

April 19 was the decisive day on the Oder front: on that day the German 9th Army disintegrated. LI Corps, which was thrown back against Eberswalde, lost all contact with LVI Panzer Corps, which was itself cut off from XI S.S. Corps; through this last breach Zhukov managed to reach Strausberg, which was about 22 miles from the New Chancellery bunker.

On the same day Konev, on the 1st Ukrainian Front, was already exploiting the situation; he crossed the Spree at Spremberg and penetrated Saxon territory at Bautzen and Hoyerswerda. The *Stavka*, which was not satisfied with Zhukov's manner of conducting his battle, urged Konev to carry out the alternative plan previously discussed.

For the last time, Hitler's dispositions favoured the enemy. Certainly neither Heinrici nor Busse opposed LI Corps' attachment to the 3rd *Panzerarmee*, but the order given to LVI Panzer Corps to reinforce the Berlin garrison without allowing the 9th Army to pull back from the Oder appeared madness to them: outflanked on its right by Konev's impetuous thrust, it was also exposed on its left. But, as always, the Führer remained deaf to these sensible objections, and Busse received the imperious order to counter-attack the 1st Ukrainian Front's columns from the north whilst Gräser attacked them from the south.

The result was that on April 22, the 1st Guards Tank Army (1st Belorussian Front), leaving the Berlin region to its north-west, identified at Königs Wusterhausen the advance guard of the 3rd Guards Tank Army (1st Ukrainian Front) which, executing Stalin's latest instruction, had veered from the west to the north from Finsterwalde. The circle had therefore closed around the German 9th Army. That evening, Lelyushenko's armoured forces pushed forward to Jüterborg, cutting the Berlin–Dresden road, whilst Zhukov, advancing through Bernau, Wandlitz, Oranienburg, and Birkenwerder (which had fallen to Lieutenant-General F. I. Perkhorovich's 47th Army and Colonel-General N. E. Berzarin's 5th Shock Army) cut the Berlin–Stettin and Berlin–Stralsund roads. The encirclement of the capital, therefore, was completed two days later when the 8th Guards and 4th Guards Tank Armies linked up in Ketzin.

Hitler's last throw

Hitler refused to abandon the city and insisted on taking personal charge of its defence. He had a little more than 90,000 men at his disposal, including the youths and 50-year-old men of the *Volkssturm*, as well as the remainder of LVI Panzer Corps. But in spite of this he did not regard

sive launched on April 20 against the 3rd *Panzerarmee* by Rokossovsky across the lower Oder. Elsewhere, as Zhukov spread out towards the west, Steiner was compelled to thin out his forces even more, some of which were entirely worn out and the rest badly undertrained. Finally on April 26, the troops of the 2nd Belorussian Front, after making a breach below Schwedt, moved towards Prenzlau. Heinrici withdrew two or three divisions from the 11th Army to stop them. As he was unable to have him shot for insubordination, Keitel could only relieve him of his command. In the present position, he would have found no one to pronounce a death sentence and have it carried out.

Meanwhile, Hitler had addressed the following order of the day to the 12th Army on April 23: "Soldiers of the Wenck Army! An immensely important order requires you to withdraw from the combat zone against our enemies in the

▽ *A concrete* Flak *tower, part of Berlin's defences. While the major threat came from the Red land forces massing to the east, the Western Allies' air forces were still very much a factor to be reckoned with.*

the battle as lost. Whilst he galvanised the resistance, Field-Marshal Keitel and Colonel-General Jodl, who had both left Berlin on his instructions, would mount the counter-attacks which would complete the enemy's defeat. The 11th Army (General F. Steiner) would emerge from the Oranienburg–Eberswalde front and crush Zhukov against the north front of the capital whilst Konev, on the south front, would meet the same fate from General W. Wenck and his 12th Army. Meanwhile, the Brandenburg *Gauleiter,* Joseph Goebbels, launched into inflammatory speeches and bloodthirsty orders:

"Your Gauleiter is with you," he shouted through the microphone, "he swears that he will of course remain in your midst with his colleagues. His wife and children are also here. He who once conquered this city with 200 men will henceforth organise the defence of the capital by all possible means." And these were the means: "Any man found not doing his duty," he decreed, "will be hanged on a lamp post after a summary judgement. Moreover, placards will be attached to the corpses stating: 'I have been hanged here because I am too cowardly to defend the capital of the Reich'–'I have been hanged because I did not believe in the Führer'–'I am a deserter and for this reason I shall not see this turning-point of destiny'." etc.

The 11th Army's counter-attack never materialised, mainly because of the offen-

A concrete Flak *tower, part of Berlin's defences. While the major threat came from the Red land forces massing to the east, the Western Allies' air forces were still very much a factor to be reckoned with.*

guns roaring. The Führer calls you! You are getting ready for the attack as before in the time of your victories. Berlin is waiting for you!"

The German 12th Army gave way to the Western Allies on the Elbe between Wittenberge and Wittenberg and carried out the regrouping and change of front prescribed. With a strength of two Panzer corps and a handful of incomplete and hastily trained divisions it moved on Berlin. During this forward movement, which brought it to Belzig, 30 miles from the bunker where Hitler was raging and fuming, it picked up the Potsdam garrison and the remnants of the 9th Army (estimated at 40,000 men), who had with great difficulty made their way from Lübben to Zossen, leaving more than 200,000 dead, wounded, and prisoners and almost all its *matériel* behind it. On April 29, however, Wenck was compelled to note that this last sudden effort had finished the 12th Army, and that it could no longer hold its positions.

In Berlin, the armies of the 1st Belorussian Front started to round on the last centres of resistance on the same day. A tremendous artillery force, under Marshal Voronov, supported the infantry's attacks. It had 25,000 guns and delivered, according to some reports, 25,600 tons of shells against the besieged city, that is, in less than a week, more than half the 45,517 tons of bombs which British and American planes had dropped on the German capital since August 25, 1940.

April 30: Hitler commits suicide

When he heard of Steiner's inability to counter-attack, Hitler flew into an uncontrollable fury; and Wenck's defeat left him with no alternative but captivity or death. In the meantime he had dismissed Hermann Göring and Heinrich Himmler from the Party, depriving them of all their offices, the former for attempting to assume power after the blockade of Berlin, the latter for trying to negotiate a cease-fire with the Western powers through Count Folke Bernadotte. On the evening of April 28, he married Eva Braun, whose brother-in-law he had just had shot for abandoning his post, made his will on the next day with Joseph Goebbels, Martin Bormann, and Generals Burgdorf

△ *Marshal of the Soviet Union I.S. Konev, commander of the 1st Ukrainian Front fighting its way westwards south of Berlin.*
△▷▷ *German troops try to rescue as much as they can from a burning S.S. vehicle outside the Anhalter Station in Berlin.*
△▷ *Part of the final exodus from the doomed capital.*
▷ *Berliners flee their homes muffled and goggled against the dust and smoke of the last battle.*

West and march East. Your mission is simple. Berlin must remain German. You must at all costs reach your planned objectives, for other operations are also in hand, designed to deal a decisive blow against the Bolsheviks in the struggle for the capital of the Reich and so to reverse the position in Germany. Berlin will never capitulate to Bolshevism. The defenders of the Reich's capital have regained their courage on hearing of your rapid approach; they are fighting bravely and stubbornly, and are firmly convinced that they will soon hear your and Krebs as witnesses, and committed suicide a little before 1600 hours on April 30, probably by firing his revolver at his right temple.

Much has been written about Hitler's "disappearance" and the various places of refuge that he reached outside Germany. But in fact Marshal Sokolovsky, the former chief-of-staff of the 1st Belorussian Front who was interviewed by Cornelius Ryan in Moscow on April 17, 1963, admitted to him that the Führer's body had been unmistakably identified by his dentist's assistants early in May 1945. Nevertheless on May 26 Stalin, who must have known this fact, assured Harry Hopkins that in his opinion Hitler was not dead and that he was hiding somewhere. When Hopkins put forward the suggestion that Hitler had escaped to a U-Boat Stalin added, according to the account of this meeting, that "this was done with the connivance of Switzerland."

May 2: Berlin falls

On May 2, 1945, after Generals Krebs and Burgdorf had also committed suicide, General H. Weidling surrendered to Chuikov, the heroic defender of Stalingrad, all that remained of the Berlin garrison, about 70,000 totally exhausted men.

Zhukov's crushing victory should not, however, appear to overshadow the equally significant successes obtained by Konev over Schörner, whom Hitler had at the eleventh hour promoted to Field-Marshal. Having routed the 4th *Panzerarmee,* Konev went on to occupy the ruins of Dresden after a last engagement at Kamenz. Two days later, his 5th Guards Army (General Zhadov) established its first contact with the American 1st Army, whilst Marshal Rybalko and General Lelyushenko's forces made off towards Prague, whose population rose up against their German "protectors" on May 4. Army Group "Centre", which had about 50 divisions, was now cut off from its communications.

Germany surrenders . . .

Grand-Admiral Dönitz, who had been invested by Hitler's last will with supreme power over what remained of Germany, now had to put an end to this war in conditions which Kaiser Wilhelm II, unbalanced as he was and a mediocre politician and strategist, had managed to spare his empire and his subjects in November 1918. In his attempt to finish off the war, the new head of state tried to save the largest possible number of German troops from Soviet captivity, and was quite ready to let the British and Americans take them prisoner.

. . . on May 3 on Lüneburg Heath . . .

On May 3, General E. Kinzel, Field-Marshal Busch's chief-of-staff, and Admiral H.-G. von Friedeburg, new head of the Kriegsmarine, presented themselves on Lüneburg Heath to Field-Marshal Montgomery and offered him the surrender of the German forces in the north of Germany, including those retreating from Marshal Rokossovsky.

They were dismissed, and on May 4, at 1820 hours, they had to accede to the conditions stipulated in Eisenhower's name by Montgomery. The instrument they signed now only related to the land and sea forces opposed to the 21st Army Group in the Netherlands, in north-west Germany, in the Friesian Islands, in

▷ Tank-eye view of the approach to the Reichstag.
▽ A Russian Stalin 3 heavy tank co-operates with infantry during the savage and costly house-to-house fighting for Berlin.
▷▷ The seal is put on Germany's defeat in the north: Montgomery signs the surrender at 1830 hours on May 4, 1945.
▽▷ General Kinzel puts his signature to the surrender document.

Heligoland, and in Schleswig-Holstein. In spite of this fair dealing, the Russians occupied the Danish island of Bornholm.

... on May 7 at Rheims ...

General Eisenhower kept to the same principle in the surrender document which put an end to the European war at 0241 hours on May 7, 1945. This merciless war had lasted a little over 68 months.

When he received the German delegation in the Rheims school which housed S.H.A.E.F., Lieutenant-General Walter Bedell Smith, Eisenhower's chief-of-staff, read out the document decided by the Allies. It ordered the simultaneous cessation of hostilities on all fronts on May 8 at 2301 hours, confirmed the total defeat of the armed forces of the Third Reich, and settled the procedure for their surrender according to the principles governing the surrender on Lüneburg Heath. Colonel-General Jodl, General Admiral Friedeburg, and Major Oxenius of the Luftwaffe signed the surrender document in Germany's name. After Bedell Smith, Lieutenant-General Sir Frederick Morgan signed for Great Britain, General Sévez for France, and Major-General Susloparov for the U.S.S.R. Finally Lieutenant-General Carl A. Spaatz, Vice Admiral Sir Harold M. Burrough, and Air Marshal Sir J. M. Robb signed for the U.S. Air Force, the Royal Navy, and the R.A.F. respectively.

... and on May 8 in Berlin

The following day, Air Chief Marshal Sir Arthur Tedder, as Eisenhower's deputy, flew to Berlin accompanied by General Spaatz for the final act of the Wehrmacht's and the Third Reich's unconditional surrender. The ceremony took place at the 1st Belorussian Front's H.Q. Field-Marshal Keitel, Admiral Friedeburg, and Colonel-General Stumpff, who signed for the Luftwaffe, appeared before Marshal Zhukov, General de Lattre de Tassigny, and the two previously mentioned officers at 0028 hours. On May 8 the European part of World War II ended.

The surrender of the German forces, with the exception of Army Group

The end of the road for Nazi
Germany.
△ The Allied delegation at the
surrender ceremony at Rheims.
Lieutenant-General Walter
Bedell Smith signs for
Eisenhower, who refused to be
present.
△▷ Colonel-General Jodl signs
for the German high command.
▷▷ Nazi Germany's last
Führer, Grand-Admiral Karl
Dönitz (centre) with Dr. Albert
Speer and Colonel-General
Alfred Jodl at the time of their
arrest in May 1945.
▷ ▽ Field-Marshal Wilhelm
Keitel ratifies the surrender
document of May 8 early in the
morning of May 9.

"Centre", took place at the time specified.
Wireless communication was irregular
between Flensburg, the seat of Dönitz's
government, and Josefov in Bohemia,
where Schörner had set up his last H.Q.
In any event, this last corner of German
resistance had given up the struggle
by May 10.

In the period between the various
stages of surrender, though it was brief,
hundreds of thousands of Wehrmacht
soldiers, even on the other side of the
Elbe, managed to get past Montgomery's
and Bradley's advance guards and surrender to the Western Allies. The Kriegsmarine also made full use of its last hours
of freedom and as far as it could evacuated
its Baltic positions.

Finally Colonel-General C. Hilpert,
commander of Army Group "Kurland"
since his colleague Rendulic's sudden
transfer to Austria, handed over to the
Russians a little less than 200,000 men,
what was left of his two armies (five corps
or 16 divisions). Similarly General Noak

surrendered XX Corps (7th, 32nd, and
239th Divisions) which still held the
Hela peninsula and the mouth of the
Vistula. The German 20th Army, occupying Norway with five corps of 14 divisions
(400,000 men and 100,000 Soviet prisoners)
surrendered at Oslo to Lieutenant-
General Sir Alfred Thorne. The 319th
Division abandoned its pointless occupation in the Channel Islands, as did the
garrisons at Dunkirk, Lorient, and Saint
Nazaire; finally the surrender at Rheims
saved la Rochelle from the tragic fate that
had befallen Royan.

Allied Control Commission

On the following June 4, at Berlin,
Marshal Zhukov, Field-Marshal Montgomery, and Generals Eisenhower
and de Lattre de Tassigny approved four
agreements governing Germany's dis-
armament, occupation, and adminis-

tration, and decreeing that the principal Nazi war leaders should appear before an international court of military justice. It should be noted with reference to these agreements that as they were not in a position to prejudge the territorial decisions of the future peace conference, the four contracting parties defined Germany as the Reich within its frontiers of December 1937.

During the last weeks of their furious pursuit, Montgomery had advanced from Wismar on the Baltic to the Elbe just below Wittenberge, and General Bradley had reached the right bank of the Elbe as far as Torgau and to the south beyond Chemnitz (now Karl Marx Stadt). Both had gone beyond the limits set out in the Yalta agreements about the British, American, and Soviet occupation zones. Montgomery had gone about 45 miles ahead, Bradley about 125 miles. In fact, in the interests of their common victory, and without arousing the Kremlin's protests, the British and the Americans

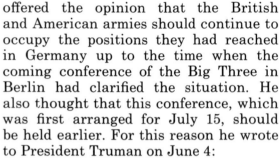

△ *A Russian points out to a party of British troops the spot where the bodies of Adolf Hitler and his last-minute wife, Eva Braun, were burned after their suicide on April 30.*

▽ *The victors: British and Russian officers inspect tanks of the 8th Hussars in Berlin. At the front, with Montgomery, are Marshals Zhukov and Rokossovsky, whom the British field-marshal had just invested with the Grand Cross of the Order of the Bath and Knight Commander of the Order of the Bath respectively.*

had exercised their "right of pursuit" beyond the demarcation line. Nevertheless on the day after the Rheims and Berlin surrenders, Stalin insisted on the precise implementation of all the promises given.

But had he kept his own promises about the constitution of a Polish government in which the various democratic factions of the nation would be represented? In London it was well known that the Soviet secret services were systematically destroying all elements opposed to the setting up of a communist régime in Poland loyal to Moscow, and that in the Kremlin the commission established by the Yalta agreements to carry out the reorganisation of the government was paralysed by Molotov's obstruction.

In these circumstances, Churchill

offered the opinion that the British and American armies should continue to occupy the positions they had reached in Germany up to the time when the coming conference of the Big Three in Berlin had clarified the situation. He also thought that this conference, which was first arranged for July 15, should be held earlier. For this reason he wrote to President Truman on June 4:

"I am sure you understand the reason why I am anxious for an earlier date, say 3rd or 4th (of July). I view with profound misgivings the retreat of the American Army to our line of occupation in the central sector, thus bringing Soviet power into the heart of Western Europe and the descent of the iron curtain between us and everything to the eastward. I hoped that this retreat, if it has to be made, would be accompanied by the settlement of many great things which would be the true foundation of world peace. Nothing really important has been settled yet, and you and I will have to bear great responsibility for the future. I still hope therefore that the date will be advanced."

On June 9, arguing that the Soviet occupation authorities' behaviour in Austria and the increasing number of irregularities against the missions of the Western powers justified his position, he returned to the charge:

"Would it not be better to refuse to withdraw on the main European front until a settlement has been reached about Austria? Surely at the very least the whole agreement about zones should be carried out at the same time?"

The Russians move in

Harry Truman turned a deaf ear to these arguments and Churchill was informed that the American troops' retreat to the demarcation line would begin on June 21 and that the military chiefs would settle questions about the quadripartite occupation of Berlin and free access to the capital by air, rail, and road between them. This was done and on July 15, when the Potsdam conference began, the Red Army had set up its advanced positions 30 miles from the centre of Hamburg, within artillery range of Kassel, and less than 80 miles from Mainz on the Rhine.

It was a "fateful decision", Churchill wrote.

CHAPTER 147
The Death Camps

Previous page: *The final appalling stages of the concentration camp system – American troops with the bodies of some of the last victims of Buchenwald camp, where some 63,500 prisoners died or were killed.*
△ *The early days: a batch of political prisoners, newly-arrived in Sachsenhausen, before changing their civilian clothes for camp uniforms.*

The Nazi concentration camp system was the most far-reaching and closely-concerted act of terror organised and carried out after January 30, 1933 by a state under the cover of legality. The terror itself was an expression of the huge breakdown of German society, of the inter-class struggle, and of the historical impasse of the 1930's. This impasse was not specifically German: it was world-wide, and because it was world-wide it made the German situation open-ended. That society's foundations were crumbling was evident from the world's increasingly rapid descent into war and from the almost simultaneous appearance of two concentration camp systems: the Soviet and the Nazi, each fed and controlled by state terror. In this wide setting the concentration camp takes on its full historical meaning: for the first time in modern history there is a very real, as opposed to an imaginary, possibility of a halt in human evolution, of humanity slipping down into organised barbarism.

The salient fact that the Nazi counter-revolution developed not before the seizure of power by the party, but after the legal installation of this power and on the legal basis of the state, plays a very important part in the development of the concentration camp system, determining its administration, its function, and its régime. Its basic function was to carry to its conclusion the state's policy of political and social violence, and it was in the very accomplishment of this task, in the thoroughness with which it was carried out, that the concentration camp somehow emancipated itself from the state which created it, becoming a social force within itself, then, by its own internal growth, profoundly altering the entire network of social relationships.

The political prisoner was to be the typical concentration camp detainee, and by political prisoner must be meant all those who, by their ideas and convictions, represented a resistance, active or passive, suspected or real, against one or the other of the activities of the establishment. He could be a communist, a socialist, a liberal, or a democrat, a trades unionist or a member of a university, a Christian, a pacifist, or merely a fanatic. They all, from the state's point of view, represented evil. Opposition was not considered as opposition but as a crime, and disagreement as heresy. This idea of evil brought in the irrationality of unbridled passions, and once society began to break down, it became irrational in all its activities, but retained an inner logic which dominated the concentration camp world.

The aim of the concentration camp was not just the death of the guilty, but a slow death by degradation. From the Nazi point of view that was one of the basic differences between the treatment of the political prisoner and the treatment of the Jew. The political prisoner was the subjective evil, conscious of himself. The Jew was the objective evil, like a poisonous plant. The plant had to be plucked out, the Jew destroyed. The problem of the destruction of the Jew was a mass problem which was to pose acute logistical questions of means and time. The humiliations the Jews were made to suffer were in the order of personal satisfaction for the oppressors. At the level of general directives, it was a question only of humiliation.

The political prisoner, on the other hand, had to be punished. The supreme punishment was to be the gradual destruction of his humanity. Death was the end, certainly, but death must be expected and prepared for in suffering. This function

of the camp was so basic that it was to remain even when the necessities of war and the personal interests of the S.S. made concentration camp prisoners into a labour force, and the camps became part of the production process. Suffering was always to have priority over production.

The death of the political prisoner demanded time, therefore—a time filled with suffering, and a time for the camps to develop into societies.

The war was to bring most of Europe into this universe.

▽ Roll-call at the Sachsenhausen camp near Berlin in February 1941. During the course of the war some 100,000 prisoners died here.
▽▽ Punishment parade in Sachsenhausen: the roll had been called three times to establish that a prisoner had escaped, and then the commandant ordered that the rest of the prisoners stand on parade ground in ten degrees of frost until the missing prisoner was found.

△ *The beginning of the mass extermination of the Jews: German troops start to round up Polish Jews for transport to the camps.*
△▷ *Humiliation as well as the threat of death: a Jewish woman, stripped and beaten by the Nazis when they entered L'vov on June 29, 1941, tries in vain to cover her nakedness.*
▷ *A Jewess forced to strip by the Nazis of L'vov.*

The system spreads

At 0600 hours on March 15, 1939, German tanks rolled into Bohemia. That same evening Hitler made a thunderous entry into Prague. "Czechoslovakia has ceased to exist." Himmler appointed Dr. Hans Frank Chief of Police of the Protectorate. On September 1, 1939 German tanks drove into the heart of Poland. On October 7 Hitler appointed *Reichsführer*-S.S. Heinrich Himmler head of a new organisation: the Reich Commissariat for the Strengthening of the German Nation (R.K.F.D.V.). Poles and Jews were to be deported from the annexed Polish provinces and replaced by Germans. On October 9 Himmler decreed that 550,000 out of the 650,000 Jews from these pro-

vinces were to be sent east of the Vistula. In one year, in fact, 1,200,000 Poles and 300,000 Jews were to disappear to the East.

The hour for mighty tasks had struck. For the first time the formidable Nazi terror apparatus had a real job to do: mass extermination. On August 22, on the eve of the Polish operation, Hitler is reported to have said, in a somewhat oracular tone, to his generals assembled at Obersalzberg, that certain things were to happen which would not be to their liking and that they were warned not to meddle. On October 18 General Halder noted in his diary a conversation Hitler had had that day with the Quartermaster General, Eduard Wagner, who reported it to him:

"The Polish intelligentsia must be prevented from rising to become a ruling class. Life must be preserved at a low level only. Cheap slaves."

Frank was appointed Governor General of Poland with a first task of eliminating the Polish intellectuals, which his directives called an "extraordinary action of pacification". It would be of no avail to seek an explanation of this policy in Hitler's psychological make-up or in the dementia characteristic of the S.S. The orders carried out were the exact replicas of Stalin's in the Baltic states and against various other national minorities.

It was therefore a general phenomenon characteristic of this period, the origins of which are to be sought in the breakdown of world society, in the spread of state-organised terror in the two countries concerned, and in the deep disturbances caused in every field of activity by the growth of the concentration camp system. Terror created the camps which, as they developed, increased the impact of the acts of terror, which in turn gave further impetus to the camp system. In the Nazi case, the phenomenon is clearly seen in its spatial development and its social effects. Each stage brought a spectacular increase in S.S. bureaucracy and a growth of its powers, so that its importance to the state increased continually and caused typical distortions of the social framework at all levels.

The suppression of the intelligentsia was no act of folly. It showed an exact understanding of modern society and its level of development. It is undeniable that the physical annihilation of the whole of the intellectual class stops social growth immediately and then leads to its rapid regression. That such a strategy can have been put into practice reveals in the most striking way the depth of barbarism of which Hitler and Stalin were the active agents. What their henchmen did not understand was that inevitably these acts were to produce a similar regression amongst themselves. The logic of terror is stronger than those who unleash it. The annihilation in Poland was to spread to Russia. The destruction of the Jews was thus only one particular case in an overall policy. Yet it is a truly extraordinary case which seems to be an exclusive product of Nazism. Nothing shows more clearly the extent to which certain circles were haunted by the Jewish question than this letter from General von Fritsch to his friend the Baroness Margot von Schutzbar in December 1938. The general hated Himmler and the S.S. By the meanest of provocations they nearly cost him his honour. They broke his career. Yet he could write: "Shortly after the War I became convinced that we would have to win three victories if we were to recover our power:

1. Against the working classes. Hitler has won this one.
2. Against the Catholic Church, or rather against the Ultramontanes.
3. Against the Jews.

"We're in the middle of the last two, and that against the Jew is the more difficult."

It was difficult because of the large numbers of Jews involved when the S.S. had to tackle it on a European scale and wipe them out. At the Nuremberg trials a

▷ One of the crematoria in the extermination camp at Maidanek, where at least 1,380,000 people were murdered by the Nazis. After being gassed, the bodies of the victims were taken down to the ovens and burned, the ashes then being crumbled, so easing the problem of disposal.
▽ Ovens in the "model" camp at Terezín in Czechoslovakia, which could take 190 corpses at a time.
▷▷ The human incinerator in the camp at Gardelegen, about 40 miles north-east of Braunschweig.
▽▷ A Polish woman weeps over the remains of some of those murdered at Maidanek.
▽▷▷ Even in death the victims of Nazi tyranny served a purpose, even if only by providing spectacles for reclamation.

directive addressed to Heydrich by Göring was produced. It was dated July 31, 1941, and expressly said: "This is to give you full powers to make preparations concerning a total solution of the Jewish question in the European territories under German control."

Heydrich was to say before 15 high-ranking civil servants on June 20, 1942: "The Final Solution of the Jewish problem in Europe affects approximately 11 million Jews." He then explained how they were to be concentrated in the East and employed on the hardest work. "The rest," he went on, "those who survive (and they will doubtless be the toughest), will have to be treated, for in them we shall have, by a process of natural selection, the germ of a new Jewish expansion."

On February 21, 1940, S.S. *Brigadeführer* Richard Glücks, head of the Concentration Camp Inspectorate, wrote to Himmler to say that he had found a suitable site near Auschwitz, a little town of some 12,000 inhabitants, lost in the marshes, with some old barrack

buildings formerly belonging to the Austrian cavalry. On June 14 Auschwitz got its first Polish political detainees, who were to be treated harshly. At the same time I. G. Farben decided to establish at Auschwitz a synthetic petrol and rubber plant. In the spring of 1940 the S.S. arrived with, at their head, two of the greatest criminals in the Nazi concentration camp world: Josef Kramer and Rudolf Franz Hoess. The latter stated with some satisfaction at Nuremberg that he had presided over the extermination of 2,500,000 people at Auschwitz, not including, he added, another half million who had had the right to starve to death.

Thus the Auschwitz zone, the most extensive and the most sinister, came into being. Then there appeared the mass extermination camps, the *Vernichtungslager*. The organisation of the vast complex of Auschwitz was exactly like that of all other concentration camp towns, surrounded by their satellites. The gas chambers introduced one more degree of terror.

Insuperable organisational problems

In their immediate, least refined, but most military objective, general terror methods aimed at annihilation raise problems of mass and speed which are difficult to solve. In 1939 Himmler and Heidrich decided in principle on the setting up of "Special Action Groups" or *Einsatzgruppen,* with four units labelled A, B, C, and D. They were to follow the troops advancing into Poland and later into Russia. Their objective would be the elimination of political commissars and Jews. They solved two minor problems: keeping the army out of it and giving the S.S. an autonomous military body, adapted to its purpose and therefore efficient. One of the leaders, Otto Ohlendorf, formerly head of *Amt* III of the Central Office of Reich Security *(Reichssicherheitshauptamt* or R.S.H.A.) then, from June 1941 to June 1942, of *Einsatzgruppe* D attached to the 2nd Army in the south Ukraine, declared at Nuremberg that his men had executed 90,000 men, women, and children. In a report seized later by the Allies, *Gruppe* A, operating in Belorussia and the Baltic states, estimated that it killed 229,052 Jews up to January 31, 1942. According to Eichmann, the *Einsatzgruppen* working in the East exterminated two million people, most of them Jews. Efficient though the special groups were in certain respects, their work could not be secret and, given the size of their task, was low in productivity.

In the spring of 1942 Himmler authorised the introduction of "gas vans" especially for the extermination of women and children. Ohlendorf explained how they worked: "You could not guess their purpose from their outside appearance," he said. "They were like closed lorries and were built so that when the engine started the exhaust fumes filled the inside, causing death in 10 to 15 minutes."

These were a step forward in the matter of secrecy, but they did not add much to the speed of the operation. There were not enough of them. Their use also brought dangerous psychological consequences on those who worked them. Even for the specialised troops it took some nerve to bring out all the bodies. The worst was that they only killed 15 to 25 at a time. The real progress came with the installation of gas chambers in Auschwitz. These meant secrecy, speed, and no psychological consequences. The loneliness of the site ensured total secrecy. The time was cut to between 3 and 15 minutes. Quantity was satisfactory: in the last period a gas chamber at Birkenau could kill 6,000 people a day. The psychological consequences were eliminated as the bodies were handled by a *Sonderkommando,* detainees who would themselves be exterminated a few months later. When the system was fully operative, however, there were bottlenecks in the transfer of the bodies from the chambers to the cremation ovens. In spite of several

▽ *The "refuse" of murder in Maidanek.*
▽▽ *Charred corpses in a mass grave.*

Ilse Förster   *Georg Krafft*   *Klara Oppitz*   *Kurt Sendsitzky*   *Martha Linke*   *Walter Otto*

suggestions no workable solution was found.

The setting-up of this procedure was clearly explained by Rudolf Hoess in his evidence. "In June 1941," he said, "I received the order to organise the extermination at Auschwitz. I went to Treblinka to see how it operated there. The commandant at Treblinka told me that he had got rid of 80,000 detainees in six months... He used carbon monoxide...

"But his methods did not seem very efficient to me. So when I set up the extermination block at Auschwitz I chose *Zyklon* B, crystallised prussic acid which we dropped into the death cells through a little hole. It took from 3 to 15 minutes according to atmospheric conditions for the gas to have effect. We also improved on Treblinka by building gas chambers holding 2,000, whereas theirs only held 200."

A Nuremberg witness spoke of the duties of the *Sonderkommando:* "The first job was to get rid of the blood and the excrement before separating the interlocked bodies which we did with hooks and nooses, before we began the horrible search for gold and the removal of hair and teeth, which the Germans considered strategic raw materials. Then the bodies were sent up by lifts or in waggons on rails to the ovens, after which the remains were crushed to a fine powder."

The gas chamber method at Auschwitz gave rise to a further refinement: selection. The detainees were selected on first arriving, then again more or less periodically within the camp and this caused an extraordinary increase in terror.

On July 22, 1941, Keitel signed two directives: "In view of the considerable extent of the area of occupation in Soviet territory," the first one ran, "the security of the German armed forces can only be assured if all resistance on the part of the civilian population is punished, not by the legal prosecution of the guilty, but by measures of terror which are the only ones which can efficiently strangle all inclination to rebel." In the second directive Keitel laid on Himmler the "special duty" of drawing up plans for the administration of Russia. To achieve this Hitler specified that he had delegated to Himmler the right to act on his own responsibility and with absolute power. Keitel then made clear the Führer's intentions by decreeing that the "occupied zones will be out of bounds during the time Himmler is carrying out his operations." No one was to be admitted, not even the highest-ranking party officials.

The concentration camp system was now in full swing. It was the basis of the social and political dominance of the S.S. The power of the S.S. was practically at its height. In the very middle of the war it was still stronger than the army. It dominated the party. It had a stranglehold on the administration. It was going to reach the peak of its power by bringing the concentration camps into the production lines.

Change of emphasis

1942 was the great turning point, the year in which the concentration camp was integrated in the production process. This was brought about by four fundamental documents:

An ordinance of March 1942 transferred the administration of the camps (*Konzentrationslager* or K.Z.) from the Central Office of Reich Security (R.S.H.A.) to the economic and administrative services of the S.S., the S.S. *Wirtschaftsverwaltungshauptamt* (W.V.H.A.), directed by S.S. *Obergruppenführer* and *General des Waffen*-S.S. Oswald Pohl.

Hildegard Lohbauer   Franz Horich   Gertrude Faist   Peter Weingartner   Elisabeth Volkenrath   Wladislaw Ostrewski

In an ordinance dated March 3 and enabling documents of April 30, Pohl set up the Concentration Camp Work Charter. The aims state: "The war has clearly changed the structure of the K.Z. and our task as far as detention is concerned. The imprisonment of detainees for sole reasons of security, correction, or prevention, is not the first object. The importance has now shifted to the field of the economy . . . This has caused certain measures to be taken which will allow the K.Z. to progress from their former purely political rôle to organisations adapted to economic tasks."

The charter had as its prime objective to "insert in the new course of events the essential and permanent function of the concentration camps as conceiving work as a means of punishment and extermination." The constraints were therefore increased, and this is the clearest difference between a concentration camp worker and a slave.

Articles 4, 5, and 6 made decisive provisions and revealed without any doubt the real spirit behind the undertaking:

"Article 4: the Camp Commandant alone is responsible for the use to which the workers are put. This can be exhausting *(erschöpfend)* in the literal sense so as to achieve the highest productivity.

"Article 5: length of work to be limitless . . . to be laid down by the Commandant alone.

"Article 6: anything which can shorten work (meal-times, roll-calls, etc.) to be reduced to the strict minimum. Movements and mid-day breaks for rest alone are forbidden."

In his comments, Pohl added that the detainees were to be "fed, accommodated, and treated in a way such as to obtain the maximum out of them with the minimum cost."

The articles are of salient interest. They are the legal basis of the S.S. ownership of the concentration camp labour force. They define the system of extermination by work: "The S.S. Commandant alone is responsible for the use to which the workers are put." Therefore the worker did not belong to the state, that is to the Minister of Labour, or of Armaments, or of War Production, and he could not be handed over by the state to private enterprise. So that the state could use him, so that a private firm could employ him, an agreement had to be reached with and a fee paid to the S.S., which, with its autonomous bureaucracy, was the sole owner of the concentration camp worker. This gave it an economic monopoly. Thus the S.S. became rooted in the production process.

"The S.S. Commandant alone is responsible for the system of work." The S.S. was thus in law the owner not only of the work force but also of the worker's whole person without restriction of any kind. This provision gave the S.S. the authority and the means to carry out its job of extermination. Minister of Justice Thierack, describing a conversation he had just had with Goebbels, explained the word *erschöpfend*. To define the new régime he used the expression "extermination through work" *(Vernichtung durch Arbeit)*. Hoess reported to the Nuremberg trial: *"Obergruppenführer Pohl told a meeting of camp leaders that every detainee must be used up to the last ounce of his strength for the armament industry."* It was Pohl also who defined for the Nuremberg jury the "Final Solution of the Jewish question" as "the extermination of Jewry".

On September 18 an agreement was reached between Himmler and Thierack on the transfer of Jews, social drop-outs, Hungarian gypsies, Russians, Ukrainians, etc. from prisons to concentration camps with a view to their "extermination through work".

△ *Guards at the Bergen-Belsen concentration camp, to which sick prisoners from other camps were sent for "recuperation". A total of about 50,000 people died here.*

These texts were preceded and prepared by a series of decisions. The decision in principle to turn the detainees into a labour force was taken on June 23, 1939, by the Council for the Defence of the Reich. Dr. Funk, Economics Minister, got the job of deciding "the work to be given to the prisoners of war and the concentration camp detainees". Himmler intervened and said: "Concentration camps will be drawn on more extensively in war-time." Yet it was not until September 29, 1941, that a first application was made, and this was only preparatory: a directive from the Inspector of Camps recommending the setting up in each camp of an *Arbeitseinsatz* service, i.e. to administer labour. A first indication of the turning-point was on November 15 when, correcting an order dated November 9 by the head of the Gestapo, Heinrich Müller, Himmler made it known that Red Army political commissars sent to the K.Z. for execution could be employed in quarries (work considered, and rightly so, as particularly hard).

These basic texts were followed by a set of executive measures, the first and most widely applicable being the ordinance of December 14, 1942, under which the numbers interned in the camps were to be increased by 35,000 able bodied detainees. The ordinance was sent to all police services on December 17. On March 23 Kaltenbrunner, who took over from Heydrich as head of the R.S.H.A., ordered this plan to be carried out.

Turning point

It is clear from Himmler's explanations to the S.S. at Poznań in 1943 that a turning point was reached with the "extermination through work" plan, and that those concerned knew it very well. Recalling 1941 (and nothing shows more clearly that until then the 1939 decision of principle had not yet been put into effect) he said: "We didn't look on this mass of humanity then in the same light as we do now: a brutish mass, a labour force. We deplore, not as a generation but as a potential work force, the loss of prisoners by the million from exhaustion and starvation." Let no one be deceived. Himmler and the S.S. had not been converted to economics.

The usual plundering of Jews' property was a by-product, not a cause, of their

deportation. Göring was able to claim: "I received a letter written by Bormann on orders from the Führer requiring a co-ordinated approach to the Jewish question. As the problem was primarily an economic one, it had to be tackled from the economic point of view." He was preaching to the wind. Selection was to go on as in the past. No examination was made of a detainee's real qualifications or state of health. Selection on arrival and inside the camps was still an act of terror. A potentially very powerful labour force continued to be sacrificed

◁ *"In Auschwitz" by H. Olomucka.*
△ △ *Female guards unload bodies from a waggon into a mass grave at Belsen.*
△ *Dead in Auschwitz.*

to the vengeance of the S.S.

The supreme criterion was still the disintegration of human beings, their abasement, and their slow death, however. Whatever the importance of this turning point, it did not affect the essential function of the camps. It merely gave them a different emphasis. The real, the crucial discovery was that through a concentration camp labour-force two key objectives were reached: production was maintained, and punishment meted out.

The second major discovery was that the labour force increased the power of the S.S. so much that it transformed it. However, right to the very end, the norms of destruction were more important than those of productivity: those who survived the camps know this well. This comes out of the statutory instruments so clearly

that these can show the difference in law between slave labour and concentration camp labour. The slave- or serf-owner took elementary precautions in his own interests, and in the interests of production, to keep the labour force alive. The concentration camp saw to it that everything was done to exterminate the labour force by wearing it out. If economic sense and logic were to prevail, this would clearly be aberrant. This constant will to destroy had one far-reaching consequence: the need for a rapid renewal of the work force. All legal decisions became null and void in the face of this need. The slightest accusation, well-founded or not, the most commonplace of court sentences could open the gates of the camps when there were numbers to make up. People would be hounded down

▽ *The ovens of Buchenwald.*

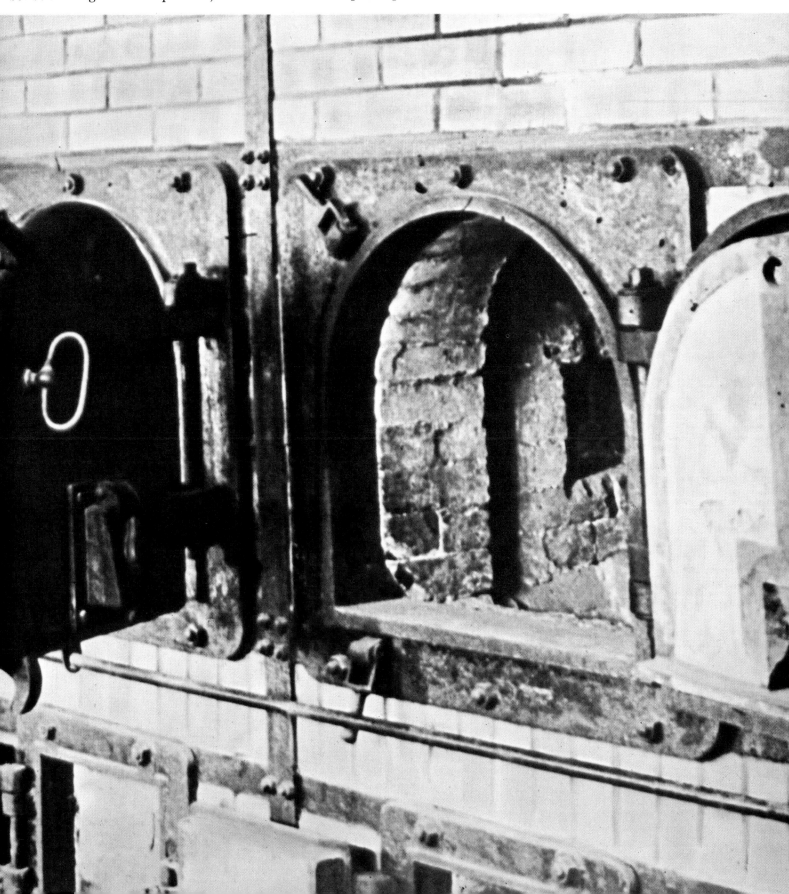

As the war lengthened and began to turn against Germany, manpower losses at the front dictated that industrial workers be conscripted into the armed forces. The only way that these workers could be replaced in the vital industrial and allied spheres was by drafting in forced, or slave, labour from occupied countries or turning the populations of the concentration camps into workers. Both systems were put into practice, and the development of the latter finally made the S.S. all but an independent state within the Reich.

Δ *Concentration camp workers clear away a hill at the edge of a new airfield.*
Δ▷ *Preparing the foundations of a new factory.*
▷ *Airfield levelling.*

by terror more than ever. Yet these swoops by the secret police had their fixed basic rules. Transport difficulties were so appalling that the losses in transit were enormous. The pressure of events was relentless.

The cause of the turning point lay completely in the unexpected prolongation of the war, in the great extent of the front, in the continuation, in spite of everything, of Blitzkrieg strategy, and in the effects of all this on manpower and industry. It was in the winter of 1941-42 that Field-Marshal Wilhelm Keitel raised the whole vital question of manpower. The army needed an annual reserve of two to two and a half million men. Normal recruitment, plus the return of the wounded and some barrel-scraping, could produce only one million. This left a million and a half to be found elsewhere. "Elsewhere" could only mean on the production lines. Factories had therefore to work at full capacity and beyond it to meet the ever-increasing needs and to make up for the now dangerous contribution to the Allied effort from the United States. So the whole of Europe had to be mobilised, and this could only be done by intensifying constraints and terror.

The general staff of the forced-labour administration consisted of Keitel, Speer, Sauckel, and Himmler. Keitel was responsible for the recruitment of army, navy, and air force reserves. Albert Speer ran the Todt Organisation from February 15, 1942, and was then put in charge of

what, on September 2, 1943, became the Ministry of Armament and War Production. Fritz Sauckel, nominated General Plenipotentiary for the Allocation of Labour, had the job of putting into effect the forced labour programme. Finally Himmler was the number one contractor.

This very considerable undertaking brought a clash between two branches of state service under Keitel and Speer on the one hand and Himmler on the other. Keitel represented military bureaucracy and Speer the joint interests of the state and powerful private enterprise, and his was a key ministry, as it brought monopolies into the state system. High-ranking management jobs were given to industrialists who at the same time remained in charge of their firms. Sauckel was merely an executive. Speer indicated to him what was wanted, Himmler provided the means. Sauckel co-ordinated. In January 1944, when Hitler ordered Sauckel to recruit four million workers, Himmler replied that to get them he would increase the number of concentration camp detainees and make them all work harder.

The matter which brought Keitel and Speer up against Himmler was the key question of who owned the forced labour gangs, and in particular the concentration camp labourers. Keitel and Speer said the state, which had sovereign rights over them. Himmler replied the S.S., and to employ them there had to be a contract with his economic service or, more

precisely, with his *Amtsgruppe* D, which ran the camps, or with the K.Z. commandants who, under the Pohl ordinance, had sole control of the use of the camp labour force. Fundamentally what was at stake was the ownership of the slave and concentration camp labour and the position of all hostile elements in production and society. At Nuremberg Keitel revealed Himmler's empire-building, his constant efforts to bring under his control prisoners-of-war, and then foreign and requisitioned workers.

In September 1942 Hitler was called upon to settle the differences between the two totally opposed sides. Speer proposed that private enterprise should take over the camp detainees. His main argument was that this was the only way to get high productivity. Himmler retorted that industries should be set up inside the camps, as only the S.S. were legally qualified to deal jointly with the needs of production and repression. Speer objected that this could not be done because of the shortage of machine tools. Himmler agreed to a compromise: some industries to be set up in the camps and some camps to be organised around existing industries. Factories would be built in regions where there were large concentration camp complexes. The ownership of the concentration camp labour force was recognised as belonging in law and in fact to the S.S. Private management and monopolies were required to pay to the S.S. a fee for each prisoner employed for the whole time he worked for them.

▷ Germany was short not only of manpower, but also of fuel and draught animals, as these men from Sachsenhausen camp harnessed to a waggon bear witness.
▽ Some of the hardest work of all for debilitated prisoners: quarrying.

Moreover, Speer had to agree to turn over to the S.S. five per cent of all the arms made by the detainees. A conflict of principles was to become a conflict of execution. Himmler got his way then, because he was indispensable. To get the workers they needed, Keitel, Speer, and Sauckel had to use the S.S. and its terror methods. They may have disliked it but they could not do without it. The logic of the system worked for the S.S.

Behind all this there were totally opposed ideas. For Speer the decisive criterion was productivity. For the Party and the S.S. it was terror, as a social function. Speer won the concession, *against the Party,* that Jews could work in arms factories. *On Hitler's order* they were to be excluded in 1943 and *in spite of this order* 100,000 Hungarian Jews were to work in underground factories in 1943. This gives Göring's letter quoted above its true meaning.

The S.S. had made its final change and become an economic power. The importance of this was not that it achieved great wealth collectively by this change, but that it obtained the final means for its independence and established its stranglehold on the state.

The only by-product of extermination which brought in huge fortunes, the gold from the Jewish corpses at Auschwitz and the valuables taken from deportees, were deposited in the *Reichsbank,* where by an agreement between Dr. Walther Funk and Himmler they were credited to the S.S. in an account entered under the name of "Max Heiliger." The deposits came so quickly and in such large quantities that to clear the vaults the bankers went to pawnbrokers and turned them into cash.

Continued growth

When the S.S. came into the production processes there was a rapid spread of the concentration camp system throughout all German society. Firstly there was a direct effort. Concentration camp labour was used everywhere: first of all in the hardest and most secret work (digging out underground factories, making V-1's and V-2's), for which it was well qualified by its isolation, cheapness, limitless exploitability, and expendability; then for all hard work in the heavy, the precision, and the peripheral in-

dustries; and then in all categories as unskilled labourers, navvies, skilled workers, technicians, and so on.

Then there was the indirect method: by contamination. Dora and Ellrich were both centres of V-1 and V-2 production and for a long time the hell of Buchenwald. By the spring of 1944 mines were being extensively used as arms factories. In April 1944 work began on the *Schacht Marie* salt mine, and soon 2,000 women were employed on the machines there. In that same month Göring asked Himmler for the largest number of concentration camp workers possible. Himmler replied that already he had 36,000 working for the air force and would examine the possibility of raising this to 90,000. Concentration camp detainees worked in the

△ *Prisoners from Oranienburg, part of the Sachsenhausen complex in Brandenburg, operating a huge cement mixer during the building of a factory in Berlin.*

overleaf above:
A Czech barber bids farewell to a friend, a Russian soldier murdered by a German guard in a labour camp.

overleaf below:
The ideal for which millions died: the safeguarding of a clean-cut Aryan future.

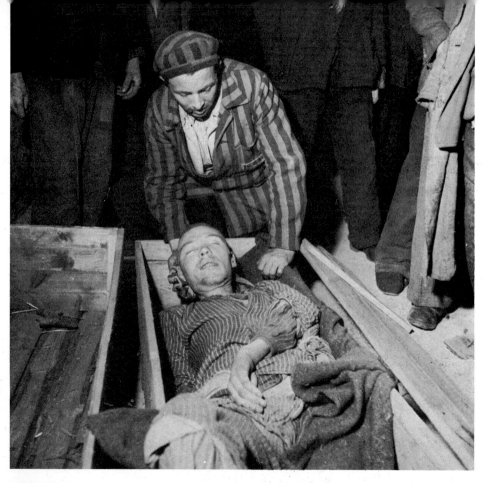

building trade in Sachsenhausen, in the brick works at Klinker, on the Annaberg motorway; they drained the marshes at Ravensbrück and Auschwitz, dug canals at Wansleben, opened up roads at Küstrin, built a submarine base near Bremen, airfields in East Prussia, made spare parts for Messerschmitts, and assembled planes at Gusen II. Amongst the documents seized in the S.S.W.V.H.A. archives, one dated November 4, 1942, was a request for specialists from the head of *Amt* III at Oranienburg to the commandant of the Natzweiler camp. Thirty-one categories were asked for (accountants, welders, oxy-acetylene welders, mechanics etc.).

The S.S. certainly took care to register a detainee's real or pretended qualifications on his arrival. The detainees themselves looked after this even more actively. To get into a factory was a much sought-after privilege. It could mean the difference between life or death. The harshest treatment in a factory was paradise compared with navvying, quarrying or the hell of the S.S. and the cold.

The numbers of workers handled were very large and the overall organisation became unwieldy and inflexible. Old-fashioned procedures such as work-books led the administrative constraints. Besides the concentration camp workers, there were seven and a half million foreign workers and two million prisoners-of-war in Germany in September 1944. At Nuremberg, Sauckel confessed that only about 200,000 out of five million foreign workers were volunteers. Albert Speer admitted that 40 per cent of the prisoners-of-war in Germany were being employed on arms and munitions production or related work in 1944. These large numbers meant an automatic change in the organisation of labour.

It is difficult to establish the proportion of concentration camp workers in the whole of the forced labour gangs. Most of the records have disappeared, and where they do exist they were so much subject to the usual camouflage and falsification that they are difficult to interpret. Krupp stated during his trial that out of his 190,000 workers half were forced labour. It has been possible to find the distribution of the latter: there were 69,898 civilians from the East, 23,076 prisoners-of-war, and 4,897 concentration camp detainees. So one in 39 of the Krupp labour force came from the concentration camp, a striking figure.

The role of Industry

The Concentration Camp system soon spread its tentacles to all German industry, with very important political ramifications. The K.Z. reacted on the S.S. by increasing the field of action of terror. This increase reached frightful proportions once the K.Z./S.S. complex was integrated in the production process. The fundamental dynamism of society provided a feedback.

It is a quite remarkable sociological phenomenon that as soon as a certain critical density was achieved, the spread of the concentration camp ethos became automatic. There was nothing abstract about the phenomenon: experience showed it in its concrete form. It can be grasped in the rise of the conflict between private monopolies and the S.S. over the legal ownership of the labour force.

The simplest and best-tried rules of productivity ought to have led the private sector, once it took in concentration camp labour, to restore normal conditions of life for the workers (food, safety at work, rest, and hygiene). Far from it: the private monopolies strove on the contrary to adapt their regulations to those of the camps.

I.G. Farben invested 250 million dollars in factories in the Auschwitz area. The labour force of a few hundred thousand came from the two million detainees who passed through Auschwitz from 1941 to 1943. It sent 100,000 of them back to the gas chambers. It paid the S.S. a fee for every worker employed, and this was remitted when the worker died or was sent back to the camp because he could work no more.

The I.G. Farben administration, on the other hand, did concern itself with the worker as soon as he left the camp. Very

△ *Woman and child in Auschwitz.*

◁ *Prisoners freed in Auschwitz-Birkenau by the Russians in January 1945. In this worst camp of all, at least two million people lost their lives.*

△ *Emaciated prisoners freed by the Allies in 1945 from the main Austrian camp, Mauthausen, where 138,500 prisoners died.*
▷ *A scene from the propaganda film "The Führer Gives the Jews a New Town", showing how well the Nazis treated the Jews. In fact these are the vegetable plots of the guards at the model camp at Theresienstadt (Terezín), all cared for by prisoners detailed for the job.*

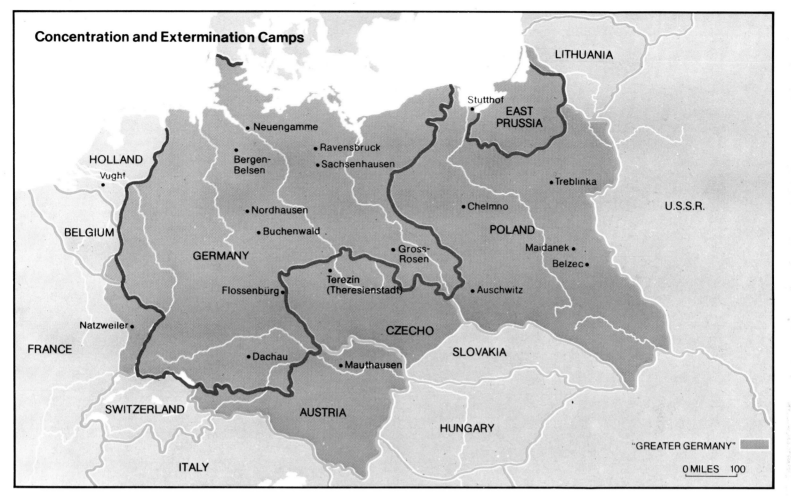

Concentration and Extermination Camps

LITHUANIA

Stutthof • EAST PRUSSIA

• Neuengamme

• Ravensbruck

HOLLAND
Vught •

Bergen- • Sachsenhausen
Belsen

• Treblinka

U.S.S.R.

BELGIUM

• Nordhausen

• Chelmno

POLAND

• Buchenwald .

Maidanek •

GERMANY

• Gross-
Rosen

Belzec •

Terezin •
(Theresienstadt)

• Auschwitz

Flossenburg •

Natzweiler •

CZECHO

FRANCE

• Dachau

SLOVAKIA

• Mauthausen

SWITZERLAND

AUSTRIA

HUNGARY

ITALY

"GREATER GERMANY"

0 MILES 100

carefully-kept records were found with entries showing a worker's behaviour, sickness, and death. The conflict between I.G. Farben and the S.S. may have been a quarrel over the amount of the fee to be paid, but it was really about the S.S.'s right to determine the kind of work and how it was to be checked. The S.S. had to be allowed into the factory: supervision of a man's work led inevitably to increased supervision of the factory itself. As the S.S. already had its own factories and workshops, as its influence on administration was enormous, and as it could act to affect all markets, to allow it to occupy a firm base inside the business itself was tantamount to giving it all up. And so I.G. stated that it would only hand back the camp worker to the S.S. either dead or dying and this the S.S. would not accept.

I.G. Farben therefore took the labour *Kommandos* in. It did not change the detainees' working conditions, but adapted its factory to meet these conditions. Towards the middle of 1942, the Buna rubber and chemicals factory was surrounded by barbed wire: the S.S. were forbidden to enter except for "very special reasons". The same thing at Monowitz,

a factory founded by I.G. Farben, now an I.G. Farben camp. This was allowed on the pretext that the daily journey to and from the concentration camp meant a loss of production. I.G. Farben therefore had to set up its own concentration camp management system. This it did on a system based on the S.S. model.

The way I.G. Farben ran its camp was identical to the K.Z. system. The S.S. actually denounced it as inhuman, saying that the mortality rate was too high–a tragic and derisory accusation. Buna (not including Leuna) had 300,000 concentration camp detainees, of whom 200,000 died. Out of the 20,000 deportees in Monowitz (which had been built to hold 5,000) 15,000 were sent to hospitals in 1943 and 10,000 "exterminated through work".

Krupp ran identical camps at Essen. They became a general feature in industrial areas and show how profoundly labour relations had changed. The process was there for all to see. The extension of the war forced Germany's leaders to seek a large and increasing number of foreign workers. Good wages and a decent standard of living were not possible. This meant a resort to force, and

△ *The concentration camp system in "greater Germany" and occupied countries.*

force was possible because the régime was founded on terror. Bureaucracy, which had the monopoly of terror, seized its chance to extend its power in and over the state. As the legally-recognised owner of the person of the deportee, it sought to increase the numbers of people it controlled, and to control the total of forced labour workers and the reserve of free workers. This it could do only by increasing its interventions and supervision. By virtue of its right over the detainee, it built up its own economic interests and gained entry to the factory. When this activity had reached a certain level its constraints over the organisation of labour became automatic. From its hold over the labour force, it passed *de facto* and *de jure* to a hold over the person of the worker. The administrative constraints structured the production processes, and were in themselves only a projection of the concentration camp system. The apparatus of terror (the social *corpus* of terror), became free of state control. The S.S. bureaucracy thus tamed the state. Only defeat broke this development before it was complete.

Camp society

The inclusion of the camp detainees in the production process greatly affected society outside the camps: but it also transformed the camps internally, making

them into societies. It brought great changes in the camp administration and diversified it. It extended the camp network in a new and original way. It increased the differences between camps. It strengthened the rôle of the centres, that is of the concentration camp complexes. It increased the outside worker *Kommandos* which tended to take root. It operated sharp distinctions between detainees and these distinctions became clearly social. The differences became based on social classes. It increased outside contacts and created complex links with firms. It consequently widened the basis of corruption and noticeably increased the detainee bureaucracy's chances of manoeuvre. It brought a radical change to this bureaucracy. Ordinary criminals gave way to political detainees. This shift of power came about through unheard-of violence, by a series of plots and a large number of murders. It split the S.S. Once the political detainees got power, the history of the camps took a new course. The great majority of detainees from Western Europe knew the camps only in this latter stage. Taken overall these consequences, so many and so serious, meant that unquestionably the camp system had undergone a revolution.

The camp network developed along two main lines of force. The central camps, powerful concentration complexes, were built along the lines of terror and its extensions. Economic necessities played no part in their foundation. They were the outcome of the increase of organised terror in Germany and of its extension, through the *Anschluss* and the war, to Central, Eastern, and Western Europe. The fixed *Kommandos,* set up as satellites to the large concentration complexes, were only for economic necessities, and their geographical distribution was dictated by the industrial infrastructure.

In 1936 the S.S. Death's Head units were restricted to fixed installations. This gave rise to the integrated complex: S.S. barracks–S.S. living quarters–concentration camp.

The three main S.S. camps were attached to the first three very powerful concentration complexes: Dachau near Munich, enlarged; Buchenwald near Weimar, founded in 1937; and Sachsenhausen, near Berlin.

The consolidation of Nazi power brought the creation of Gross Rosen in the Lausitz region; Flossenburg near Weiden in Bavaria; Neuengamme near Hamburg; and Ravensbrück in Mecklenburg. The *Anschluss* brought Mauthausen near Linz.

The war brought the development of the concentration camp network in Eastern Europe (Auschwitz, Treblinka, Sobibor, Maidanek, Belzek, Stutthof near Danzig), Natzweiler in the Vosges, Bergen-Belsen near Hannover, and Neubremm near Saarbrücken.

The crisis year of 1942 resulted in a network of satellite camps all over Ger-

△ *Mass burial for the bodies of those who died just before Auschwitz was liberated.*
◁ *The scene in Dachau when it was liberated by men of the U.S. 42nd (Rainbow) Division of the 7th Army early in May 1945. This camp, which served Bavaria, was one of the earliest to be set up, and here about 70,000 people had met their end. When the Americans entered the camp, they found many thousands of bodies lying there unburied.*

All that remained of the bodies of several hundred victims killed and cremated in Buchenwald.

taken of the "final solution". The true figure would appear to be between nine and ten million, probably nearer the latter.

Buchenwald was a typical large concentration camp complex. In April 1945 it had 47,500 detainees from 30 different countries and by that time several evacuations had taken place.

The camp at Lublin was the first to be freed by the Allies. Orders for the extermination of all camp inmates were sent out from Berlin, but there was such incoherence and confusion that they could not be complied with in the majority of cases. On January 18 Auschwitz was emptied. There was a slow exodus westwards to Buchenwald, Oranienburg, Mauthausen, Ravensbrück, Dachau, and Bergen-Belsen in open waggons and a temperature of minus 30 degrees Centigrade. The breakdown of relations with the outside and the influx of a fresh, harassed, and demented population completely disorganised the administration of the concentration camp complexes. There was total confusion as convoys of detainees, civilians, and troops crossed each other all over Germany. Famine spread and exanthematous typhus appeared. The S.S. went on killing. They killed on the roads all those who, in haggard columns, showed any signs of weakness. They killed indiscriminately. Even in its death-throes the world of the concentration camp accomplished its basic mission. The Nazi concentration camp system was broken when it was at its height. It did not collapse under the weight of the crumbling régime. It was broken from without by force of arms. The S.S. went down with Auschwitz and Buchenwald.

In *L'Univers concentrationnaire* and *Les Jours de notre Mort* I have described in detail life inside the camps. Here I have merely traced the outline of their history. From the outside I have seen them as one sees a comet. Here they belong to history and they make this history. The important thing is their genesis and their action on society. The lesson speaks to our intelligence. To understand this genesis and the changes brought about by the growth of the concentration camp system is of tremendous importance.

The sum of unspeakable sufferings cannot be weighed. It has nothing to do with historical analysis. It is not a social factor. It is the very depth of the camps' meaning. On this threshold the reader must listen to the witnesses.

many. There were about 900 in 1945 attached to 15 large centres.

The numbers of those detained are difficult to estimate because of the lack of sufficient documents. Eugen Kogon gives eight million, of whom seven and a half million died; he also says that in 12 years only 200,000 were set free.

Olga Wormser states that from 1933 to 1939 there were no more than 100,000 and that the total eventually reached five to six million, including survivors from Auschwitz (in 1945 these numbered only 65,000). She does not give figures for the victims of the "final solution", i.e. deportees who were gassed. Compared with Wormser's, Kogon's figures would appear to be high, but low if account is

GERMANY'S SECRET WEAPONS

The words "Secret Weapons" have an emotive ring which disguises the fact that they are generally unusual weapons developed secretly whose employment comes as a nasty surprise to the enemy.

German research in World War II was affected by the early victories in the opening years: it seemed that the Reich would be able to win the war with her conventional weapons, and so there was little call for research in new equipment. Thus many of the projects which were developed

Previous page
The Bachem Ba 349A "Natter" (Adder) on its launching rails (left) and just after launching (right). This was designed late in 1944 as a last-ditch interceptor fighter. Powered by four rocket engines, the Natter had a top speed of 560 mph and a climb rate of 35,800 feet per minute. Armament was twenty-four 55-mm rockets under a detachable nose cone. None was used operationally.

▷ *German groundcrew make last-minute adjustments to a V-2 in preparation for an operational firing against southern England.*
▽ *The motor of the 10th experimental A4 blows up after 2½ seconds of running, as a result of a servicing error, on January 7, 1943 at Test Stand No. 7.*
▽▽ *Moments later the wrecked missile topples over onto its side. The quartered black and white markings were to aid the photo-telemetry equipment.*

were done on a freelance basis by German companies.

It is an awesome thought that in 1939 the Germans had already established a research group into the possibilities of atomic power and, moreover, that they had a three-year advantage over the Allies. Rivalry between the physicists and a failure to "sell" their work to *Reichsminister* Speer meant that they never received the massive backing which was accorded the "Manhattan Project" Up to 1942 both sides had reached the same point in their work, but from there on the Germans marked time.

In rocketry, however, they made major advances. In 1945, when V-2's were falling on Britain, a British Government statement admitted that "the design and the construction of the V2 is undoubtedly a considerable achievement", but added "the military value of the weapon at present is extremely doubtful". Had a V-2 been armed with an atomic warhead, the missile would certainly have caused the panic that Hitler had envisaged.

Research had begun before the war, but unlike the work of the nuclear physicists it was centralised and under firm leadership. Walter Dornberger, an experienced artillery officer and a professional engineer who became head of the rocket research project, laid down the missile's specifications. It was to have a payload of about a ton and a range of at least 160 miles, so representing an advance on the largest guns of World War I.

German work was interrupted by heavy air raids on the research centre at Peenemünde, and earlier in 1943 when Hitler ordered a cutback in supplies after suffering from a bad dream on the subject of rockets.

There were two major projects, the A4 (V-2) ballistic missile and the FZG 76 (V-1) flying bomb. The V-2 has always attracted more interest than the V-1 as it was a proper rocket, whereas the V-1 was a pulse-jet-powered pilotless aeroplane with a 1,870-pound warhead. However, in value for

▽ *The high command inspects progress at Peenemünde in 1944. From left to right: General W. Warlimont (with binoculars), Field-Marshal W. Keitel, General F. Fromm, and Major-General Dr. W. Dornberger, head of the Peenemünde establishment.*

◁ *The early days at Peenemünde: a* Waffenamt *(Army Weapons Department) inspection in 1942. Among those present are Dornberger (back to camera), Dr. W. Herrmann, in charge of the supersonic wind tunnel (background, in civilian clothes), Lieutenant-General Schneider, head of the* Waffenamt *(with binoculars), and Dr. Wernher von Braun, the rocket engine designer (foreground, in civilian clothes).*

2210

◁ *A V-2 lifts off and accelerates swiftly into its ballistic trajectory. Control of the missile was dependent on a stable platform in the nose. This contained two gyroscopes, one defining the pitch axis and the other the yaw and roll axes. Any deviation from the planned trajectory was detected by these gyroscopes, and corrections to reduce the error to zero fed to the control vanes on the fins and in the rocket efflux.*
▽ *V-2 launch site.*

money the V-1 more than repaid the German efforts. Germany expended an estimated £12,600,670 on the manufacture and launching of V-1's and the erection and defence of the sites. The flying-bomb offensive between June 12 and September 1, 1944 cost the British £47,635,190 in lost production, loss of aircraft and crews, in extra A.A. defences, in clearance of damage, and in the bombing attacks on the launching sites. In addition, permanent repairs to housing damaged by the V-1's cost at least another £25,000,000. The V-1 had a very high blast effect when filled with *Trialen*, an explosive with almost twice the power of the conventional RDX-type.

A V-2 cost £12,000 compared with a V-1's £125. The most serious damage done by the V-2 was in fact inflicted on the Germans: "The A4 project critically invaded Germany's aircraft production capacity; the induced shortage of electrical components from the summer of 1943 onwards not only crippled the fighter-aircraft industry, but interfered severely with both submarine and radar requirements." Moreover, Speer refused to allow work to expand on the anti-aircraft rocket projects late in 1944 unless the V-2 programme was cut back to provide the necessary components.

Had the resources used on the V-2 been diverted to an anti-aircraft missile, Allied bombers would have sustained very heavy losses. In December 1944 a committee under Dornberger reviewed the work on anti-aircraft missiles. They awarded three contracts, for the "*Wasserfall*", "*Schmetterling*" and Ruhrstahl X-4.

This last missile was to have been used by German fighters against B-17 formations. It was a wire-guided liquid-fuelled rocket with a 44-lb warhead. One of its major features was the use of non-strategic materials and components which could be constructed and assembled by unskilled labour. The metal sheets had simple tabs which, like a metal toy, could be slotted together. The wings were of plywood and were secured to aluminium supports by nuts and bolts.

By February 1945, some 1,300 missiles were on the production lines when the engines at the BMW factory at Stargard were destroyed in an air raid. The work that was necessary to re-build the plant was so great that the project was allowed to lapse.

2211

2212

◁◁ *British troops examine a* Reichenberg *suicide aircraft captured at Tramm, near Danneberg. This was a piloted V-1 "doodlebug". None was flown operationally, although 175 were built.*

△ *V-1 launching site overrun by the Canadians in Holland. Inspecting the ramp are Lance-Corporal Don Stover of Moose Jaw, Saskatchewan, and Sergeant R. Clarke of Forestdale, B.C.*

◁ *Launching ramp taken by the British in France.*

▽ *Underground V-1 (FZG-76) factory at Nordhausen, captured by the 1st Army in April 1945.*

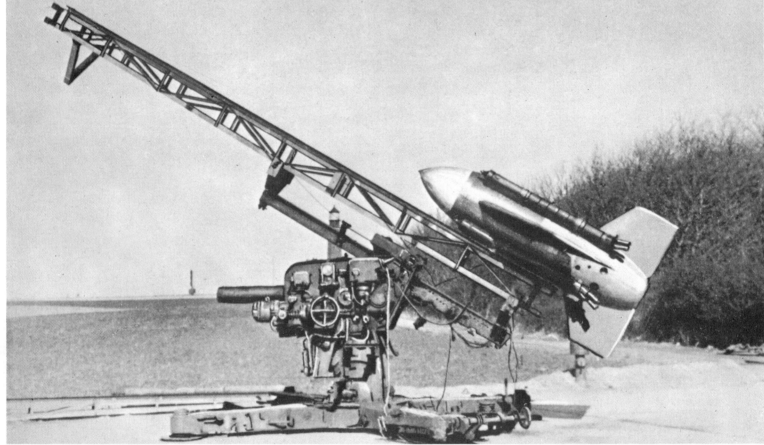

The "*Wasserfall*" missile was designed by the Peenemünde team which had worked on the V-2. It was liquid-fuelled and could reach a maximum altitude of 55,000 feet.

The "*Schmetterling*" anti-aircraft missile incorporated features of the Hs 293 glider bomb. It had two solid-fuel booster rockets and a liquid-fuel engine which could take it to a maximum altitude of 45,000 feet. With a 51-lb warhead it was intended to be the standard anti-aircraft missile for the Reich.

As the war swung against Germany there was an increased emphasis on the use of non-strategic materials. The Me 262 had demonstrated the effectiveness of jet-propelled fighters to the *Reichsluftfahrtministerium* (Air Ministry). In September 1944 the R.L.M. called for a high-performance fighter utilising a minimum of strategic materials and suitable for mass production by semi-skilled labour, and which could be ready for production by January 1945.

The Heinkel He 162A "Salamander", popularly known as the "*Volksjäger*" or People's Fighter, was submitted to the Ministry. A scale mock-up was inspected on September 23, 1944, and five days later a quantity order was awarded. The prototype flew for the first time on December 6, 1944. In a demonstration four days later it crashed in front of Party functionaries and members of the Ministry, but despite this development continued.

Its components reflect the raw materials' famine that existed in Germany at the end of the war. The one-piece wing was of wooden construction and the fuselage had duralumin formers and skin with a plywood nose and a tail of duralumin, steel, and wood.

Not only was there a lack of raw materials, but the Reich had a shrinking labour force as men were drafted into the Army. Unlike Britain, Germany never fully mobilised its considerable pool of female labour. Instead she employed foreign workers, the bulk of whom had been shipped against their will from occupied countries. Predictably, the quality of the workmanship was low.

At the far end of the scale from the V-2, a rocket which served to further political rather than tactical ends, there was a wide variety of field rocket equipment.

Chemical warfare units equipped with the 10-cm *Nebelwerfer*

35 had participated in the invasion of Poland. At the beginning of the war there were few *Nebeltruppen*, but the low cost of rocket artillery made it attractive to the Germans. Moreover, rocket batteries had an impressive rate of fire: a brigade could fire 108 rounds in ten seconds or 648 rounds in 90 seconds.

The Germans developed a variety of rocket projectiles, from the 181-pound 28-cm *Wurfkörper Spreng* which could be fired from its crate or a mobile launcher, to the anti-tank *Panzerfaust*. This weapon was a small hollow-charge rocket fired from a tube.

The hollow charge principle had attracted Hitler before the war and he had suggested that it could be employed against the bunkers and emplacements in Eben Emaël, the fort which was in 1940 the key to the Belgian defences.

Hitler's interference in German research led to considerable funds being diverted to prestige projects. At a demonstration of the 80-cm railway gun "*Gustav*", Guderian was horrified to hear Dr. Müller of Krupps tell Hitler that the massive gun could be used against tanks. "For a moment I was dumbfounded as I

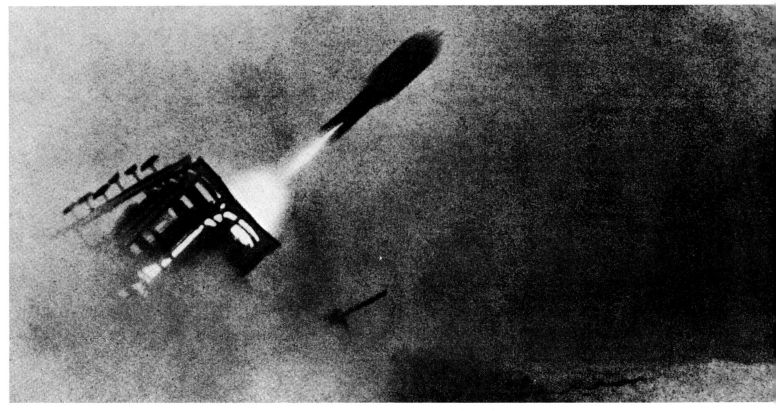

envisaged the mass-production of 'Gustavs'." He hurriedly explained to Hitler that the gun could be fired, but could certainly never hit a tank and moreover needed 45 minutes to reload between shots.

"Gustav" was a good example of the German interest in superheavy versions of conventional weapons. The gun, which required a crew of 1,420 for its operation and defence, was commanded by a major-general. It had two types of shell: a four-ton anti-personnel projectile with a range of 29 miles, and a 17-ton concrete-piercing shell with a range of 23 miles. The gun was employed at Sevastopol' and Warsaw and fired a total of about 60 or 70 shots.

As a piece of ordnance engineering it was undeniably a considerable achievement, but it was also a waste of resources, for a bomber could have achieved the same results at less cost.

One artillery project which might have paid for the effort which was expended on it was the "V-3" "High-Pressure Pump". Sited at Mimoyecques on the French coast, the gun was designed to fire a finned 550-pound shell at London. It was unusual in that the powder for the charge was distributed in a series of breeches

△ ◁ ◁ *Superheavy German ordnance. With a good railway system at her disposal, Germany found the development of such monsters worthwhile.*
△ ◁ *Three views of a German rocket gun in action.*
◁ *Rocket artillery, in which the Germans led the world all through the war.*
△ ▷ *An American soldier poses beside an experimental rocket launcher abandoned by the Germans. It was a very neat piece of design, and had a plastic shield to protect the firer from the blast.*
▷ *The incredible* Hochdruckpumpe *long-range gun. This was built into the ground at a fixed elevation and bearing, and used arrow-shaped projectiles, 8 feet long and 550 lbs in weight. The barrel was in 40 sections, and there were 28 powder chambers distributed along the bore. The intention was that as the projectile moved up the barrel, the extra powder chambers would fire in succession, to boost the shell to a muzzle velocity of 4,500 feet per second. Range was about 80 miles. The barrel burst about every third shot, however.*

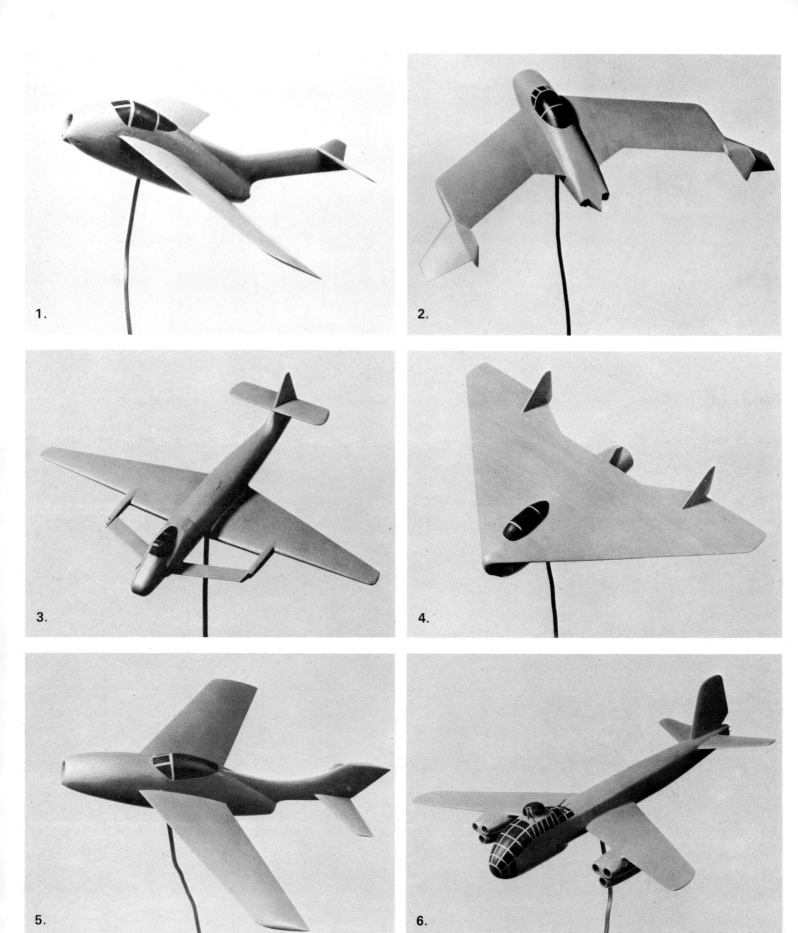

1. *The Focke-Wulf Ta 183 fighter (4 × 30-mm cannon; 597 mph), about to enter production as the war ended.* 2. *The Blohm & Voss P.215 bad weather fighter* (7 × 30- and 1 × 20-mm cannon and 2 × 1,100-lb bombs; 594 mph).* 3. *Blohm & Voss P.192 ground-attack aircraft (2 × 30- and 2 × 20-mm cannon and 1 ×* 1,100-lb bomb) with the propeller behind the cockpit.* 4. *The Arado E.581.4 fighter (2 × 30-mm cannon).* 5. *The Focke-Wulf Ta 183 (Project II) fighter, with a* more conventional empennage.* 6. *The Junkers 287 bomber (8,800 lbs of bombs; 550 mph).*

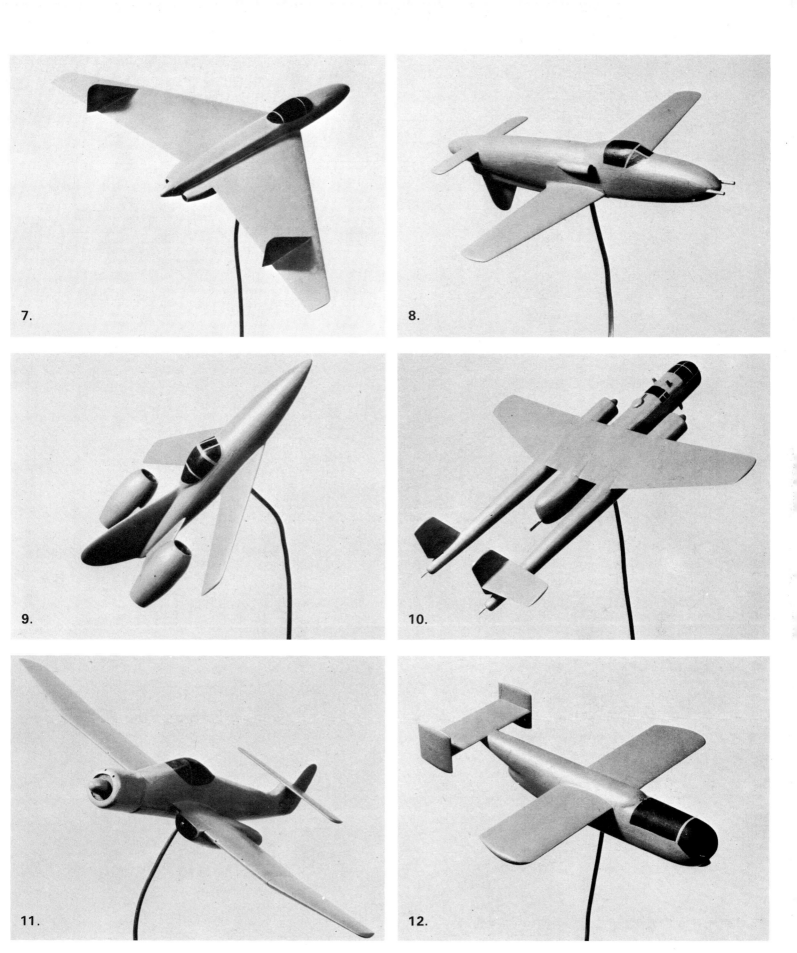

7. *The Arado bad weather fighter Project I (6 × 30-mm cannon and 2 × 1,100-lb bombs; 503 mph).* 8. *The Blohm & Voss P.207.03 pusher fighter (3 × 30-mm cannon; 490 mph).* 9. *The Focke-Wulf Ta 283 athodyd fighter (2 × 30-mm cannon; 682 mph).* 10. *The Arado E.340 bomber (3,300 lbs of bombs; 388 mph).* 11. *The Blohm & Voss P.194 attack aircraft (2 × 30- and 2 × 20-mm cannon and 1 × 2,200-lb bomb; 482 mph).* 12. *The Arado miniature fighter, carried by the Ar 234C bomber (1 × 30-mm cannon). Span was 16 feet 5 inches.*

△ *The remarkable Heinkel He 111Z* Zwilling *glider tug. This was an amalgamation of two He 111H-6 bombers, joined by a new centre section carrying a fifth engine, to tow the mammoth Me 321 Gigant transport glider. The crew was in the port fuselage of the* Zwilling. *The basic H-6 variant was also used for the launching of various air-launched missiles such as the* Fritz X *and* Hagelhorn. *It was also used for trials with the* Friedensengel *experimental winged torpedo.*

along the barrel. As the shell moved up the barrel each charge would be fired to increase the shell's speed. This was not only economical in propellant, but the barrels suffered less wear.

The original scheme had called for 25 barrels located on the French coast, firing one round every 12 seconds.

Work was well advanced on the site at Mimoyecques: 100 feet down in the limestone hill there was a warren of tunnels and galleries served by a railway line.

In tests, however, the barrel had a tendency to burst after several rounds had been fired. The shells, too, proved to be unstable when they reached velocities above 3,300

feet per second. *Reichsminister* Speer was confident that with better materials and workmanship, and more wind tunnel experiments on the shell, the gun could be made a viable weapon. This confidence, however, was not shared by some of the army artillery experts.

German inventiveness was extremely fertile before and during the war. Some of the projects were pursued to a successful, if expensive conclusion, while others were either left on the drawing board or remained to be captured as mock-ups or prototypes. Among these ideas were the artificial creation of an aerial vortex to destroy Allied bombers. An amplifier which would project sound waves of high power and low frequency was built and tested. (The noise was intended to kill or disorientate.) A piloted version of the V-1 was constructed and a squadron of dedicated pilots was formed. They were not employed because no target worth their sacrifice appeared before the end of the war. The "Do" missile, a submarine-launched solid-fuelled rocket, was successfully fired from a submerged U-boat. There were plans for U-boats to tow V-2's to positions off the United States coast and fire them from special canis-

ters. A more modest weapon was developed for close quarter fighting in tanks. The *Sturmgewehr* 44, in itself an important advance in small arms technology, was fitted with a periscope. With this special sight the gun incorporated a curved barrel. Tests, however, showed that the bullets were distorted by the barrel.

Hitler's interference in German research misdirected several projects, but his interest in the jet-propelled Me 262 was disastrous.

The aircraft was designed to be a high-speed interceptor. With two Junkers Jumo 004B-1, 2, or 3 turbojets it had a maximum speed of 538 mph, which put it out of range of the fastest conventional fighters the Allies possessed. Its four 30-mm cannon and 24 R4M air-to-air missiles gave it a fire-power which could have restored control of the skies over Germany to the Luftwaffe.

Hitler, however, saw this fighter as a new revenge weapon. "This will be my Blitz bomber," he said when he was told that it could carry bombs. From the "Schwalbe" it became the "Sturmvogel", from speeding "Swallow" to lumbering "Storm Bird" loaded with two 550-pound bombs. This load not only made the aircraft difficult to handle, but put back the project

by at least four months. When the *Sturmvogel* was employed in action it was slow enough to be pursued and attacked by piston-engined fighters.

The Luftwaffe eventually received a real jet bomber in the Arado Ar 234 *"Blitz"*. It arrived too late to affect the fighting in Europe, though one was reported to have flown a photo-reconnaissance mission along Britain's east coast.

Germany's research and development programme was diffuse and ill co-ordinated, suffering from interference by Hitler and no proper central scientific control. Many projects received backing only because their originators were able to "sell" them to some government ministry. Party functionaries in some unusual ministries fancied themselves as the patrons of scientific research and granted money and resources to German inventors.

However, some of the fruits of German war-time research remain with us today. The V-2's which were shipped to the United States in 1945 were the beginning of the American space programme. The "short" 7.62-mm round for the MP43 and 44 assault rifles, became the basis for the current Russian AK 47 assault rifle.

CHAPTER 148

Germany in defeat

In the early days of May 1945, Prime Minister Churchill was in a profoundly worried mood. True, the struggle against Hitler was finished when Germany surrendered on May 8. But Churchill could not join fully in the rejoicing of the London crowds on V.E. Day. Japan was still unconquered, and now the West was faced with a new threat: the tide of Soviet imperialism was running unchecked across Eastern Europe. Communist or pro-Communist puppet governments had been set up by the Russians in Bulgaria and in Rumania in violation of the Yalta agreement, and Western news reports were suppressed. "An iron curtain is drawn down upon their front," Churchill wrote on May 12, "We do not know what is going on behind."

The Prime Minister felt that it was necessary to have a showdown with Stalin immediately. The United States were preparing to withdraw their troops in Germany back to the predetermined occupation zone. This would give the Russians another large chunk of Germany, 300-400 miles long and 120 miles wide. "This would be an event which, if it occured, would be one of the most melancholy in history," Churchill wrote. The territory under Russian control would include "all the great capitals of middle Europe including Berlin, Vienna, Budapest, Belgrade, Bucharest and Sofia." Only Greece would be saved. If Churchill and President Truman did not confront Stalin before the American withdrawal, the Western Allies would have little bargaining power. As early as May 6, therefore, Churchill sent an urgent telegram to Truman asking for a conference of the "Big Three" as soon as possible.

Truman agreed that the Three should meet soon, but said that he himself could not attend until July, after Congress had approved

his new budget programme. He had been president for less than a month, and did not share Churchill's dread of Russian domination in eastern Europe. But Truman agreed that a conference of the three heads of state would help clear up outstanding differences over the procedure for drafting peace treaties, the occupation of Germany, and the question of reparations, as well as the eastern Europe question. He suggested that the conference might meet in Alaska, or perhaps Vienna, and that he and Churchill should arrive separately, to avoid giving Stalin the impression that

Page 2221: *The last "Big Three" Conference, at Potsdam in July 1945. But this time there were two new faces – Clement Attlee of Great Britain and Harry S Truman of the U.S.*
△ ◁ ◁ *German civilians loot a liquor store.*
△ ◁ *German girls make their way home with the spoils from a looted distillery in Lippstadt.*
◁ *With the strengthening of law enforcement in the months after Germany's surrender, black marketeers found the going more difficult, as these women have found to their cost.*
△ *Hitler's portrait comes down.*

△ ◁ The team that steered Britain to victory, seen on May 7, 1945. Standing: Major-General L. C. Hollis (left) and General Sir Hastings Ismay; seated, left to right: Air Chief Marshal Sir Charles Portal, Field-Marshal Sir Alan Brooke, Winston Churchill, and Admiral of the Fleet Sir Andrew Cunningham.

△ But while the Allies celebrated V. E. Day, in Germany the position was somewhat different. Although most were glad that the war was over, there was now the heart-breaking job of picking up the pieces—under Allied occupation.

◁ ◁ Not least of Germany's problems was the reconstruction of industry, so that she could pay her way in the world, after the ministrations of Allied strategic bombing.

◁ The new, non-Nazi Germany in the making: German children on their way to school under the watchful eyes of one British and two Belgian soldiers.

Overleaf: The shell of Cologne.

Apart from the moral and social problems of rebuilding Germany, there was also the vast effort required to clear up the actual physical debris of war before reconstruction work could start. The best tool for the job was manpower, and Germany's people weighed into the problem with a vengeance – not least because their food rations were dependent on it.

△ *Rationalising the skeleton of gutted Dresden.*

△▷ *A Berliner in the old business quarter, now in the Russian sector.*

▷ *Body count in Dresden, under the supervision of Russian officers. But how could an accurate figure be arrived at when thousands of bodies were reduced to nothing but fine dust by the fire-storms?*

the Anglo-Saxon leaders were "ganging up" on him.

Stalin himself suggested that the meeting take place near Berlin, and agreed with Truman that July 15 should be the date.

The codename for the conference was to be ˈTerminalˈ; each delegation would have a separate headquarters at Babelsberg, a suburb of Berlin just south of Potsdam. The meetings themselves would take place in the Cecilienhof Palace, a former home of the German Crown Prince. The heads of state would be accompanied by their foreign ministers and other top officials, but the press would not be invited.

As the date of the conference approached, President Truman and his staff produced dozens of notes, agendas, and memoranda for their use at Potsdam. Churchill, on the other hand, did not set his plans down on paper, but took a short holiday.

The two Western leaders both

arrived at Babelsberg on July 15. Churchill drove to the house that was to be his headquarters, a large home in the former film colony of Germany. President Truman's residence, near Churchill's, was similar and soon became known as the "Little White House". It lacked screens, however, and the American delegation was to suffer mosquito bites for the first few days until the weather cooled. Stalin's house was about a mile away, much closer to the actual conference centre – the Russians had arranged that.

The Soviet leader, recently promoted from Marshal to Generalissimo, arrived on July 17, and the first conference session took place that evening. Truman was named chairman, at Stalin's suggestion. He immediately proposed that a Council of Foreign Ministers be set up to draft peace treaties and deal with other problems after the end of hostilities.

This proposal was quickly approved, although there was some debate over whether China and France should be included.

The prompt agreement on the first proposal raised hopes that other issues could also be resolved without difficulty. This optimism was soon dispelled as the three leaders debated the situation in eastern Europe. Churchill and Truman denounced the Russian violation of the Yalta terms in setting up puppet governments in the East. Instead of allowing all democratic groups to join the caretaker governments, the Soviets had restricted participation to those known to be friendly to Moscow. There was also evidence that the Soviets did not intend to hold free and unfettered elections. Then there was Stalin's demand for reparations from Italy. The Western leaders wanted special treaty arrangements for Italy, which had eventually joined the Allies and promised help

2228

△ *While the Americans and the British were restricted in their social activities by non-fraternisation orders, no such worries hindered Russian soldiers.*

▷ *French prisoners-of-war discuss how best to get home to France.*

▷▷ *One of the legion of female "rubble workers" of Berlin takes her meagre mid-day meal.*

NORWAY

SWEDEN

FINLAND
Helsinki

Lake Ladoga

Leningrad

Tallinn

ESTONIA

NORTH SEA

DENMARK

Copenhagen

Riga   LATVIA

Memel   LITHUANIA

Baltic Sea   Niemen

Königsberg

Danzig

EAST PRUSSIA

RUSSIA

HOLLAND

Hamburg

Berlin

Oder   Neisse

Vistula   Bug

Warsaw   Brest-Litovsk

Pripet

BELGIUM

Bonn

LUXEM-BOURG

Frankfurt

POLAND

Kiev

Metz

Rhine

Prague

Vinnitsa

FRANCE

Munich

CZECHOSLOVAKIA

Dniestr   Bug

Basle

Berne

Vienna

Dniepr

SWITZERLAND

AUSTRIA

HUNGARY

Budapest

Odessa

Po

RUMANIA

ITALY

CORSICA

Adriatic Sea

Belgrade

Bucharest

Black Sea

YUGOSLAVIA

Danube

BULGARIA

Sofia

Istanbul

SARDINIA

ALBANIA

GREECE

TURKEY

(inset map) NORWAY   RUSSIA   FINLAND   Helsinki   Leningrad

PRE-WAR FRONTIERS
POST-WAR FRONTIERS
ALLIED OCCUPATION ZONES:
BRITISH
AMERICAN
FRENCH
RUSSIAN

△ *Post-war Europe.*

△▷ *and* ▷ *The non-fraternisation order is lifted. The order on British troops had been imposed before the end of the war, but on June 12 the order was lifted to allow soldiers to speak to and play with children, and from July 1 the troops were allowed to speak to Germans in public places. Finally, in September, the rest of the ban was lifted. The only things not permitted were accommodation in German homes and marriage.*

against Japan; Stalin would not grant favours to Italy which would not be shared by Hungary, Rumania, and Bulgaria. The Three did not reach a definite agreement on these questions at Potsdam, merely referring them to the attention of the new Council of Foreign Ministers. Similar decisions were made concerning the question of what "war booty" each Ally could legitimately confiscate, and the Soviet desire for trusteeship over some of the colonies of the

defeated Axis powers.

The conference was interrupted temporarily on July 25. Churchill and the Leader of the Opposition, Clement Attlee, returned to Britain to await the outcome of the recent general election. The actual voting had taken place on July 5, but the final results were not known until the 26th. Churchill had brought Attlee to the conference to ensure continuity in the British position, regardless of the outcome of the election, and on one occasion,

with Attlee at his side, Churchill had toasted "The Leader of the Opposition–whoever he may be." On July 26, the result was announced: the voters had chosen Attlee's Labour Government. Two days later, Prime Minister Attlee returned to Potsdam and took his place beside Truman and Stalin.

The last four meetings at Potsdam were concerned with Germany. All agreed that the nation must be denazified and disarmed. In the words of the official com-

The damage to Germany was comprehensive, embracing industry, urban areas, transport, and historic monuments.

△ ◁ ◁ Cologne.

△ ◁ The Propaganda Ministry in Berlin.

△ Combat engineers of the U.S. Army salvage steel from the Fallersleben factory, which had been turned from Volkswagen to V-1 production during the war.

◁ ◁ The Foreign Ministry in Berlin, pictured on August 21, 1945.

◁ The Henschel aircraft engine factory at Altenbaun near Kassel, completely destroyed by two U.S.A.A.F. raids.

△ *Refugees in Vienna's main station.*
◁ *A measure of comfort: released after 13 years in a Russian camp, Count Bismarck greets his mother. Years in Russian labour camps was the fate that awaited many thousands of German fighting men taken by the Russians.*
▷ *Cologne's Hohenzollern Bridge across the Rhine.*

muniqué, "all German land, sea and air forces, the SS, SA, SD and Gestapo, with all their organisations, staffs and institutions, including the General Staff, Officers' Corps, Reserve Corps, military schools, war veterans' organisations, and all other military and quasi-military organisations, together with all clubs and associations which serve to keep alive the military tradition in Germany, are to be completely and finally abolished . . ." War criminals were to be arrested and tried, and high-ranking Nazis interned. All more-than-nominal members of the Nazi Party were to be removed from public office and positions of responsibility in private undertakings and enterprises.

The question of reparations was more difficult. The Three had previously agreed to treat Germany as an economic unit, and reparations were to be drawn from the nation as a whole. But the Western leaders had learned that the Red Army was confiscating all manner of goods (including household furniture) in the Russian-occupied zone. No agreement could be reached on the value of these goods, and this made it impossible to make a fair division of reparations. This thorny problem was ingeniously solved by an American proposal: each occupying power should collect its share of reparations from its own zone of occupation, rather than from Germany as a whole. This idea was accepted, with provisions for trading coal and food supplies in the Russian zone for industrial equipment from the Western areas.

The last great question at Potsdam concerned the Polish border. It had been agreed already that the Russians were to receive Polish territory east of the Curzon Line, and that Poland would eventually receive German territory in compensation.

No decision had been made as to where this western boundary would be fixed. But the Russians had unilaterally transferred a huge chunk of conquered German territory, as far west as the Oder and Western Neisse, to the Polish Government which Churchill described as the "ardent puppet" of the Soviet Union. This meant that the richest agricultural and coal-producing area of Germany was not to be included in the debate on reparations, and millions of hungry Germans would have to be repatriated to the western zones. The Potsdam conference thus marked the real birth of the Cold War, in this clear display of Stalin's determination to consolidate his position in eastern Europe, excluding Western influence.

The most important decision at Potsdam was not, strictly speaking, part of the conference. On July 17, Churchill had been told that the test at Alamogordo, New Mexico, had been successful: the atomic bomb was a reality. Truman and Churchill agreed that a final opportunity must be given to the Japanese to surrender. If they refused, the new weapon must be used to end the war. On July 26, therefore, the two leaders, together with China's Chiang Kai-shek – the Soviet Union was not then at war with Japan – issued the Potsdam Declaration. "We call upon the Government of Japan to proclaim now the unconditional surrender of all the Japanese armed forces," the declaration said. ". . . The alternative for Japan is prompt and utter destruction."

△ ◁ *Justice is meted out: the scene in a Vienna court as the sentences on four men convicted of murdering over 100 Jews are passed. The man crying has been given eight years' gaol. The other three were sentenced to death.*

◁ *Cossacks serving with the Wehrmacht, rounded up by the British in Austria.*

△ *The Yugoslav partisan forces pull out of Klagenfurt after reaching agreement with the British about occupation zones and the fact that the Yugoslavs had none.*

▷ *Germans read the first edition of a Hamburg newspaper printed under the control of the Allied Military Government.*
▽ *An American private checks the papers of two civilians accused of murdering a Russian slave labourer.*